The NUDE

COMPLETE PHOTOGRAPHY COURSE

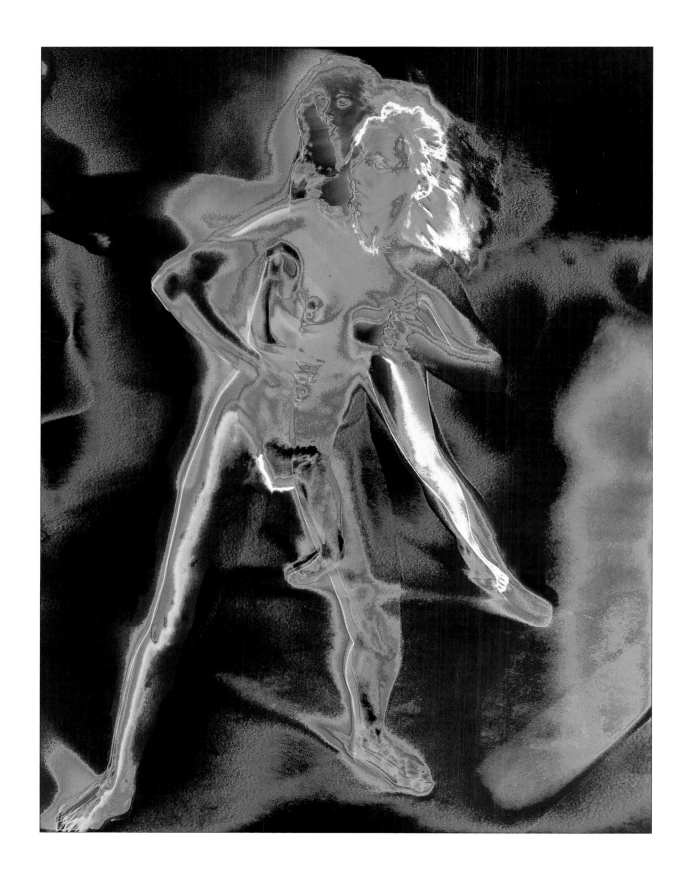

The Nude

COMPLETE PHOTOGRAPHY COURSE

TEXT & PHOTOGRAPHS BY

Bruce Pinkard

SILVER
PIXEL
PRESS®

Rochester, NY

*To Didi, whose help, love, and understanding have
made all things possible.*

First North American Edition, 1999

Published by

Silver Pixel Press®
A Tiffen® Company
21 Jet View Drive
Rochester, NY 14624 USA
Fax: (716) 328-5078

ISBN 1-883403-60-X

©Fountain Press Ltd. 1999

Text & Photographs ©Bruce Pinkard
Cover Design by Andrea Zocchi Design
Design & Layout by Grant Bradford
Printed in Belgium by Die Keure n.v.

Library of Congress Cataloging-in-Publication Data
Pinkard, Bruce, 1932-
    The nude / Bruce Pinkard. -- 1st North American ed.
        p.   cm.
    Includes index.
    ISBN 1-883403-60-X
    1. Photography of the nude--Handbooks, manuals, etc.   I. Title.
TR674.P5624 1999
778.9'21--dc21
                                                99–14005
                                                CIP

FOREWORD

When I began this book, I was very conscious that for centuries artists have used the nude female form as a classic symbol of purity and truth. The nude gives no clue to its social status or point in time allowing the image to be examined before the identity of the subject becomes apparent.

As a photographer, I also knew that my chosen medium was one noted for its optical specificity in terms of subject matter ... that in millions of pairs of hands around the world, the camera is used every day to reveal factual events and define objects. That this attribute could easily destroy the anonymity of the models I had chosen and therefore intrude on the creative structure I wished to impose in the name of art, was self-evident. However, factual photography of a naked woman is a comparatively easy activity and at that simple level, quite without soul. In this book, readers are encouraged to believe, that this need not be the only option. Photographers who use the female nude to demonstrate craft skills, poetic concepts or frank eroticism follow in the footsteps of many masters, both painters and photographers and have no need to dabble in ordinary reportage.

This book has been carefully structured. First to introduce elementary essentials of photographic skills; then the choosing of the model and directing her; understanding creative lighting and imaginative concepts; special effects in the darkroom and the magic of digital photography. The Masterclass features some of my most advanced work, but much of it springs from very simple disciplines which I discuss very early in the main book and which suggests I hope, a level of aspiration which may be attempted by either amateur or experienced professional.

It should not be forgotten that the often ambiguous and enigmatic pictures to be found in the Masterclass, are all machine made images using conventional photography and that there are no computer manipulations involved. They are of the female nude, in action or repose and are intended to present generic and possibly unromantic statements about their beauty, activity and felinity.

Voluptuous tonality and sensual colour in these images endows the best of them with innate feminine sexuality and decorum, rather than with provocative attitudes. Perhaps my images of women are more for women than for men, symbolising as they do, wordless mysteries which lie deep within the essence of the female psyche and therefore, are best understood by them.

In some of my work in this book, the appearance of the naked body has been intellectualised deliberately and coded by the use of a Metagraph*. This is an invention of my own whereby the optical purity and colour fidelity which is inherent in normal photography, has been changed by the use of arbitrary graphic techniques and masking.

Where I have given a picture a title, it has been used as a device to assist entry into the labyrinthine visual structures of the image and to lead the viewer towards another and separate reality of my own devising, an existence outside time, no longer recording an event, but an event itself.

If the text and images in my book are thoughtfully studied and practised, I believe readers can expect to reach exceptionally high levels in what is probably the most creative of all photographic art forms.

Bruce Pinkard

*Metagraph is a registered trademark

CONTENTS

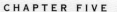

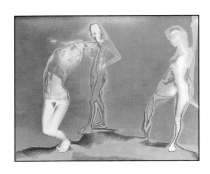

CHAPTER ONE

Perspectives

Artists initially begin to assess their chosen subjects by an intuitive reference to their own figure and any other human figures present. This provides scale, proportion and a relationship to the creative ego. Those artists who contemplate and theorise about art as a philosophical pursuit and try to fit their own artistic efforts into that timeless scale usually seek a continual simplification of the means of expression. They generally employ subjects which in themselves are not visually complex or do not carry any identity that anchors them in any particular moment of history

Of these artists, those whose interests lie in a major exploration of humanity often seek the ultimate simplicity which is provided only by the naked figure. Humanity clothed is humanity identified along with class, race, historical era, habits and aspirations, which can intrude upon an elemental study of the subject. The nude figure has much of the fundamental simplicity of the straight line. It has no exact historical determination, it has infinite movement, is irreducible and is charged with symbolism. It is also largely de-personalised but not de-humanised… a perfect subject to challenge the mechanics of the artist's craft in painting, sculpture or photography.

For 2,500 years, western civilisation has been influenced by the Greek concept of ideal harmonic beauty to be found in the nude, the subjects were usually male, always well proportioned and athletic. Early artists who thought to express these ideals used closely controlled mathematical data to arrive at the final execution and there arose an established custom of proportion. Before the birth of Christ, and perhaps for some time after, the classic proportions of the nude female were assumed to be found when the measurement between the nipples, equalled that between the breast and the navel, as well as that between the navel and the crotch.

Artists in later centuries, including Dürer, Leonardo da Vinci and Michelangelo, continued to attempt to present pure, harmonic form in the nude, both male and female, by an idealisation of the figure and a mathematical formula in respect of proportion. They would generally reach their final imagery by achieving a synthesis of anatomical parts from various live models. Even today, calendar artists tend sometimes towards this synthetic ideal, using several models to provide the reference for the final 'perfect' female.

The ethics of the early Greek and Roman artists clearly led them to use the nude female subject to produce art works which expressed an intellectual and Olympian interest in physical culture, spiritualism and idealised confidence to the exclusion of sin or eroticism.

In the exotic cultures of pre-Christian India however, the nude female form was used in the contemporary art of that time to deify the sexual processes and arouse the viewer. As in other areas of our history, twin streams of eastern and western artistic practice have joined in influencing our culture, giving rise to the duality which exists today in respect of the art of the nude: intellectualised abstraction versus earthy sensuality.

In the centuries dominated by the Arabian conquest, not only the nude figure but all artistic representation of living things, ceased to be central to European art. The Jewish influence in early Christian philosophy also defined the imagery of living things as idolatry, with any rendering of the nude body clearly identified with evil. The strong religious persuasion of both Islam and Christianity was brought to bear on what was considered to be rampant paganism and remains a powerful factor influencing the exhibition of any representation of the nude, particularly the female nude.

In the waning influence of the departing Muslim conquerors and the fragmentation of the Christian movement into less authoritarian segments, artists began once more to find a legitimate area in which to explore the representation of the nude. Strangely, this arises from the Catholic Church. In early medieval times, all artists were trained by the friars. There was no other formal tuition and any young boy with any evidence of artistic promise was inducted into the seminary where his growing years were spent in the scriptorium, studying the technique of applying ink and paint to paper, mostly to illuminate manuscripts.

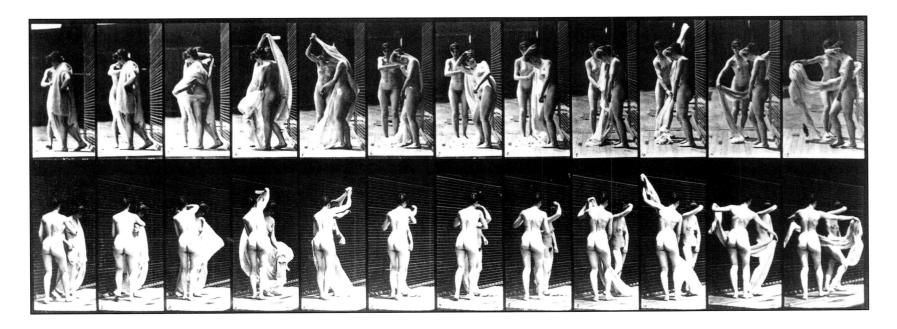

Eadweard Muybridge, an English born photographer working in the USA, used nude figures to demonstrate his photographic analysis of human locomotion. In 1887 he published this multi-image illustration in his book Animal Locomotion.
COURTESY KODAK MUSEUM, HARROW

The rising need to symbolise Christian events in lush imagery often led to the necessity of using the totally or semi-naked human body as the central part of that narration. The near-naked body of Christ, the nudity of Eve (even if chastely draped), restored to the nude a powerful connotation of innocence and spiritualism. For centuries the Church of Rome was the sole master of the artist and under its censorial eye these young artists learned to purify the nude image even while they strove for more and more realism by employing the newly discovered rules of perspective. Again the artist faced a duality: a struggle for the improved natural rendering and therefore the sensuality of the figure but, at the same time, a need to satisfy the intensely controlled ethics of their patrons.

By Renaissance times, the naked body in art became inextricably tied to religion, while it also became the supreme symbol in officially sanctioned culture. Strangely, the nude survived the demonic activities of the sixteenth-century inquisitors – possibly because of the enlightenment of one particularly powerful prince of the Church, possibly also because of the heroic reputation of Michelangelo. The baser elements inherent in nude imagery vanished from the secular scene at this time but, in a few and very select apartments within the Church administration, the robust sensuality of the nude, as presented by the virtuoso artists of that time, found its place. Eroticism, as found in the image, became a most private affair and painting a holy vocation.

Reinforced by the sensual lyricism of Botticelli's 'Birth of Venus' and the deep conviction and reality of Leonardo da Vinci's masterpieces in the fifteenth century, the sixteenth century dawned with the promise of a dramatic change in the way the nude body was to appear in art.

The genius of Michelangelo presented the nude figure in architectural and formal terms but with these attributes it brought also a breathtaking realism. Raphael, who died before the age of 40, produced seemingly effortless examples of the nude, full of poetry and sensuality; he rarely painted a study from life, although successfully striving for realism, and took his inspiration from the 'mind's eye'. He presented beauty as a concept, the figure as something to be aware of for its own idealised values.

The Venetian, Titian, with his masterly control of paint, brought to the naked female body a lush sensuality which must have caused some concern amongst the holy patrons of his art, and Correggio produced a pagan sensuality in some of his figures which further diffused the fine dividing line between the sacred and the profane.

In the northern countries, building on the anguished exercises of the great master Albrecht Dürer, painters had already reached the point where their portrayal of the nude was often for itself alone, with only a thin allusion to religious themes. The provocative nude in art became a decorative and public subject for the first time. The German painter Lucas Cranach (1472-1553), exemplified this trend, producing for his patrons sensual renditions of the female figure, full of delicacy and romance.

Two artistic giants contributed historically vital images of the nude in the seventeenth century: Rubens and Rembrandt. Rubens (1577-1640) at the age of 31 returned to Antwerp full of energy and skill and in the first decades of the century, although his patrons were mostly Jesuits and Kings, he endowed his nudes with immense energy and life. The figures were richly modelled, the flesh wholly tactile. His images remained conceptually spiritual, but in their execution they displayed breathtaking naturalism.

Rembrandt's moody and moving work, enormously influential on all artists who followed him, contained illustrations of the nude of such searing honesty that he was often taken to task by the critics for his neglect of conventional idealisation. In his handling of line and colour, and his masterly control of light, he provides photographers with marvellous examples to study.

Rembrandt chose to document the human body when it was something past perfection. Women, their bodies fat and wrinkled, stood in thought; heavy young girls disclosed a naturalism that was so honest as to be almost documentary. With Rembrandt, the portrayal of the nude reached a new compromise with reality, while spiritualism tended to lose most of its emphasis.

The greatest painters of the nude in the eighteenth century were probably a Venetian and a Frenchman. Tiepolo was a great master decorator who finished an astonishing number of churches and palaces in Venice, Milan, Verona, Wurzburg and Madrid with witty and sophisticated visual spectacles for wall and ceiling. He made no secret of his fascination with the female nude, endowing his figures with keenly observed textures and startling personality. His sacred subjects contained some of the most joyous and voluptuous angels in painting so far, and with his prodigious techniques, his art was a rich pleasure for the eye, where happiness and beauty were paramount.

Francois Boucher, whose patron was Madame de Pompadour and who seemingly painted from the viewpoint of graceful femininity rather than any masculine concept, nevertheless was responsible for some of the most richly erotic female nudes up to that point in time. Never bawdy, but always sensuous, his paintings were often dismissed for their 'elegant vulgarity' and he himself for being 'merely a decorator'.

In the history of art, Boucher was not considered the equal of Tiepolo. He was thought to impose too little of his own character on the product of his patrons' commissions, but in his illustrations of the female nude, he had left his contemporaries far behind, and in many ways could be said to summarise the lessons to be found in Rubens' fleshy rendering of that subject and from which all painters that followed that genre drew so much profit.

Photographers who wish to improve their concepts and understanding of illustrating the nude need to research a little through a few art books and reflect upon the changes in the eighteenth century's western art which preceded the discovery of photography. The supreme patronage of the Church of Rome gave way slowly to the secular influences of the Protestant north, bringing increased naturalism and therefore allowing the ascendance of sensuality over spirituality.

As the photographic age dawned in the nineteenth century, France was, indisputably, the principal influence in illustrations of the female nude, which was not treated by itself as the sole subject within the frame and was beginning to be used by many artists as the preferred vehicle for displaying their technical virtuosity and innovation. In 1799 an army coup, led by Napoleon had effectively ended the revolutionary period which began ten years before, bringing stability to France. The lessons in ideology of the French Revolution now could surface without pressure and the public could have access to the new understanding of the fact that life and freedom were available to the common man.

The emphasis on improving the human condition in a worldwide sense was not lost on art students, the painters or their public. The imagery of the time reflected the revolutionary spirit, the painter David, chief visual propagandist for the revolution, executed his work with cool detachment and marked absence of brilliant colouring, demonstrating the dynamism of the naturalistic image.

These were pictures of the people and for the people, not for the privileged princes of church or state. Such art became wholly accessible to the untrained eye. To make this public art required immense study and discipline, particularly of the traditional mainstream of art which had arisen from Rome and the well

By mid-Victorian times when slow wet plates still dictated very static poses, the female nude was being revealed as never before.
COURTESY B.T. BATSFORD LTD.

springs of the centuries. Technical tradition was not lost, but incorporated in the structure of revolutionary painting.

However, concepts became more liberal, more human and therefore more sensual. David's pupil, Jean-Dominique Ingres (1780-1867), painting with great intellectual vigour, used his pictures of the female nude as technical set pieces in their own right. Yet, because of their simplicity and romanticism, they caught the imagination of a wide public. His efforts solidly anchored the nude into academic art, and particularly with 'Baigneuse de Valpincon' (1808), 'La Grande Odalisque' (1814), 'Venu, Anadyomene' (1848) and 'La Source' (1856), he produced some of the most famous nudes ever painted.

In 1820, on the Greek island of Milos, archaeologists uncovered a marble statue of a young woman of great classical beauty. She was half naked, chastely draped from the hips and lacking arms, yet no woman in art became so widely known or as influential in establishing in the public mind both commendable beauty and socially acceptable nudity. Venus de Milo, long resident in the Louvre in Paris, was probably sculpted a century before the birth of Christ and revived the interest in classical formulae for the portrayal of the naked body. Because of her feminine delicacy and naturalism, she aroused in the public a consensus about permitted sensuality and covert voyeurism. Venus de Milo, only one of hundreds of the visualisations of the goddess Aphrodite, has somehow stuck in our minds as the most important. In modern times she has become the symbol, almost the ideogram, of commerce wherever it is connected to female beauty. Strangely, too, in the collective mind of the masses of the world's population, this particular Venus has become symbolic of 'ART', with a pretentious capital 'A'.

The stage then, in the early decades of the nineteenth century had been set for the climactic arrival of that other staggering influence on the means of portraying the nude in art (and art in general): the invention of photography. If the French Revolution altered very basic concepts in art and made it concerned with the contemporary, rather than classical problems of mankind, the Industrial Revolution had begun a serious diffusion of the quality of hand craftsmanship. The machine, even in art was King, and the camera – machine, waiting in the wings, was about to take centre stage in the drama of high art.

New principles and theories about perception awakened in the artist an interest in science and how it affected painting. The camera created a furore in Paris where it was first announced to the world in 1839. Paris, home of the new intellectualism in art

***Dry plates and faster emulsions
in the late Victorian era,
encouraged the photographer to
seek a relaxed natural attitude
and explore more dynamic poses
from the nude model.***
<small>Courtesy B. T. Batsford Ltd.</small>

and birthplace of art's new preoccupation with the earthy humanities which stood before the easels in both studio and field, was faced with a very different revolution.

Just when artists felt that their 2,000 year quest for naturalism and deeper reality was drawing to a successful close, they were confronted with an upstart technology which used a machine which in seconds could accomplish a far more realistic image of the world than could be completed by hand in many days. No wonder the painter Paul de la Roche exclaimed: *'from this moment painting is dead'* and a leading Leipzig newspaper denounced photography a *'blasphemy'*!

Whatever chasms and cracks opened up in the academies of art (and they were to cause agonising and probably fatal divisions), when the full scope of the camera was understood as it related to the portrayal of the nude figure, photography gave mankind an ideal means for its realisation. Sensuous reality was available at the touch of a button, voyeuristic sexuality could be indelibly recorded with complete discretion and privacy. The revolution in easel art insisted on a study from life and here was such a study so mechanical yet so documentary and realistic, so easily obtained, that the coyness, prudery and spiritual camouflage previously accompanying any illustration of the female nude would soon vanish.

The great painters of the nineteenth and twentieth centuries still used the nude as a means of presenting their ideals of form, colour, line and concept. Photographers who wish to specialise in the nude, may obtain inspiration from the work of Courbet, Renoir (who began his famous work of the nude at the age of 40), Manet, Degas, Cezanne, Gauguin, Matisse and Picasso.

The unspoken promise of photography, since its invention, has always been that it would be a democratic art; that it would put into the hands of millions the means of making a satisfying and accomplished image. It is true that the means have been made available; millions and millions of people own and operate cameras, but, sadly, little of the marvellous machines' billions of outpourings ever crystallise into an art object. In the photographic rendition of the female nude, the success rate is even lower.

As the age of the mechanical image dawned, painters of the nude were still largely inhibited by a prudent awareness of classical taboos and the academic idealisation of the female figure. If artists were to eat and pay the rent, they had to understand that these were the pictures required by society. The magic box, which appeared in 1839 under the auspices of the

French government who gave it to the world free of charge, was to change all that.

Monsieur L.J.M. Daguerre had invented an intensely private instrument whereby two consenting adults could enter into worlds of lyric, erotic or even obscene imagery without any censorship and with very little practical skill needed. The camera was to begin its attack on prudery and false modesty just as it had commenced its assault on inadequacy in easel painting, by the use of the compelling naturalness of its image and by the simple but sophisticated realism which the machine could produce in the hands of the talented layman.

In the beginning artists saw the best use of the camera as a means to provide artists' reference, to support their latest studio painting of the subject in depth. Eugene Delacroix was one painter who was excited by the Daguerreotype nude and frankly admitted it by becoming a founder member of the Photographic Society of France.

Both he and Courbet used photographic nudes from which to construct famous paintings, Delacroix especially revelling in the frankness and beauty of the new imagery which was handed to him by various photographers, including Durieu and Ziegler and he refused to indict the new invention as non-art, as many other leading painters of the time felt obliged to do.

In the great explosion of photographic activity in the three decades following the introduction of the machine image and the philosophical uproar which swirled about it, photography and its startling realism began to be used in the services of obscenity, particularly in Britain. Caustic criticism from art experts and the intransigence of hypocritical Victorian moralists who detested even the most innocent of nude photographs, helped to drive these pictures of the nude underground, to the extent that such photographs were even banned from the Royal Mail. The trade in this cruder type of image still survives today, in a much shabbier form than 120 years ago.

However, slightly more acceptable commerce was more publicly maintained under the euphemism 'Etudes Academiques' these being a series of discreetly erotic pictures of nude young ladies, carefully locked in academic poses and smothered in banal settings of fake, classical antiquity. Such pictures were also highly regarded by the poorest artists of the day as source material for their paintings and studies of the nude, because they saved them the considerable fees of live models.

So photography of the nude began its early years, still inextricably linked with painting, vilified to some degree,

By Edwardian times in pre-war England, photographer and model co-operated in producing very open and frank pictures of the nude. These images were soon arriving in discreet art shops all over the country.

This is probably one of the earliest colour photographs of the nude, taken by the Lumiere process about 1912.
COURTESY CIBA-GEIGY, SWITZERLAND.

exploited by pornographers, obliquely praised by the majority - many of whom beheld honest attempts to use its beautiful clarity and frankness. It was only openly championed by a few far-sighted members of the art community, such as Ingres, Delacroix, Degas, Renoir and Cezanne, who all saw in the new medium the ideal means to portray the naked body with all its poetry and humanity.

Eadweard Muybridge, a gifted English landscape photographer who settled in the USA in the 1880s, explored the scientific analysis of locomotion using the nude and under the auspices of the University of Pennsylvania, where the artist Thomas Eakins, himself interested in creating very realistic nude photographs, was influential as Professor in Anatomy in Art. Muybridge's

work was to guide all who were interested in an analysis of human and animal movement and his work became a vital factor in the slowly growing public acceptance of the nude.

The arrival in the 1890s of the ubiquitous Kodak camera, with roll film and hand-held 'snap' shot exposures, took the popularisation of photography a giant stride forward. This mass-produced machine gave promise of a genuinely democratic imagery within the means and skill of all.

During this energetic re-appraisal of photography and its truly machine-made images, art was again greatly affected. As the nineteenth century closed and the magical twentieth century dawned, nude photography was seen again in slightly less than a socially acceptable role. Guarded distribution began of what was for the times, boldly erotic postcards, some tinged with sly humour, paying no homage to art as the earlier 'Etudes' had done. It became fashionable among young ladies of social status to collect pictures of their female friends in the nude, even though these were almost always taken by lady photographers.

Slowly the nude photograph was becoming an acceptable social acquisition for public display. The relaxing of some moral strictures against this public display of the nude in photographs allowed more people to accept the sensational realism of the camera when it was turned to stare at such hitherto private subjects. The new understanding of such images, however over sentimentalised and optically discreet they may have been, helped the photographers and artists to continue their studies of the nude with some chance of patronage.

One of the most sensitive of these was Alfonse Mucha, working in Paris from about 1900. His figure studies were mostly to become references for his paintings but today, viewed simply as photographs in their own right, they have a shining delicacy about them which becomes a candid celebration of femininity in the best of taste. They are fine examples for any modern photographer who chooses to photograph the nude.

Two giants of the photographic salons, Alvin Langdon Coburn and Edward Steichen, became interested in the nude. Coburn even photographed George Bernard Shaw, who was deeply interested in photography, in a somewhat self-conscious and shadowy, but totally nude, pose and obtained a public showing of the result.

In the early years of this century, the whirlpool of energy around the photographer Alfred Stieglitz in the USA, was to bring to North America the shattering images of French modern art and the public saw, for the first time, the startling work of Matisse, Rodin, Picasso, Brancusi, Picabia, Braque and other extraordinary artists.

At the same time Stieglitz organised the Photo-secession which was to begin the maturation of photography as art and was to attract to its best images, the status of high art. These influential events began to reawaken serious photographers' interest in realism and to win many away from the Salon trail where muted and manipulated images clogged the senses with viscous sentimentality, particularly where the female nude was concerned.

Clarence White, working with Stieglitz, produced a series of simple, unaffected nudes; Edward Steichen contributed a few

This nonchalant pose from the post-war 1920's shows a very different attitude to posing and a noticeable change in the body shape.
COURTESY B. T. BATSFORD LTD.

overtly romantic examples of his somewhat overblown style of the time, but it was left to Stieglitz himself, the photo-realist supreme, to show the way, with an incisive collection of images of Georgia O'Keefe. Many of these were frankly erotic, all were crystal clear. They foreshadowed the modern approach to the nude of such later master photographers as Edward Weston, Imogen Cunningham and the modern Americans, Harry Callahan and Ralph Gibson. Unfortunately, these important photographs by Stieglitz are never publicly exhibited.

Of all the impressionable young photographers who came under the influence of Stieglitz and his New York gallery, '291', two were to change the art world's photographic approach to the female nude. Edward Weston, later to be a founder member of the F64 School, after some heart searching and some years of compulsive asceticism, evolved the silvery beauty of his famous brand of realism and his images of the nude include some of the most satisfying examples of the subject in all art.

His brilliant examples of uncompromisingly pure photography, set the Salon world into a spin and linking up fortuitously with the successes of the New Objectivity movement in Europe, he effectively laid the foundations and created the influences which are responsible for much of modern photography, both in the commercial and art field. His influence on photography of the nude was enormous.

The other great influence to come out of this photographic hothouse was very different. Young, determined to fulfil a destiny as a painter, yet fascinated by photography, he would visit '291' in his lunch hours, soaking up the images lining the walls. His name was Man Ray. Stieglitz certainly influenced his photographic thinking, but Man Ray was very much an originator. Later, when he became deeply involved as a painter in Paris, particularly in the Dadaist and Surrealist periods after the First World War, he managed to step neatly across the divide between the two disciplines and perform brilliantly as both a photographer and an artist.

Where Weston was concerned with optical purity, especially with his nudes, Man Ray was an entrepreneur, bent on the excitement of discovery and the alteration of the purely mechanical image. He made a remarkable series of solarised nudes and was probably the first photographer to project light onto the female torso to mask the form and to confuse contours. He also showed some of his subjects clearly and realistically, yet with such elegance and taste that the photograph appeared as not intrusive and the photographer and viewers were not cast as voyeurs. His early interest in graphic devices in his photographs and his skilful technique did not

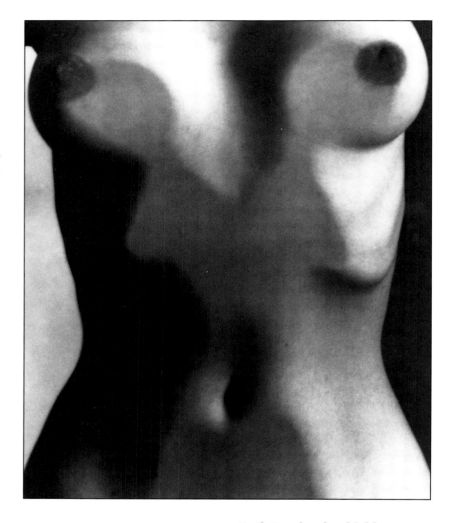

Ruth Bernhard, a highly respected fine art photographer was exploring very different aspects of nude photography. This was taken in 1947.
COURTESY OF RUTH BERNHARD

have a vast impact at the time, except perhaps with a few kindred spirits such as Lazlo Moholy-Nagy, but today's practising photographers in the fine art field neglect him at their peril.

Moholy-Nagy, genius of the Bauhaus and the New Bauhaus when it shifted to Chicago in the late 1930s, did not contribute many examples of the photographic nude. But he did force the growth of the new modernity which swept through America in the 1940s and therefore later changed the photographic style of the entire world, creating suitable techniques and philosophies to allow the nude photograph to become a part of our culture.

The famous documentalist, Andre Kertesz, tried his hand only once at photographing nudes, in 1933, and intrigued and startled the art establishment with a series of complex distortions, most fastidiously controlled but still obviously documentary in their inspiration. These photographs probably arose from his earliest distortion, 'The Underwater Swimmer' taken in 1917. Here the glinting surface of the water created the effect, much copied by later photographers, but in his studio distortions, the twisted reflections from a funfair mirror produced a benign sense of comedy which is rarely present in any other photographs of the nude.

The next watershed in the history of the nude was without doubt the work of Bill Brandt, the British photographer. In 1945 he began a long study of the way deep focus and sculptural lighting could be used with the female body and 15 years later presented the startled art world with a book of unforgettable examples entitled *Perspectives of Nudes*. Moody, intensely structural, the pictures invade the body of the subject with boldness and detachment, yet achieve a subtle eroticism which is unmatched in the work of any other photographer.

To compare the work of Weston, Man Ray, Kertesz and Brandt, when the subject of the female nude is considered, offers four opposing points of the compass from which to begin a journey, which travels entirely different country, yet reaches the same safe haven of deeply thoughtful concept, of brilliant technique, and universal empathy with the femininity of the subject.

Of the modern photographers who chose to have some considerable interest in the female nude as a photographic subject, those particularly worthy of study include Harry Callahan, USA; Lucien Clergue, France; Grooteclaes, Belgium; Eikoh Hosoe, Japan; Eric Hartman, USA; Duane Michaels, USA; Sam Haskins, Britain; Ruth Bernhard, USA; Helmut Newton, France and, of course, the great masters mentioned above: Man Ray, Edward Weston and Bill Brandt.

In 1953, Bill Brandt startled the world with a book of nudes which were completely unlike any previous images seen before or since, in either art or photography. This image is just one of a dazzling and powerful series of female nudes, which even half a century later still resonate in the art world consciousness as one of the watersheds in photographic imagery.

COURTESY OF THE LATE BILL BRANDT

In the sixties, candid and explicit poses of the nude were found to be acceptable to a growing number of fashion editors. This photograph is of those times and is as refreshing and strong today as it was then. It is the work of Helmut Newton, an outstanding photographer of women in general and the nude in particular.

The changed social status of women, the relaxation of many taboos on the public display of nudity and the wider understanding of the nude's place in the photo-art movement, offer many opportunities for photographers to create innovative and important images of the female nude. But before you begin it may be a useful exercise to consider two points of view from different periods of our history. The first comes from The Encyclopaedia of Photography, published in early 1905:

Nude, Photography of the

'The nude figure, male and female, is extensively and successfully treated by painters and draughtsmen. To photographers, however, this particular class of work offers less opportunity for successful effects. In some hands results have been secured that are quite pleasing and satisfactory, but in the ordinary way the chances of complete success are remote. The great difficulty lies in the fact that the photographer does not possess the unlimited facilities of the artist for idealising, for combining, modifying, emphasising and suppressing to secure the final satisfactory result. For purposes of figure study, good photographs of the nude have a real value and use. The introduction of nude figures into landscapes has also been successfully accomplished in some cases. But the treatment of the single nude figure for pictorial purposes is seldom satisfactory in the photographer's hands, although this is not because photography is not eminently capable of rendering the beautiful contours, texture and delicate light and shade of the human body. The difficulty lies rather in first securing the perfectly artistic model and then rendering it by photographic means with that ideal perfection and purity which should characterise all renderings of the nude figure. Too often the result is mere nakedness, which is a different thing altogether. On the whole therefore, this class of work is better left alone by the ordinary photographer.'

By 1968, Ruth Bernhard although still actively photographing the female nude had considerably changed both style and concept.
This photograph, entitled The Bride, enrobes the model in a veil of plastic, using the drape, a perennial prop of nude photographers since nude photography began, but with an entirely new and fresh approach.
COURTESY OF RUTH BERNHARD

This picture, completed in 1972 by Jerry Uelsman, an American photographer working with special effects and surrealism long before computers allowed easy manipulation of images, demonstrates a growing interest by photographic artists in personal and inner visions of the nude.

COURTESY OF JERRY UELSMAN

Some 70 years later, Ruth Bernhard, a famous teacher of photography and renowned exhibitor and photographic artist from California, had this to say:

'Our terrestrial human body as organic form and personal expression, intensely attracted me in sculpture and painting long before I began photography. It represents to me the same universal innocence, timelessness and purity as do all seed pods (suggesting the mother as well as the child, the parental as well as the descendant), conceived according to nature's longing. The human body implies its reproductive function, its vitality and its continuity.

With my photographs I try to exalt this power of life. It is my aim to transform the complexities of the figure into harmonies of simplified forms revealing the innate reality, the life force, the spirit, the inherent symbolism as well as the underlying remarkable bone structure. Minimising the face or even at times not including it emphasises the human body's universality. Often parts represent the whole, revealing a fresh view of a commonplace experience.

I have approached the nude much as I would a still life – with patience and reverence. My aim is to isolate and give emphasis to form with the greatest clarity, to indicate a sense of ideal proportion and to reveal the sculptural mass by the magic of light and shadow. In fact, light is my supreme inspiration. It is as vital as the model herself. By recognising the model's presence as an eternal, sensual symbol of life and all existence, I experience my own identity.'

CHAPTER TWO

Photo-basics

For those who have decided to specialise in the subject or at least to undertake a fairly serious programme of nude photography, certain practical matters must be settled before even beginning to search for model or concept. The camera and ancilliary equipment must be carefully considered to provide the basic path to good technique. Processing and printing standards should be elevated to very high levels indeed.

Comfortable working conditions must be established for both model and photographer. A secure space where the model can feel relaxed and confident, must be found where photography can take place in sessions lasting two to four hours each.

CAMERAS

The most practical camera for this work is the reflex type and of this type, the SLR (single lens reflex) is the ideal. A normal and medium long focal length lens is needed, together with suitable accessories – filters, lens hoods, cable release, tripod and separate narrow angle (spot) exposure meter.

Many photographers will already possess a 35mm SLR and for these cameras a lens of 50-60mm, plus a 135mm lens, is sufficient for most work. Wide angle lenses are rarely used, at least in the beginning, because distortions of the nude body are less acceptable to most viewers. As technique and concept improves later on, experiments may be made with shorter focal length, but wide angle lenses are not usually considered basic equipment for this kind of work.

The 35mm SLR is a fast, comfortable machine for making quick images and wherever mood is paramount, as it often is with this subject, there can be no better choice than this type of camera. It is useful to equip it with a motor drive. Suitable brand names of 35mm SLR cameras include Canon, Contax, Leicaflex, Minolta, Nikon, Olympus, Pentax. Dozens of other SLR brands will also be suited to this work and they are too numerous to detail here, but the photographer searching for a new camera should visit several suppliers and choose the camera which is most comfortable to handle and is equipped with the best lenses affordable.

This is an ideal 35mm camera to use for nude photography. The Contax is fully automated, motor driven and also manual when desired. Fitted as here, with a Zeiss zoom lens covering a range from 80mm to 200mm, continuous selection can be made of an image at varying scale. A support lens of fixed focal length is a good idea, in this case a superb Zeiss Macro-Planar lens of 60mm focal length. With this, close-up textures of the body may be photographed with extreme resolution.

My own personal choice is the Contax RX equipped with a Zeiss Macro-Planar 2.8 60mm lens and a Zeiss Vario-Sonnar 4.5 zoom lens covering 80-200mm focal lengths. This is a wonderfully refined yet very robust camera platform produced by an excellent combination of German lenses and Japanese electronics and made by Kyocera - Yashica of Japan. The camera is fully featured, motor driven with an integral centre weighted exposure metre plus a spot meter option. Also this totally automated camera can be operated in manual mode.

Nude photography tends to depend on very precise control of lighting, often by the use of small areas of sharp rim lights and accent lights falling on the body and the use to some degree of back lighting. In these circumstances, it is not wise to trust to the 'through the lens' (TTL) metering systems of most

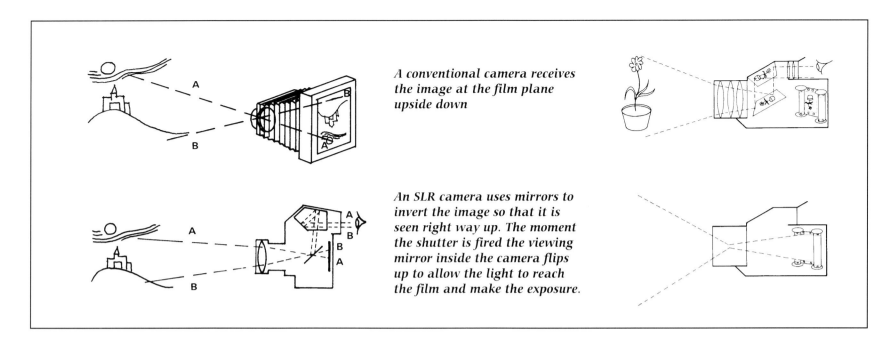

A conventional camera receives the image at the film plane upside down

An SLR camera uses mirrors to invert the image so that it is seen right way up. The moment the shutter is fired the viewing mirror inside the camera flips up to allow the light to reach the film and make the exposure.

automatic cameras unless they are as sophisticated as the Contax RX. Even on memory mode with ordinary automated cameras, many inaccuracies can creep in and it is much wiser to rely on a separate hand-held meter. An auto-flash meter is an excellent choice, being most effective in measuring flash, daylight, tungsten or a combination of needs. For very accurate measurement of skin tones under daylight or tungsten conditions, a spot meter with an angle of 1° may be useful.

The very nature of nude photography often includes a primary interest in texture, contour and body structure and these attributes sometimes become the sole reason for making the picture. Where this occurs a camera larger than 35mm will often be needed. When working with live models, where considerable direction must be given, the photographer has to snapshoot to some degree, so fast, easily focused 6 x 6cm ($2\frac{1}{2}$ x $2\frac{1}{2}$in) or 6 x 7cm ($2\frac{1}{2}$ x $2\frac{3}{4}$in) cameras will be found to be ideal. If these also have a Polaroid capability so much the better. This family of cameras would include Bronica, Mamiya, Hasselblad and Pentax which have formats between 6 x 4.5cm, 6 x 6cm and 6 x 7cm, all of them using 120 film.

In this film format, a wide range of emulsion types exists giving the photographer a choice which is possibly better than in any other format. The 6 x 6cm lens systems will include a normal 80mm lens, although this will distort slightly on head and torso close-ups and a 105mm lens with extension tubes to permit close working where skin texture is vital.

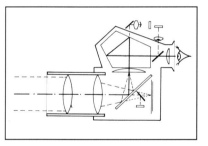

A diagram of the internal mirrors, prisms and lenses in a conventional SLR. This arrangement allows the photographer to see the subject until a fraction of a second before recording it on film. When photographing the nude this is the ideal camera to use.

If only one lens is to be used, ideally it would be about 150mm in focal length. For the 6 x 7cm format a 90mm lens is normal and a 180mm as a longer focal length would be ideal. It would be essential to use a good lens hood, preferably of the sliding compendium type, to reduce the chance of flare or desaturation.

Of the other camera types, the only other serious possibility is the big view camera, either 9 x 12cm (4 x 5in), 13 x 18cm (5 x 7in), and 18 x 24cm (7 x 10in), all used on a suitably stable tripod. Of course, such camera systems, using large format sheet film deliver superlative texture and optical results and there are many famous photographers who have used them with magical effect. The nudes of Edward Weston, Ruth Bernhard, Bill Brandt, Irving Penn, Richard Avedon, should all be studied to see where these large cameras have been used to contribute spectacularly to the main collection of work.

The view camera cannot be operated at great speed and this requires a considerable level of photographic skill and extra

Serious photographers will often need to work on a tripod, which must be equipped with a pan & tilt head such as this. They are expensive but it is advisable to buy the best affordable from reputable manufacturers such as Gitzo, Manfrotto or Quickset.

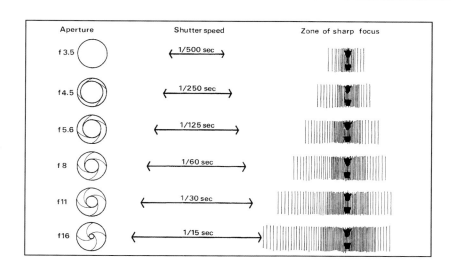

Understanding depth of field is important for all photographers. For any given exposure to be kept constant as the lens is stopped down, the shutter must be slowed to allow more light to reach the film. Slow shutter speeds allow the movement of subject or camera to affect the image. Stopping down the lens (going to higher numbers), reduces light but increases depth of field which extends the band of sharp focus behind and in front of the subject.

patience from the model before good results are achieved. Also when using expensive sheet film it is not possible to use a great deal of material on repeated changes of camera angle or body positions, so the photographer must think most carefully before making an exposure and be very confident in what he wishes the model to do. Obviously this deepens the concentration of the photographer and the model and sharpens the concept of the picture considerably.

Should a photographer decide to confine his work to the art and exhibition fields of nude photography, I would suggest making a beginning with such a camera, preferably using daylight as a source of illumination. The discipline needed for this approach is formidable, but results can be superb. It will take infinitely longer to acquire the polished techniques so essential for this work, but by using a large format from the start the photographer will invest the work with much more optical and aesthetic meaning. The disciplines acquired from using these large format cameras in live situations also will be found invaluable if and when the photographer begins to work with smaller formats in volatile situations.

A view camera needs a heavy tripod, preferably with a geared centre post, such as those made by Gitzo or Manfrotto of Europe or Quickset of the USA, also a large and effective universal joint to connect camera to tripod, a compendium lens hood which takes gelatin filters and at least six double-film holders with which to load the sheet film. Only one lens is likely to be needed and that would ideally be an apochromatic type (fully corrected for all colours) and for a 9 x 12cm (4 x 5in) format, be of 150mm focal length. For a format of 13 x 18 cm (5 x 7in) a lens of 210mm is suitable and for 18 x 24 cm (7 x 10in) cameras a focal length of 360–450mm would be ideal.

Using such cameras does require basic training and this could be obtained from any willing professional photographer in a few concentrated hours of practical demonstration or the reader could obtain clear and practical information from a short course at an advanced photo school.

It has now become commonplace for most professional photographers to check final lighting set-ups and exposures by the use of Polaroid and this is to be highly recommended wherever possible when working with the nude. Black and white Polaroid tends to be more accurate for estimating lighting values and if the original camera film stock is chosen with a speed closely matching the ISO speed of the Polaroid film, black and white Polaroid is far more accurate in assessing both colour and black and white exposures.

However, such is the nature of nude photography in matters of security and privacy, Polaroid is often used for its own sake for the final camera image. Each Polaroid is unique as an image and in colour only the ideal images need be kept. Very beautiful results can be obtained with black and white Polaroid materials and in available light conditions there is almost no film to match the 3000 ISO type for speed and quality.

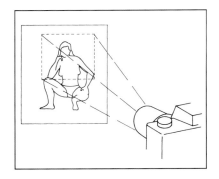

Using a telephoto lens allows the photographer to select areas of the body from a remote distance and be a less intrusive presence in the session. Remember however, that long lenses will add apparent weight to a figure.

When working with 9 x 12cm (4 x 5in) Polaroid, my preference is to use a Speed Graphic camera fitted with a Polaroid film back, and loaded with Type 55 (P/N) or Polapan Pro 100. This is a rangefinder press camera from the 1940-50 era and provides superb definition when fitted with a 135 Ektar lens. It is very easy to use with live models either in the studio or on location and with Polaroid sheet film there is an inexhaustible supply of film in either colour or black & white.

FILM

All photography of the nude should be accompanied by a flawless technique, whether working in colour or in black and white, as anything less than outstanding competence in lighting and processing can often present an ugly and abject rendering of nakedness instead of the highly motivated aesthetic pictorial which the good nude photograph must become.

Considerable help and study may be needed in order to acquire these skills, but certain priorities will be essential for this particular subject matter. Lighting is discussed in detail later in this book but in finding a suitable film and developer combination, the serious photographer will want to experiment before settling on a routine.

When using either 35mm or 120mm formats, the photographer should become familiar with slow film (Agfa APX 25- ISO) and medium speed film (Agfa APX100- ISO) and a fast film (Agfa APX400- ISO) all black and white film for professionals. Agfaortho 25 Professional is a film without red sensitivity and can be processed to give very creamy skin tones from which blemishes tend to disappear. Choices for colour film range from Kodachrome 25 ISO 35mm (a superb film), to the Agfachrome Professional RSX films with speeds of 50, 100, or 200 ISO. Agfa films have been used throughout this book.

Changing the speed of the film will create two immediately apparent effects: graininess increases as film speed increases;

contrast increases as film speed gets slower. This is true both of colour and monochrome emulsions. In black and white, the film developer will also have considerable impact particularly in the matter of edge sharpness in the image (acutance) and also contrast being enhanced or otherwise by the choice of developer and its dilution and temperature.

Because of the nature of the subject and because it is sometimes a condition of models who value privacy and control over the results of a nude session, it is almost essential that the photographer himself processes all films. This avoids any problems with commercial processing houses who often have strict limits to what they will process when the subject is the nude. Should it be necessary to use commercial processing, it is preferable to pay the slightly extra charge and send the work to

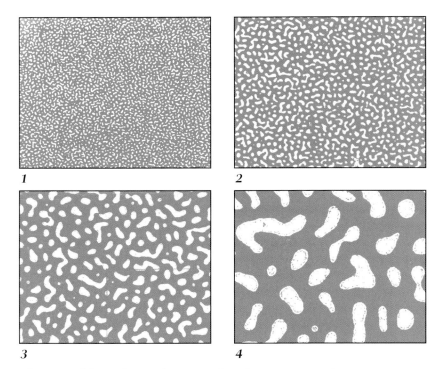

Photographic grain can be a creative element or a nuisance. The greater the film speed the coarser the grain. Slower films have no visible grain when properly processed and produce high resolution negatives. In the diagram above 1 is an example of very fine grain film ISO 25-50; 2 represents a film rated at 100 ISO; 3 suggests a film rated at double that speed, 200 ISO; 4 is a representation of 400 ISO when pushed one stop to a film rating of 800 ISO. The diagrams refer to black and white films and are greatly magnified.

a good custom laboratory such as used by professional photographers, where very different standards are exercised in respect of such subjects. In the case of film processed only by the manufacturer it may be wise to accompany such film with a short letter explaining the nature of the subject.

Serious work with the nude would never be subject to censorship but any hint of obscenity in the pictorial matter submitted for processing could lead to confiscation. Each country and society has its own strict legal requirements in this matter by which film processors must abide and it is a far simpler solution to learn the easy steps of self-processing and avoid those films which cannot be used in this way.

If professional photography is your business, of course, there would be no inhibiting problems and self-processing is generally not an option. Kodachrome 25 is an exception and is always processed by Kodak or a few licencees. It is possibly the finest colour film available and may very well be a suitable standard on which the whole technique of nude photography could be based. When sending films to Kodak for processing which contain nude pictures, it is advisable to include a note of explanation to the lab manager.

PROCESSING

In black and white processing elementary techniques should be learned by starting work with a medium speed film of 100- ISO and a basic developer such as Kodak D76, Ilford ID11 or Agfa Rodinal. Follow the manufacturer's instructions and use the standard working strength and normal rated film speed. Bracket the exposures in sets of three: one under-exposed, one normally exposed and one over-exposed. Process strictly by time and temperature using a good thermometer, accurate to plus or minus half a degree and a dark room timer calibrated in seconds and minutes. Note these developing times in a dark room log book and let it become routine to so list every change of processing or film, with a commentary on the results.

After some experiment with the above, the photographer may again begin testing, using the same developer but diluted (at least 1:1 in the case of D76). Over-expose the film by 20-25 per cent and reduce development by 30-40 per cent, again working most strictly to time and temperature. Note the results in the log book and inspect the dried negatives with a good magnifier. It will be found that on comparison with the first set of negatives, the new test will show sharp edges, decreased grain in the shadow detail, together with lower contrast.

HINTS ON DEVELOPING

Step 1: Be careful and precise in measuring liquids.

Step 2: Bring temperatures exactly to those recommended by manufacturers.

Step 3: In total darkness cut an end section from the film and process it as a test. Reserve the remainder of the film in a light proof box.

Step 4: If the clip test is satisfactory, process the balance of film with any modifications thought to be desirable.

Step 5: Always time processing exactly with a professional timer.

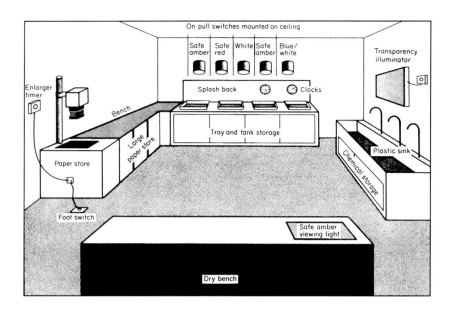

A typical layout for a darkroom

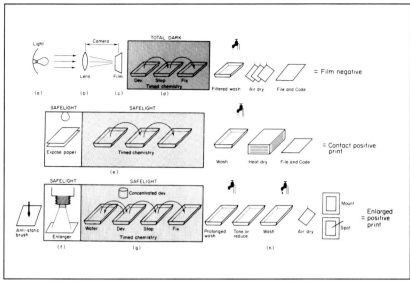

A flow diagram of the wet process steps needed in conventional photography.

The practical results of achieving these attributes in the black and white negative will be to obtain a startling improvement in the rendering of flesh textures in the final print and this is a very desirable point of departure for any illustration of the nude figure.

Tests with negative processing can be further expanded by tests on printing paper and in each case it would be wise to carry out parallel tests against a black background, a white background and a daylight environment. When the figure is to be lit by tungsten light only it may be necessary to revise the listed ISO speed downward (slower than normal) and increase development by 15 per cent. Again tests will be needed.

After establishing a considerable routine with a medium speed film and a preferred developer, the photographer should explore the slower films (more contrast, less graininess) and the very fast films where pictorial use is deliberately made of the grain structure and where lower contrast in film emulsion can offset harsh existing lighting conditions, such as may be found in normal interiors which are not given any augmented light by use of photographic floodlights or flash.

An exploration of other developers, particularly the compensating type such as Kodak D-25, Paterson Acuspecial, dilute Rodinal, 2-bath Emofin from Tetenal, PMK Pyro developer or any panthermic developer, will be found of great interest.

Most professional suppliers will have a range of developers and in Britain, Silverprint Ltd, (website address: http//www.silverprint.co.uk) is a good place to start.

Fine grain developers which deliver improved edge sharpness will allow greater enlargements particularly from the smaller film formats. Formulae could include D-25 diluted 1:2, Edwal Super 20, Rodinal (Agfa) diluted to 1:50, Ethol UFG diluted 1:3 and Paterson Acutol. These should be coupled with fine grain film for maximum effect.

Where grain is wanted for its own sake (and it is particularly beautiful where large expanses of neutral grey areas of tone also appear in the image), a very fast film is best, slightly under-exposed and over-developed. Developers suitable for these effects include Kodak DK50, D-76, diluted 1:20 or Agfa Rodinal diluted 1:25. On all tests follow the manufacturer's instructions, then institute your own test procedures compare the results carefully in the dark room log book and keep a detailed record and commentary.

All processed negatives should be washed thoroughly and given a final rinse in a suitable wetting agent such as Kodak Photoflo or Paterson Acuwet. This will help films to dry without water marking. Because of the inherent delicacy of tone in any photograph of the nude, every opportunity must be taken to acquire most perfect negatives, totally without surface abrasion

CALIBRATION TEST FOR B&W NEGATIVE PROCESSING

Every time you are faced with an unfamiliar film stock, a new developer type or both, it may be advisable to calibrate the new specifications with your own processing techniques. Unless you do this before starting an expensive photographic session it may not be possible to produce the desired quality of final print.

METHOD

Make up a test card of grey tones as indicated. It should consist of black at one end of the scale and white at the other, with 9 graduated steps of grey from dark to light. This 'greyscale' should be about 50 cm long and mounted on a card support. Ask some one to hold this in front of the camera, together with a white card with exposure and development information. Light the person with a side left key light and no fill. The best camera to use on this test is a 4x5 sheet film studio type, on a tripod. Processing should be strictly to time and temperature as per developer recommendations.

1) **THREE NEGATIVES SHOULD BE GIVEN A NORMAL METER-MEASURED EXPOSURE.**
2) **THREE NEGATIVES ARE GIVEN 30% OVER EXPOSURE.**
3) **THREE NEGATIVES ARE GIVEN 50% UNDER EXPOSURE.**

Develop each set of 3 negatives individually – one at normal development, one at 30% under development and one at 50% over development. This will produce nine negatives in total and the scale opposite indicates the probable tones that will result. Notice how some dark areas are lost and some light tones fail to separate.

Notes relating from printing out these negatives with normal processing.
a) Gives good average tones
b) Causes darks to clog, but separates highlights
c) Gives better separation in darks, but highlights begin blocking up
d) Weak dark tones, low contrast
e) Low contrast, low density
f) Improved rendering of scale, slightly lower contrast. Excellent printing negative.
g) Low contrast in shadows, highlights blocking up
h) Extends printing scale with good separation, but shadow detail may be lost
i) Low contrast condensed scale of tones into mid tones. Effective for making high key images

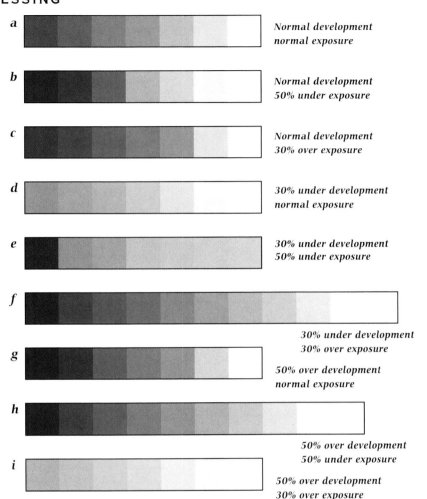

a — Normal development / normal exposure
b — Normal development / 50% under exposure
c — Normal development / 30% over exposure
d — 30% under development / normal exposure
e — 30% under development / 50% under exposure
f — 30% under development / 30% over exposure
g — 50% over development / normal exposure
h — 50% over development / 50% under exposure
i — 50% over development / 30% over exposure

or marks. On an otherwise perfect body contour with correct texture, a single water droplet drying badly can produce a scar effect which often means the negative is useless.

Provided the final rinse bath contains wetting agent of the right dilution and a very soft photographic sponge or chamois leather is used to remove excess water before hanging the film in the drying cupboard, these problems should be avoided, particularly with black and white film.

Dried negatives should be encased in the clear proofing type film envelopes which permit contact proofs to be made without removal of the negatives. This will mean all handling, searching, proofing, editing and frame notation can be made with negatives fully protected.

TEMPERATURE CONVERSION

Equation: $F = \frac{9}{5}(C) + 32$ **Practical:** F= Celsius x 1.8, then +32.
$C = \frac{5}{9}(F-32)$ C=Fahrenheit -32 then divide by 1.8

Celsius	–18°	–10		0	10	20	30	40
Fahrenheit	0°	10	20	32 40	50	60 70	80	90 100 110

An extended contemplation of the processed image is needed when working with the nude subject as the body shape interacts to a considerable degree with the frame format and this means that after contact proofs have been searched and edited of bad

DIFFUSION ENLARGER

CONDENSER ENLARGER

Condensing Lenses

Negative Carrier

Diffusion Glass

Multi directional Light

Mono directional Light

Softer Image — Focus Plane — Harder Image

On the left of the diagram is a diffusion enlarger. This produces a softer light and lowers print contrast and minimises any scratches on the negative. On the right a condenser

enlarger is shown. This enlarger gives higher contrast for prints, requires perfectly clean negatives, but is the expert's choice for making repro or fine art prints.

PROOFING

Step 1: Put dry negatives into clear plastic polyethylene archival film sleeves.

Step 2: Clean a sheet of heavy plate glass large enough to cover negatives.

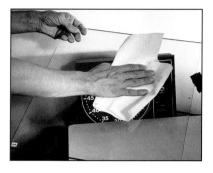

Step 3: Put negatives on photo paper (in safelight) and trap these with the glass sheet. Expose under the enlarger using a precise timer.

SETTING UP THE ENLARGER

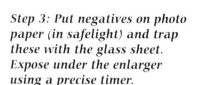

After the enlarger has been installed correctly, occasionally all levels should be checked with a small spirit level.

Before making a print, dust must be blown from the negative before insertion into the enlarger. Use a pressure can of air.

work, likely negatives should be printed up to 13 x 18cm (7 x 5in) size, to allow cropping to be marked up carefully for the final print. This is called the work print system of evaluation and is essential for this type of subject, and many models withhold publishing consent until they have seen these enlargements of the image.

The work print should be made on a medium contrast, resin-coated enlarging paper which dries very rapidly, using the entire negative area to make the print. Then cropping 'L's' are made of black card and the final composition is defined by tracing the masked-out border with a film marking pen, such as the Stabilo Overhead Projection Marker, or by using a wax pencil.

Only after this stage has been reached would the serious photographer make the final reproduction or exhibition print. Reproduction prints could be made also on RC (resin coated) paper as these dry quickly and need not be permanent but, for the finest prints with the greatest nuances of tone and certainly for all exhibition prints, RC paper must not be used.

Agfa, Ilford, Kodak and Kentmere make excellent fibre-based papers which, when processed correctly, have totally archival

Examine the contact sheet with care and mark your selection.

MAKING THE WORK PRINT

Step 1: Remove the selected negative from its sleeve, clean and dust it.

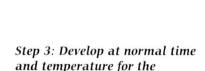

Step 2: Use a grain magnifier to get the negative absolutely sharp on the enlarger.

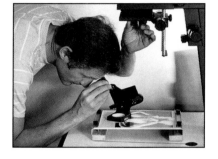

Step 3: Develop at normal time and temperature for the chemistry and paper. Time it.

Make the work print and mark possible cropping.

life, which at the time of writing, is certainly not true of RC papers. However, fibre-based papers are more difficult to dry and take longer to wash and this must be allowed for.

For quality exhibition prints of the nude an excellent fibre-based paper with a high silver content is Kentmere Art Classic, a specialist black and white enlarging paper marketed by Kentmere Ltd, Staveley, Kendal, Cumbria LA8 9PB, United Kingdom and giving deep lustrous blacks, long scale and creamy highlights. Other excellent fibre-based enlarging papers are made by Ilford: the superb Ilfobrom Galerie FB, in a matt surface and their warm tone variable contrast MGFB Warmtone.

It should be noted that most prints for reproduction will require a slightly higher contrast than those for exhibition, and this is especially true where images are to be reproduced in magazines with poor quality paper and a high speed print run. Even with higher contrast, adequate shadow detail must be present where needed and, in most cases, over-emphasised. This can sometimes

be achieved in the dark room, but may also require augmented fill light in the original take. Reproduction prints should be on glossy paper with a 1cm ($^3/_8$in) border of white around the image. The photographer's name and address and copyright details should be stamped on the back of each print. Prints must be unmounted and approximately 18 x 24cm (8 x 10in) unless otherwise indicated by the editorial staff who have requested the picture.

When working editorially with colour material, most use can be made of reversal or transparency film. There tends to be a high wastage of pictures from nude photographic work and editing is cheaper, faster and more critical if it is done from transparency material (reversal film), rather than from colour negative films. Excellent prints from reversal film may easily be made by using print material such as Agfachrome 63 professional paper.

If archival fine art prints are required, Ilfochrome Classic CLM1K, supplied by Ilford Limited, is the best print material for

MAKING THE FINAL PRINT

Step 1: Gently but thoroughly clean the front of the negative with film cleaner. Do not clean the emulsion side. Dust both sides of the film with an anti-static device and use canned air.

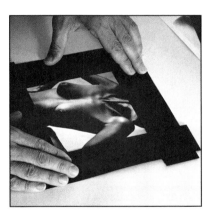

Step 2: Frame the image carefully on the enlarging easel, use a grain magnifier to get it perfectly sharp. Expose and process, timing every step precisely.

Step 3: When the print is dry, check cropping again and if intended for reproduction, tape a tissue overlay to the print, with the cropped area clearly marked.

Make a further workprint from a selected cropping.

printing from transparencies and has an infinitely long dark life. Under controlled exhibition lighting, protected by UV lamination and mounted on aluminium, the life expectancy without colour shifts is probably over 30 years, up to possibly 100 years or more.

PRODUCTION NOTES FOR THIS BOOK

As a matter of practical interest, this book was produced using a wide range of equipment and film. Cameras included: Rollei SLX; Hasselblad 6x6; Makina 6x7; Nikon 35mm; Contax RX 35mm camera, fitted with Zeiss lenses.

For black and white medium format film, most work was standardised on Agfa materials. In 120 formats, 400 Agfapan APX Professional film was used. In 35mm format, a wider range of emulsions was chosen, including Agfapan APX 25, Ilford Pan-F,

50 ISO, and the slow 25 ISO speed Agfa Ortho for special effects. Development was in Agfa Rodinal, Kodak D-76, Paterson Accutol or a custom made Windisch compensating developer.

Most of the colour images were made on Agfachrome RSX 100 reversal film with an ISO speed of 100. This film proved to be exceptional for correct colour rendering of skin tones. Dupes to 5 x 4in format were made on the excellent Agfachrome Duplicating film.

Work prints and final reproduction prints were made on Ilford Multigrade IV RC Deluxe, a full range, glossy resin-coated paper, but exhibition prints or those for public relations purposes were made on Ilford Galerie FB paper or Kentmere Art Classic, both of which have a high silver content, are fibre based and can be archivally processed to fine art standards.

Make an exhibition print to the final size.

CHAPTER THREE

The Full Colour Nude

Only comparatively recently has colour photography reached a state of sufficient reliability to be considered of value to the serious photographer of the nude. The painter has always known that this subject, above all, requires absolute control of colour so that visual concepts may be defined with the necessary precision.

The colour of the human body is one of the first visual clues to be assessed by any beholder of an image of the nude and this of course relates to our assessment of the health of ourselves and strangers, in real life. Chalky white skin could indicate pallor or sickness, reddish skin the first signs of fever, golden brown the desirable flush of sun-drenched vitality and so on.

But these colours could indicate other things. A creamy pale skin could indicate delicacy and femininity, a ruddy glow could suggest robust health and pastoral themes, blue could suggest, not the frozen mystique of death, but the elusive and elliptical ambiguity of latent emotion.

Now that it is technically so easy, colour photography often becomes amazingly trite and, it seems, never so banal as when it is applied to the nude figure. Our little memories of reality, our celebrations, our holidays and family events are, of course, best perceived in full colour and if this is often a little less than faithful to actual life experience, it is of no great consequence; but apply this careless standard to a carefully executed photograph of the nude and the results may be disastrous. There are good reasons for any deviation from truly natural colour in a photograph and once these are known, and steps are taken to control any technical problems, precise and predictable colour can be produced by the photographer with just as much certainty as the painter.

COLOUR FILM

Manufacturers of colour film have today reached an extraordinary level of quality compared to that only 20 years ago, but the assessment of colour is subjective and varies from person to person to a considerable degree. It is important therefore, to experiment with what is available on the market, to test various selections of film, and choose one or two types which are personally pleasing.

Testing must include pictures of landscape, a colour swatch of pure red, yellow, blue, green, white and black and a series of pictures of people to assess flesh tone. Flesh tone is the most difficult colour mix for the manufacturers to produce on film, because it is so easily understood by the customer and is subject to such intense emotional evaluation, most of which is unconscious. Agfa, Fuji and Kodak all make professional films of varying speeds and colour balance.

Having selected suitable film, the rules of the professional photographer who must have dependable and exact colour results at all times, now apply. Buy film direct from the manufacturer if possible, rather than a local stockist, or buy from a reputable photographic dealer who has a quick turnover of stock and who keeps all colour film under refrigeration.

Heat and humidity cause immediate changes in even fresh film, and film which has sat on a sunny shelf, for even one week, must be suspect. Once bought, keep the film unopened for as long as possible and always in cool or refrigerated storage. Very long term storage is best in a deep freeze, but this must only be for completely sealed packages. Do not deep freeze any opened rolls and allow 2-3 hours for deep frozen film to warm up.

Warm up times for photographic material held in cold storage

Film	From a Refrigerator 10°C (50°F)	From a Deep freeze -18°C (0°F)	Paper	From a Refrigerator 10°C (50°F)	From a Deep freeze -18°C (0°F)
135mm cassettes	1 hour	2 hours	100 sheet box 20x25cm (8x10in)	2 hours	4 hours
135mm bulk roll	3 hours	5 hours			
120 roll	1 hour	2 hours	50 sheet box 40x50cm (16x20in)	2 hours	3 hours
Polaroid s x 70	1 hours	2 hour			
Polaroid other packs	1 hour	2 hours	50 metre roll, any width	4 hours	10 hours
25 sheet box large-format film	1 hour	2 hours			
50 sheet box large-format film	2 hours	3 hours	Lay all packages out individually, with some space between each, while thawing takes place.		

On location or vacation keep loaded cameras out of the sun as much as possible, out of glove compartments in the car, or away from room heaters. Keeping film fresh and cool are perhaps the two most vital needs in making good colour photographs. The camera will offer another variable. Lenses will alter colour most noticeably - some tend to make pictures warmer, others cooler. Tests will indicate this and especially if the same film type is run through two different cameras or photographs are taken with different lenses on the same camera with the same film.

PROCESSING

All of these preliminaries are simple attempts at setting up a standard of expected performance from a combination of camera, lens and films. Processing is of course particularly important and bargains in this area may be a false economy. For the sake of commercial prudence, amateur film processors will process colour film and print material to an average standard, which may vary considerably from week to week. If this standard is found to be acceptable, the photographer may not yet be critical enough in judgement of colour performance and therefore any elaborate routine for achieving colour balance may be wasted as an exercise until experience and judgement has improved.

However, discerning photographers will generally see a need for precise processing and will either take the material to a professional colour laboratory, where colour material is processed to a much higher standard (and the price is much more than that which the drug store processors charge), or steps will be taken to learn how to process colour in the photographer's own dark room. One exception to the averaging performance of bulk processors is when the film is returned to the manufacturer for processing. Here it will be given optimum treatment, particularly if it is reversal or transparency film such as Kodachrome.

Self-processing of colour material is now a very simple matter. As in black and white work, care and cleanliness in the dark room are major essentials. Developing a colour film requires precision timing, exact temperature control, and avoidance of cross-contamination in the various solutions. Very little scope exists for creative tinkering with standard procedures as the results are usually far less pleasing than creative processing of black and white.

A routine should be acquired: read the manufacturer's data sheet carefully before beginning any session in the dark room; assemble all equipment; mix solutions with absolute accuracy adjust temperatures of solutions and the room itself, so that the processing is carried out within a plus or minus half a degree of correct solution temperature; time all processing to the second, or split second, using a large electric timer with luminous numbers; rinse hands in running water after touching a solution and be fanatical with cleanliness in all procedures.

ENLARGING

With the simple precautions suggested above, excellent and consistently repeatable results will soon be obtained. Colour enlarging is also a matter of clinically clean routines, attention to the manufacturer's data sheets, and very accurate time and temperature controls of each step. A colour enlarger needs a facility for interposing printing filters into the light beam and this is an easy task if the enlarger is equipped with a bank of rotating filters in the lamp house itself. Colour printing (cp) filters are available in the photographic primaries of magenta (pinkish-red), cyan (blue) and yellow, in density ranges from 0.05 to 200.

Suitable enlargers for colour printing include Leitz, Durst, Omega, Besseler and Berkey, all of whom make both professional and amateur equipment of the highest standard. Lenses should be colour corrected and be the best affordable. These could include brand names such as Schneider, Rodenstock or Nikkor and must be flat field, apochromatic lenses specially made for enlarging. Do not use camera lenses in the enlarger.

By the use of these filters with one or two primaries (never use three primaries as these mixed together produce neutral density and increase exposures without adding any useful changes in colour filtration), print colour may be changed subtly or dramatically. This is basically the only difference when comparing colour enlarging with black and white. For making colour prints from transparencies I usually specify Agfachrome 63 Reversal Paper.

One extra tool, which may be found helpful by those who print colour enlargements of the nude, is a set of 'dodgers' made from CP filter material. Dodging in enlarging (see diagram), is a matter of holding back areas of the print by placing a small wand with a black disc attached to it in the enlarger light beam during exposure. This casts a shadow in any selected area, reducing the exposure and so darkening the area.

If a CP filter is used instead of the black disc, the area will be shadowed slightly, but colour will be changed considerably. This means that any areas of the nude can be selectively altered in

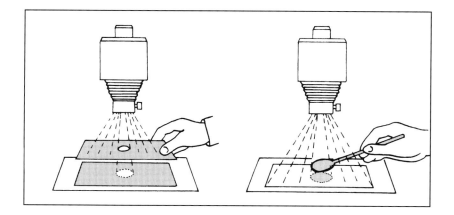

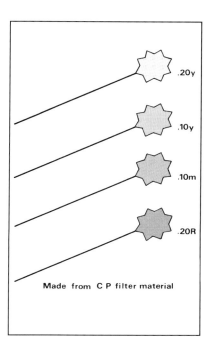

Colour enlarging may require the simple density controls of dodging (on the right of the diagram), or burning in, pictured on the left. By moving a thin wire wand fitted with a coin sized opaque disk, in the enlarger beam, its cast shadow reduces the density in that area. Burning in, however has the opposite effect: a large black card with a hole in the centre is used in the enlarger beam to direct more of the exposing light to selected areas of the print. The hole must have a serrated edge so that the extra light is applied with a soft transition at the edges.

If the wand is fitted with discs made from Colour Print filter material, wherever it is held in the enlarger beam it will cast a colour balancing shadow which only effects the area over which it is held. Selected areas of the print can be improved dramatically with this method.

colour balance, shadows may be warmed or cooled, or the background can be given a different colour balance to the main subject. These delicate shifts of colour are most useful for those who wish to pay critical attention to final prints, particularly if an exhibition print is being made.

For those who require archival quality in colour prints made from transparencies, but who do not wish to explore the esoteric processes of carbro or dye transfer, Ilfochrome Classic is bound to be of interest. This is marketed worldwide by Ilford Limited of the UK, and made by Ciba-Geigy of Switzerland. This print material has been improved over the years. Once thought to be excessively contrasty and unsuitable for delicate subjects, the CLM1K emulsion is of medium contrast and will give excellent results, particularly of flesh tones.

By choosing an Ilford polyester film base rather than a paper based RC alternative, very long exhibition life (probably in excess of 50 years) is achievable. Keeping the print mostly in the dark and in low humidities and temperatures could extend the life to hundreds of years. Naturally such life spans for colour prints are only possible if processing is perfectly performed according to Ilford's recommendations and the print is never displayed for lengthy periods in the sun or in light levels which are excessive, or those which contain large amounts of ultraviolet energy.

Neg/Pos vs Reversal Films

There is probably no real theoretical or technical advantage one way or the other in choosing between colour negative film or transparency (reversal film) when a standard material is being sought for photography of the nude. But in practice, working with the nude may be easier with transparency material. There is usually considerable wastage in any one roll of such subjects, as editing must be very stringent indeed and it is far easier to decide on discards where the photographer is faced with something close to the real scene.

Subtle changes, particularly flesh tones, are far more easily noticed on transparencies and, of course, only those transparencies need be printed which reach the necessary standards, saving time and money when compared to negative/positive processing which requires the whole roll to be printed before editing can begin.

Because of the conditions under which nude photography may take place, often in under-lit locations or in interiors with insufficient natural light, under-exposure is a constant hazard. Negative colour film does not respond to push-processing, whereby compensation is made during development for under-exposure in the camera by increasing the time of first development of the film. But with transparency film, real gains in film speed are obtained by altered processing. Transparency film has the further benefit of being suitable for Ilfochrome print making and therefore long life colour prints.

FILM TYPES

Manufacturers of colour film generally provide two main categories: that which is used in daylight or with the bluish flash from electronic flash units, or film which must be used in artificial tungsten light such as domestic lighting or photographic floodlighting. Films are usually designated 'daylight' for bluish light and natural light and 'Type B' for use in artificial light.

To help reach standards needed by photographers who try and match their results to the remembered scene, or for those professionals who must be absolutely accurate with colour results, manufacturers indicate both ISO speeds of the film and the colour temperature at which it must be exposed for optimum colour accuracy.

COLOUR TEMPERATURE

Colour temperature is a phenomenon identified by the British physicist, Lord Kelvin, and it is expressed in degrees Kelvin. He indicated that when a black body of, for example, iron, was at ambient temperature, colour was not present, but if such an object was heated to a certain temperature the object not only radiated heat but visible light as well, the colour of the light being yellowish at low temperatures and bluish to white at high temperatures. A precise correlation was possible between the colour of the light emitted and the temperature of the radiating source of energy and so the Kelvin scale was established.

Daylight colour film is balanced to a standard of 5-5500K, if used for normal noon sunlight with a Kelvin rating of 5200, good, accurate colour results are obtained. Afternoon reflected sky light, however, could rise easily to 20,000K, a light far too blue for good colour results, unless compensating filters are used. Tungsten or Type B film is rated for balance at 3200K and this is the precise colour of photographic flood lights if they are equipped with tungsten halogen lamps.

Approximate colour temperature of common light in degrees Kelvin

Fire light	1000°
Candle flame	1500
House lamps	2500-3000
100 watt, tungsten-filament lamp	2850
500 watt, tungsten-filament lamp	3000
500 watt projection lamp	3200
3200° Kelvin floodlamp	3200
White, No. 2 Photo flood, reflector flood	3400
Reflector floods (except R 32)	3400
Warm, white, fluorescent lamp	3500
Foil filled flash lamp	3800
Cool, white fluorescent lamp	4500
White-flame carbon arc	5000
Noon sunlight temperate zone	5200
High-intensity sun arc	5500
Direct sunlight between 10 am to 3 pm (average)	6000
Blue expendable flash lamp	6000
Daylight fluorescent lamp	6500
Sunlight plus light from blue sky at noon	6500
Light from overcast sky	6800-7000
High speed electronic flash tubes	5800-7000
Light from hazy sky	7500
Light from clear blue sky in afternoon	10,000-27,000

Colour Temperature is expressed in kelvin and guides the photographer when mixing light sources or balancing colour filtration. Film is either balanced for 3200 K, exposures being made by tungsten photographic lamps, or 5200-5500 K for exposures to electronic flash or noon sunlight. Interesting effects are possible when film is deliberately exposed to warmer or cooler light sources than the suggested norm.

COLOUR FILTERS

Between these two ideals are many variations and it is often necessary to alter colour balance by the use of colour compensating (CC) filters on the camera lens. The industry standard is the Kodak Wratten cc series of gelatin squares, obtainable in red, green, blue, brown, yellow, cyan, magenta, UV (ultra violet absorption) and ND (neutral density) filters for reducing density without changing colours. They are provided in densities from 0.05 to 0.50 and are used delicately to alter colour balance when needed.

Two strong filters are also used by colour photographers to make large colour balance shifts when artificial light film is used in daylight or vice-versa. To convert Type B film for use in daylight, an 85B (amber) filter is used and one needs to increase exposures by two f stops, while to convert daylight film for use in artificial light or with photographic flood lights, an 80A (bluish) filter, is used and needs exposure increases of one stop.

Corrective filters for colour films

Conversion filters for large shifts in colour temperature

Filter number	Exposure increase	Degrees K	Filter colour
*80A	2	+2300	BLUE
80B	$1^2/_3$	+2100	BLUE
80C	1	+1700	BLUE
80D	$1/_3$	+1300	BLUE
85C	$1/_3$	-1700	AMBER
85	$2/_3$	-2100	AMBER
‡85B	$2/_3$	-2300	AMBER

*converts daylight film for tungsten use
‡converts Type B film for daylight use

Conversion filters for small shifts in colour temperature

82	$1/_3$	+100	PALE BLUE
82A	$1/_3$	+200	PALE BLUE
82B	$2/_3$	+300	PALE BLUE
82C	$2/_3$	+400	PALE BLUE
81	$1/_3$	-100	BROWNISH YELLOW
81A	$1/_3$	-200	BROWNISH YELLOW
81B	$1/_3$	-300	BROWNISH YELLOW
81C	$1/_3$	-400	BROWNISH YELLOW
81D	$2/_3$	-500	BROWNISH YELLOW
81EF	$2/_3$	-650	BROWN

Where cold or bluish light (daylight) is used to expose type B colour film, use the minus filters to balance colour correctly.

Where warm or reddish yellow light (tungsten) is used to expose daylight colour film, use the plus filters to achieve colour balance.

This is a guide table for using CC (colour correcting) filters in plus or minus kelvin ratings to either achieve optimum balance or special effects.

Trial filter packs for exposures to fluorescent light

Tube colour	Daylight film	f stop increase	Tungsten 3200K film	f stop increase
Cold blue	50C+30M	$1^2/_3$	85B+15Y+20M	2
Daylight spectrum	40C+20M or FLD filter	$1^1/_2$	50M+50Y+80B	2
Blue-white	30M	$2/_3$	40M+50Y	$1^1/_2$
White	15C+30M	1	40M+40Y	$1^1/_3$
Warm white	20B+10M	$1/_2$	30M+20Y	1

Note: Table is based on shutter speeds of $^1/_{30}$ second and is for tubes in diffusers. Kodak Wratten cc filters are indicated.

Exposing to indoor situations lit by fluorescents will require special filters if correct film balance is required.

For the photographer of the nude in colour this slightly complex matter of colour temperature, colour balance and colour compensation by the use of cc filters must be understood. It will be found that under certain conditions of light the body takes on an unhealthy bluish tinge or, in other lighting situations, perhaps a garish yellow colour cast and these may easily be changed by filtration.

By using the Kelvin scale shown, it will be seen that the colour temperature of some light sources may be left unfiltered and therefore will affect the film in a biased way. This may be aesthetically undesirable or, conversely, could be excellent for creative effects, or perhaps may be filtered to accord more closely to normal. Many electronic flash units produce a very cold blue light of 6500K or more, and this light is too blue for good skin tones on most colour film. A warming filter must be added to decrease colour temperature. The filter can be on the camera lens or on the flash head itself.

Where light sources are too bright and are preventing the use of wide apertures or slow shutter speeds for special effects, a neutral density filter may be necessary.

Neutral Density Filter Chart and f. Stop Increases

Density	Transmission by factor	Increase in %	f. Stop	
0.10	80.0	1.2	x	$1/_4$
0.20	65.0	1.5	x	$1/_2$
0.301	50.0	2.0	x	
0.40	40.0	2.5	x	$1^1/_3$
0.50	32.0	3.1	x	$1^2/_3$
0.604	25.0	4.0	x	2
0.70	20.0	5.0	x	$2^1/_3$
0.80	16.0	6.2	x	$2^1/_2$
0.91	13.0	7.7	x	3
1.00	10.0	10.0	x	$3^1/_3$
1.20	6.3	15.8	x	4
1.50	3.2	31.2	x	5

COLOUR BALANCING

The photographer working in a studio with colour will have a far easier task in correcting colour balance as the shifts in colour temperature are usually small and once a batch of film is tested, the same filtration may be used for the whole time that that batch is being used. The other way to achieve altered colour balance, but this time subjectively, is to use colour printing (CP) filters over the light source or light-balancing, non-flammable filters.

These alter the light only for each lighting unit so treated, allowing extra control in mixing delicate changes of colour or, if theatrical effects are wanted, dramatic and vivid colour harmonies may be made. Many studio photographers of the

Obtaining perfect colour balance requires patience and discipline. Once a suitable film type has been tested and provided it is kept under optimum storage conditions, exhaustive tests are only needed for first time use.

nude will treat the reflector behind the main key light with gold foil or gold paint and this throws an attractively warm light, but only on the body highlights. Other lights and fill lights remain cooler, therefore promoting an impression of depth.

For the location photographer who uses interiors which are sometimes lit by very cold bluish light from the sky, especially if there are windows facing north, it is advisable to use thin polyester gauze over the entire window to diffuse it softly, but in a champagne colour shade. This material comes in widths up to 3m (10ft) and is very sheer. It is possible to use tea to dye plain white curtains to a warm colour or to use creamy parachute silk. This off white colour will guarantee that the key light from the window will not be too cold.

Further compensation may still be needed, however, on the camera lens, using CC filters. Tests must be made. When the photographer works with natural light outside, the figure will reflect colour from the sky and from its immediate surroundings. A trained eye can identify even subtle shifts of colour and if good skin tone is wanted, concentration will be needed to correct the colour balance.

In shadows, under trees or near buildings, a warming filter of minus 200 to 400K may be all that is needed and will change the close surroundings very little. This would be a brownish filter from the 81 series, probably an 81A. Warm light could also be thrown in from a gold foil reflector. If photography is taking place with overcast skies or in mist, light falling on the body will be exceedingly blue and an 81EF or even an 85B may be needed unless the blue effect is wanted for creative purposes.

If the model is being photographed in the last rays of sunset, the light may be too red, giving the body an unpleasant red flush. Here the 82 series of the light blue filters will be found useful or, for really excessive problems, an 80c correction filter may be necessary, adding about 2000K to the colour of the light reaching the film.

Should the model be in a thickly wooded forest, or near large green shrubs, the body may take on a greenish tinge which would be removed by the CC red filters or 81 brownish-yellow series. These filters are best attached to the camera by slipping them into a compendium lens hood or special box filter hood without cutting the filter squares. Always handle the gelatin filters by the edges or the corners and never use more than two filters at one time if maximum lens performance is important.

The ultra violet filters 1A to 2B, sometimes called skylight filters, are almost indispensable and these should be obtained in glass from a reputable camera or filter manufacturer and left permanently screwed to the front of the lens. Every lens should be given its own filter. This protects the optics from scratches, finger marks, rain or sea spray, and by removing the bluish UV from the light, gives a more natural skin tone to the model without increasing camera exposure.

Assessing results of tests and filtration requires that transparencies are viewed under the correct conditions. Use a black mask slightly larger than the transparency being viewed to obtain the best judgement of densities and colour balance.

POLARISING FILTERS

One other filter is important to colour photographers of the nude: the polariser. This is a filter composed of minute crystals arranged to form a grating which will pass polarised light only, when it is polarised in the same plane as the direction of the grid. As the filter is rotated towards 90 degrees, polarised light is slowly extinguished, until at 90 degrees from the original position no polarised light can pass into the lens, but all other light may do so.

Polarised light is reflected from all shiny surfaces including glass, metal and water and is present in sky light when sunlight is scattered by the atmosphere. Such polarised sky light travels at right angles to the direction of sunlight and, with the judicious use of a rotating polariser, the colour of the sky may change from deep blue to black. Clouds remain white, colours are more deeply saturated but remain true. Rotating polarisers can be used as a variable neutral density filter also.

A practical example of the use of a polariser would be where the model is needed in a pool or just beneath the water but surface reflections prevent good visibility or colour saturation and the body cannot properly be seen. A polariser on the lens will remove the unwanted reflections and any action beneath the water surface may be photographed clearly.

COLOUR SHIFTS WITH LIGHTING

Another possibility in colour photography of the nude is deliberately to throw colour film out of balance with the main key or ambient light, in order to obtain special effects or interesting colour mixes. For example, if Type B film (3200K) is used in a daylight interior situation (6000K) all those areas lit only by daylight will be rendered as striking blue. If the model is then separately lit by a 3200K tungsten halogen floodlight, and the beam is controlled tightly to prevent this warm light spilling into daylight areas, a very dramatic picture will result. Using daylight film and a mixture of electronic flash (5500K) and tungsten light (3200K), any areas lit by tungsten light will turn reddish-brown, while those only affected by flash will be rendered in natural colour.

When deciding on exposures for mixed lighting units, tungsten light is controlled by means of a shutter and aperture combination and is calculated first, while the flash is so placed that the chosen f stop for the tungsten exposure also will give correct exposures for flash. Naturally the shutter speed chosen must not exceed the maximum at which the camera flash synchronisation works.

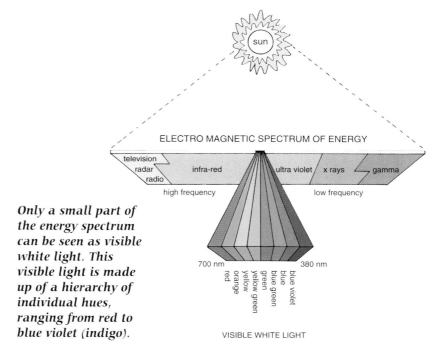

Only a small part of the energy spectrum can be seen as visible white light. This visible light is made up of a hierarchy of individual hues, ranging from red to blue violet (indigo).

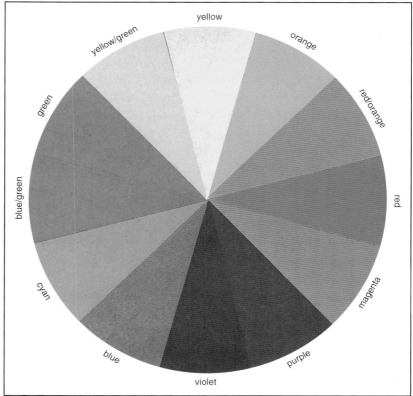

This is an example of a simple colour wheel. With its help, harmonies and colour planning for photograph may be considered beforehand.

SUBJECTIVE COLOUR

Modern colour photography is now very controllable and it should be quite possible to produce any photograph in colour with all the nuances, subtleties or saturation needed to increase depth of communication with the beholder. The saturation of colour and colour contrast are primary elements in colour compositions and fortunately the technology of manufacturers provides us with excellent means of rendering them.

Saturation, of course, can be achieved merely by under-exposing slightly, say one-third or half a stop, or using a polariser on the lens; while colour contrast is a matter of the juxtaposition of hues, used at full saturation to produce the effect desired.

SPREAD OF COLOUR

Spread of colour within the format is also connected with both saturation and contrast, when certain colours which are a significant part of the main subject are repeated and distributed to other parts of the picture. For example, the image of a model wearing a red towel would be very much improved for colour reproduction in magazines or calendars, if small areas of the same colour are to be found elsewhere within the format.

These colours lead the eye away from the main subject, but because recognition of the colour is instant and the area of it is small and exactly matches the main colour in the subject, no decoding of that part of the image is needed, and the eye moves back once more to the main subject. This eye movement creates deeper interest in the visual concept and increases the involvement of the beholder.

COLOUR SYMBOLISM

Colour symbolism may be used in the environment around the subject or it can be attached as a prop to the figure. Some of the more general symbolic meanings for basic colours are:

RED – a positive, advancing colour, masculine and active. Although it is stable within its own area, not expanding laterally into other colours, it is a colour which generates feelings of excitement, vigour and daring, symbolising sensuality, love and consummation. It can also symbolise anarchy, anger, hate, cruelty and disgust.

ORANGE – a passionate, unstable colour signifying confidence, domination and stress. It also symbolises ribaldry and rebellion.

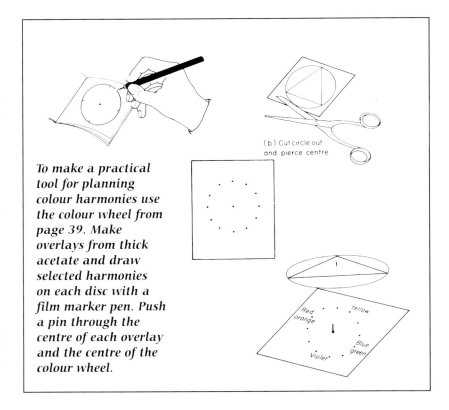

To make a practical tool for planning colour harmonies use the colour wheel from page 39. Make overlays from thick acetate and draw selected harmonies on each disc with a film marker pen. Push a pin through the centre of each overlay and the centre of the colour wheel.

PINK – because it is red diminished by a neutral hue, it represents the gentler side of red symbolism. It easily suggests innocence but can suggest inflexibility and fool-hardiness.

YELLOW – a very exciting, constantly advancing colour, and the most eye-catching of all colours. It can symbolise liberation, wisdom, energy, imagination, but can also suggest tension, instability and scandal.

GREEN – the psychologically stable colour suggesting refuge, naturalness, naiveté, compassion or innocence. It can indicate ambivalence, inactivity or boredom. Light green indicates youth, hope, sympathy and latent energy but these are suggested along with the possibility of weakness and immaturity.

BLUE-GREEN – the colour of turquoise and the most flattering of all colours near the nude body. It advances strongly, particularly among other blues and suggests confidence, femininity and discretion. Also it can symbolise self-indulgent narcissism and inattention.

BLUE – most people's preference above all other colours. It is a receding colour, contracting within its own area and creating spatial planes of depth in the picture. It symbolises devotion, peace, logic, harmony and honourable sexuality. Conversely it can suggest despair, unhappiness and introversion.

PURPLE – this colour signifies hidden power, vanity, exclusivity, royalty, death and anger.

BROWN – suggests wholesome healthy self-sufficiency accompanied by wisdom. It can also indicate avarice, obstinacy and exhaustion.

BLACK – the absence of colour creates memories and fantasies of colours in the past and those yet to come, creating a haunting, majestic air of incompleteness and mystery. Very feminine as a symbol, because of its suggested, suppressed sensuality. This colour can also indicate conflict, horror, lust or malice.

WHITE – a unifying, advancing colour which symbolises fragility, unity and innocence, but also negation and boredom.

GREY – accepts a bias from other colours and be warm or cool. Greys suggest sophisticated femininity, elegance and faith, but also symbolise fear, exhaustion and sadness.

NEUTRALS

Photographers will often need to work with monochromes or greys and these delicate backgrounds near the female nude can create intense introspection on the part of the viewer and therefore amplify the visual concept. These neutrals will usually have a slight bias towards a known colour and harmonies may be built up around sympathetic or contrasting colours once this basic shift from neutral is identified.

Neutrals can act as screens for small areas of bright colour or create effects such as 'after-imaging' when the primary colours are used on grey. The body itself can often be classed as a neutral and this fact can offer the photographer many advantages when building simple colour harmonies.

THE COLOUR WHEEL

Colour harmonies may be constructed by the use of a colour wheel, and the use of overlays which help identify major harmonic themes. Nature often favours the reassurance of analogous harmony, where all the colours in the scheme are taken from the same small segment of the colour wheel. Simple dramatic harmonies can be produced by using a colour scheme which uses small, sharp areas of accents taken from the opposite side of the colour wheel to the model's skin colour.

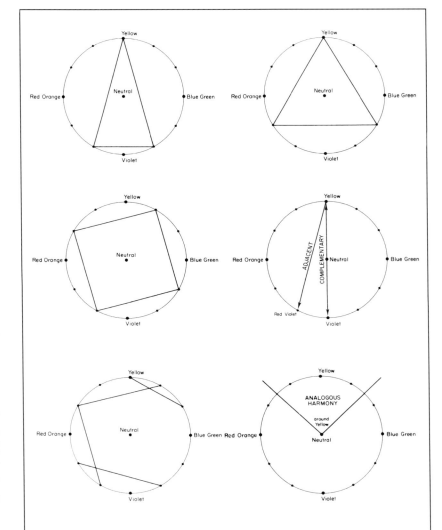

Above is a suggestion for six harmonic plans. Harmonies using adjacents on the wheel, for example reds, oranges and yellows, produce analogous harmonies or tone-on-tone. These are refined and soothing. Harmonies chosen from opposites on the colour wheel use complementary colours, which create vibrant and sometimes harsh colour schemes, which can draw the eye instantly. Balanced harmonies, based on triangles, create strong unequivocable statements, especially if a triadic harmony is built upon an equilateral triangle. When selected colours on the wheel form rhomboids, some of those points can be bright accent colours, others can be analogous, thus forming an interesting and subjective harmonic plan, which is very suitable for an environment for the nude figure.

Simple props and bright colour can be used to create an editorial picture.

If no props are being used by the model on her body but coloured objects are wanted as an environment, it is first wise to identify on the colour wheel the position of the skin colour or the hair if this is to occupy a large area of the image. Then it may be decided which harmonic pattern is to be employed and this can be read off the colours on the wheel. Distribute these colours between background and other objects and a pleasing harmony will result. It is often desirable to surround light areas with dark areas so that the light areas advance to meet the eye. In the case of the nude when it is the main subject and is to occupy the largest and lightest part of the image, this is almost always the wisest plan.

COLOUR DESIGN

The photographer who uses colour must always be aware of this when designing the image. It will help if the aesthetic manipulation of colour within an image is accompanied by excellent photographic technique and a full understanding of the way in which basic image management skills support the added dimension of colour.

The decision to work in colour for nude photography must only be taken if colour will add more valuable information or impact than would be possible using black and white.

CHAPTER FOUR

Lighting Plans

The sun gives light and life to this planet and as far back as the shrouded memories of earliest history, the sun was known as a male god, striding across the heavens with blazing gait. But anyone who has taken time to consider and contemplate the light which falls from this mythical mystery, cannot help but be impressed by the many female qualities to be found in its character.

Light is measurable, an absolute fact, one of the few provable constants to be found among natural phenomena. Light is a law. It is inviolate: however much it is absorbed, refracted, transmitted or turned, it re-constitutes itself and sweeps back to its original speed of 300,000 kilometres per second.

Light has character and mood and its femininity cannot be denied. The fresh caress of golden light at sunrise, streaking out to explore the world with long, raking fingers and gentle urgency. The frank, revealing light of mid-morning and mid-afternoon; the relentless austerity and crisp reality of noon light; the sensual sexuality of the late day, exploring and displaying hidden contours to those who know how to see; the sympathy of the evening light, a mist of rose and blue to recall intimate memories and then the dark sweep of dusk, when the absence of light indicates more hauntingly, its earlier presence.

To the average photographer, light is only one of the major elements in his technique; to the photographer of the nude, light is the sovereign ingredient in his art. There is no better way to begin the study of lighting the figure than to perceive and appraise light as it is created in nature.

The contemplation of light, as it changes moods and activity throughout the day and seasons, can easily be translated in practical terms when the time comes to work with the camera and photographic lighting. It will be seen that the low light, soon after dawn, sweeps across contours and discloses texture and form, the mid morning light also models the forms but with a lighter, more open mood. At noon, the short, sharp shadows are always closely attached to the subject's form and texture, while this light brings an unsentimental veracity to all it encompasses. The evening light, again, is a low contour revealing phenomenon, but with a darker, autumnal mood.

Broad and short lighting are terms for distinctive but basic types of lighting for an individual person.
Step 1: Broad lighting illuminates the side of the body which faces the camera. It reveals both contour and texture and is used often in nude photography.
Step 2: Short lighting falls on the part of the body which faces away from camera. This light separates form from its background and is often used to light profiles.

THE KEY LIGHT

It is helpful for photographers to classify these natural changes in light and develop an understanding of the relationship between the lighting angle and the information it discloses in respect of form, as well as the atmosphere it creates. Consider that the subject lies within a hemisphere at the centre and that a key light can be located laterally around the circle or anywhere on the meridian lines above.

The main or key light, like the sun, dominates the subject in both direction and character and the photographer's key light must always appear to be the only source in the picture.

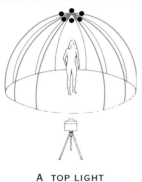

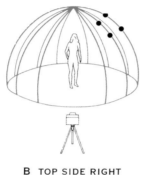

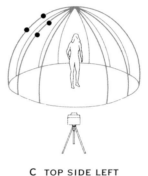

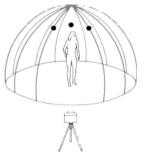

A TOP LIGHT   **B** TOP SIDE RIGHT   **C** TOP SIDE LEFT   **D** TOP FRONT

The lights placed within the imaginary hemisphere can be simplified for photographers of the nude into 12 categories:

A TOP LIGHT	**B** TOP SIDE RIGHT	**C** TOP SIDE LEFT
D TOP FRONT	**E** TOP BACK	**F** SIDE RIGHT
G SIDE LEFT	**H** BACK LIGHT	**I** AXIS LIGHT
J OFF-AXIS BACKGROUND	**K** OFF-AXIS LEFT	**L** OFF-AXIS RIGHT

These are indicated in the diagrams. How they relate to the practical lighting of a figure in the studio is shown in the main diagram. There is a further lighting position used for some theatrical reasons or special effects, where the light is placed below horizon level. This is called a 'grotesque' light, but is not greatly used because it has no counterpart in nature and is especially unsuitable for nude photography.

The key light can be sub-divided into two main categories when lighting a figure: broad lighting, where the side of the body closest to the camera receives the most light, or short lighting, where the side of the body furthest from the camera receives the key light.

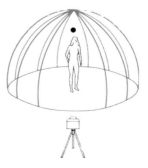

J OFF-AXIS BACKGROUND   **I** AXIS LIGHT

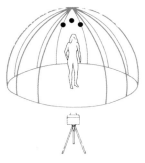

E TOP BACK

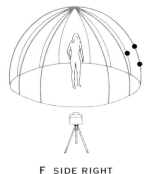

F SIDE RIGHT

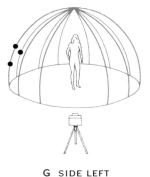

G SIDE LEFT

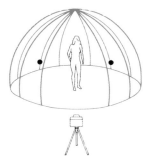

H BACK LIGHT

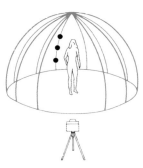

K OFF-AXIS LEFT

L OFF-AXIS RIGHT

LIGHTING SET-UPS WITH A MANNEQUIN

Because model charges are very high, and the tedium of standing naked in front of a camera while the photographer experiments with lighting, can cause even friends embarrassment and boredom, a helpful accessory, as stated earlier, is the display mannequin. These can be obtained from shop window display suppliers, sometimes second hand, and the companies Adel Rootstein Ltd, Shawfield House, Shawfield Street, London, SW3 and Adel Rootstein (USA) Inc, 451 West Broadway, New York City, NY 10012 will rent them out for reasonable charges.

The more expensive articulated dummies which allow the limbs and head to be moved are not particularly useful and a static model will suffice. The cost of the mannequin is soon recovered in the saving of model fees, and in early lighting training it is much easier to observe and photograph ideal lighting plans on an unmoving and uncomplaining subject.

Even when lighting has become more advanced and the photographer proceeds with considerable confidence, it is often a time-saving idea to set up lighting on the stand-in dummy before the real model arrives.

STEP ONE

STEP TWO

STEP THREE

Building a lighting plan using a mannequin.
Step 1: Place an accent light to separate the model from her background
Step 2: Next place the Key light
Step 3: Add a diffuse fill light in a large reflector

LIGHTS & REFLECTORS

Lighting the nude figure in the studio will require equipment which delivers specular light from tight reflectors, or snoots, and broad source lighting which provides a very large reflected light source, soft but with brilliant highlights.

Specular light comes from tungsten halogen spotlights or floodlights, equipped with barn doors to control the fall of light. Such light throws hard shadows, emphasising texture and contour and is particularly interesting when posing the model on dark backgrounds or when rim lighting is needed to outline the body for later use in dark room graphics. This hard-edged light has the character of noon sunlight and it is important to use the effects of the shadows as an integral part of the picture. Such light brings a strong highlight to any part of the body which is oiled or is perspiring and dramatises any action which is evident in the pose.

Specular light can also be delivered by flashlight, either by the small electronic units which are usually camera mounted or by large studio equipment which has its own stands. For accurate placement of lights, flash lighting should have a modelling light, which indicates the fall of light from the reflector and its intensity. The type that has a variable switch over a two-stop range for both modelling light and flash is ideal. These allow great precision in balancing the key light to fill light and in placing accent lights with complete accuracy. They do not, however, recharge as rapidly as the big studio units and therefore may cause some inconvenience.

Those who do not wish to work with tungsten light or the larger flash systems with a modelling light can operate quite successfully with multiple flash units of the small electronic kind. However, considerable practice may be needed before really well lit photographs are taken with these. At least three lamps will be needed for most work, synchronised to the camera with a multiple cord connector, slave cells, or using a provision in the flash unit for plugging in extension units.

The key light should usually be placed off-camera so some degree of modelling can be seen in contours and it will be necessary to have each flash unit on separate stands or

(a)

(b)

(a) This is a reflector with a snoot – a narrow cylinder which directs the light into a small area and lights the subject with a hard direct light. Very useful for accent lights or rim lights.
(b) For large areas of the body and to provide diffuse light for fill lights or to minimise contour or texture, a softbox is used. Usually a metre square, sometimes much larger these have flame-proof translucent foil covering the light source.

A

B

C

D

E

F

Types of light which suggest mood.

(A) An accent light is used to highlight hair or to separate dark forms from dark backgrounds.

(B) A chisel light is so called because it carves out form over a narrow area of the model's body, revealing contours and textures. It is, like the accent light, usually a direct, undiffused light.

(C) This illustrates the effect of adding a diffuse fill light to the set up in (B).

(D) Another way to suggest mood, this time with grotesque lighting, so called because it reaches the body from below the camera level, casting dark shadows upward. It has no counterpart in nature, but is very theatrical, suggesting that the model is lit by stage footlights. Another low key lighting plan.

(E) A very moody low key lighting plan, with only one light used to illuminate both model and background.

(F) This is a moody light with the model on a dark background. Short Lighting is used with an accent light to separate the head and shoulders from the background. This is an example of low key lighting.

lightweight tripods. The use of a guide number to calculate exposure for multiple flash is no more difficult than working with a single camera-mounted flash unit. Some means of bouncing these flash lights into small reflectors such as the Reflectasol or the Soff-Shoulder will be found most useful and where no modelling light is built into the flash unit, this broader spread of light can eliminate many errors of aiming.

Lighting a full length figure will frequently use a light that gives an even illumination of the total head-to-toe area. This can only come from a light source of the same general height and proportion to the body and those photographers who

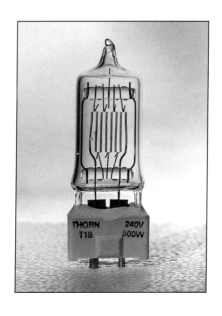

This is a typical tungsten halogen photo lamp.
When re-lamping, use a tissue to hold the lamp. Grease from the skin on the glass envelope will shorten the life of such hot lamps. Use a wire guard over these units as on very rare occasions they have been known to explode.

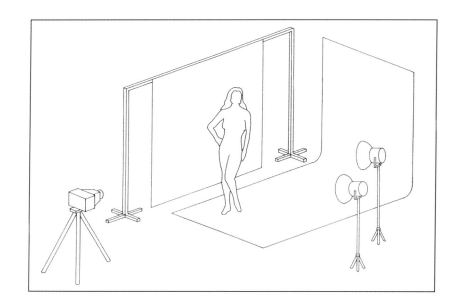

This is a basic lighting arrangement for a complete figure. The model is placed well forward of the background and is lit by a strong side light.

A multi-flash connector – which is an essential.

intend to specialise in pictures of the nude are advised to construct a 2m trench light as shown in the diagram.

This light should be narrow, highly reflective and directional but soft, distributing evenly over its whole length. It should be highly mobile and powerful enough to give low f stops on small cameras using medium speed film in the range of f8, f11 and f16 if it is from a flash unit, or shutter speeds of at least $\frac{1}{60}$ second, if tungsten light is being used. The trench light can contain a flash system, tungsten only, or both. This is not of course powerful enough as a light for some close up work with large format cameras, but these require sophisticated, expensive studio flash units of the professional type.

SILHOUETTES & RIM LIGHTING

Unlike those who photograph conventional subjects, the photographer of the nude may be advised to start with the handling of the back light, as it is applied to the full length figure. If this light is placed precisely along the lens axis and behind the full length model, a silhouette results. Of course, the light must be small enough to be hidden, or holes may be cut in the background to conceal the stand. If the background is light in colour, a good separation will result between the dark form of the model and the ground (background).

From the beginning of time it has been known in art that figure and ground must separate, and the silhouette is the simplest example of that precept. With correct alignment of the light in relation to the model and camera, some edge illumination will also be apparent and a rim light will be obtained. This amplifies

Direct lighting (specular light) without diffusion.

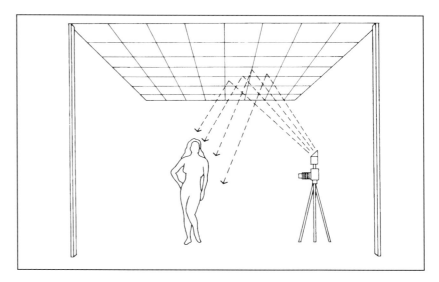

Flash or flood lights can be diffused with a metal scrim. Particularly used to diffuse very hot lights such as tungsten - halogen 500-2000 watt lights.

Flash can be diffused effectively by covering the flash head with half a thickness of 2 ply face tissue.

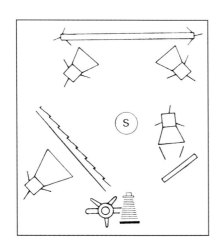

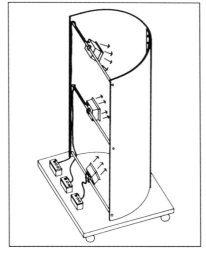

An easy method of diffusing light either with flash or tungsten flood lights, is to bounce the light from a ceiling and open the lens two stops to compensate for the lower light values. If using hot lights,

watch that they do not get close to ceiling tiles or paintwork, and if working in colour, be aware that even slightly off-white shades of painted surfaces will shift colour balance towards that colour.

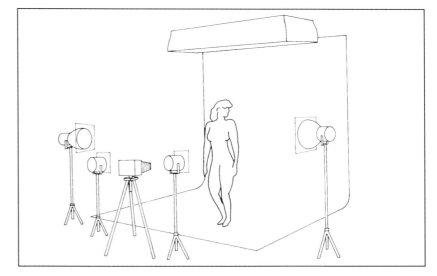

This is a floor plan for diffusing with four lights. S is the subject. Two lights are bounced on to the background. On the right of camera, one light is bounced on to a small reflector and on the left of camera, a large light source is beamed through a large diffusing screen to provide a broad source fill light.

To light the model from head to toe, build a trench light about 2 metres in height. This is made by bending a white painted plywood sheet into a U-shape and tensioning it with wires. When not in use it can be dismantled and stored flat. Three floods or flash lights are beamed into the reflector to provide a soft but directional light.

Making a wraparound light. Where a model must move frequently, highly directional light is not appropriate. A bright overall light is needed from all around the model. This lighting set up is made with a strong and large top

light and two lights on either side of camera. Additionally, a strong side light is positioned both left and right of camera and the model is posed on a white limbo paperfall. All lights are fitted with diffusers.

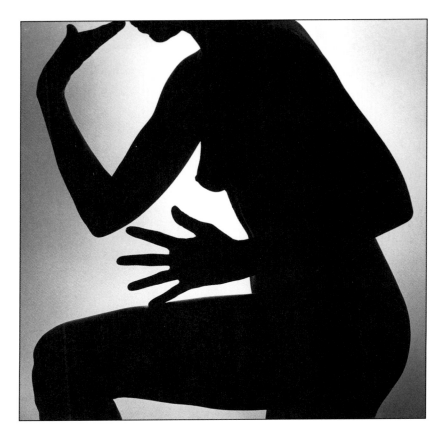

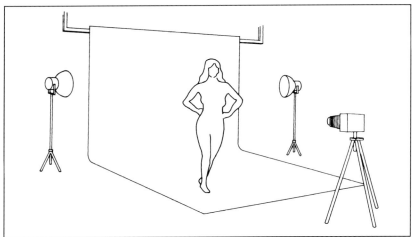

Very simple but artistic photographs can be made by using very simple lighting plans. Here the model poses against a brightly lit background to create a silhouette.

A diagram of the lighting plan.

the edge of the form and creates flat, cut-out shapes. However, if the background is dark or black, a rim light has to be extensive enough to light the entire figure and it is rarely possible to conceal such a large source of light by placing it behind the model.

The answer to this problem is to move the light off-axis, out of camera range and to place another on the opposite side of the model. These should be tall, broad-source lights or strip lights, or at least two small flood lights on each side of the figure, one at one metre height pointing at the model's waist and one at two metre height pointing at her shoulder. It is essential to use a long lens, two-and-a-half times the normal focal length, and a good lens hood to prevent flare. Now the entire body can be outlined in a brilliant edge of light.

Obviously, this type of light suppresses form and contour and whether it is decided to work figures on light or dark backgrounds, it will be found easier to begin at this point. The model feels more secure, shrouded in such a rich lighting

scheme and the photographer can learn to control the edges of the figure in relation to his frame of reference, that is to say, the camera viewfinder.

BACK-LIT SCREENS

Once this lighting approach to the nude figure is mastered an alternative may be tried. Place a large, bright source behind a translucent screen of cotton sheeting, which has been stretched over a frame. This now gives an effect of true, flat silhouette, reminiscent of the Indonesian puppet theatre. If it is not convenient to work with the translucent screen, two strong light's may be beamed onto a large white background either side of the model, and exposure can be adjusted so that the body is very much under-exposed. Silhouette and rim lighting are all improved by under-exposure of at least one stop and 50 to 100 per cent over-development in a crisp developer such as Kodak DK50,or Ilford PQ Universal. Another variation of screen could be obscure glass or plastic which has been partially obscured by ripples or bubbles.

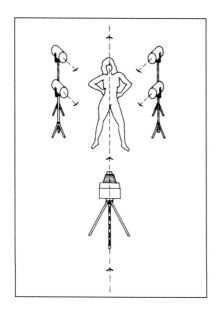

Rim lighting diagram when only an outline of the body is wanted. Four lights are used in tight reflectors positioned slightly off the lens axis.

This is the photographic result of such a lighting set up.

SINGLE LIGHTS

Having explored these key lights the photographer can move on to the extreme side lights and top side light from right or left. These lights, skimming at right angles across the lens axis, reveal contour to its maximum degree and if placed with precision, a single light source will also adequately light the background. This is a moody, theatrical lighting if rendered in a slightly under-exposed value; it is low key and forms the basis of one of the most important lighting plans in figure photography.

This single key light can be delicately filled from the camera position to enhance the shadows, or be given fully lit shadows to make a superbly modelled form. When fill light is added, a supplementary background light is needed behind the darkest side of the model to eliminate double shadows and to create good separation of figure from ground.

The single top light is a dramatic light also, particularly if the model lifts her chin and looks up at the light. The top back light is rarely used by still photographers except to delineate the shoulders and neck from a dark background.

The top front lighting is, in nude photography, what it is in portraiture, a glamour light. If the face is important to the photograph, then this is a benign light yet reveals body contours strongly. It is not very effective for a full length figure. Where it is used on even a waist length figure it must be filled adequately, either with a broad diffused floodlight from the camera position, or a large one metre square white card, used as a reflector, so that the lower part of the body is not too deeply in shadow.

One other, somewhat unusual light, may find its place in the nude photographer's repertoire, and that is the axis light, delivered along the lens axis by a ring light around the lens. This light models form in a delicate but definite way, creating a highlight on any contour projecting directly towards the camera, but a dark shadow on the extreme outer edge of the body. It can be an excellent beginning to a graphic special effects image and tends to create interest in the edge of the figure, just as the silhouette does, yet without entirely losing form as does the silhouette lighting plan. It is essentially a high-key light, to be used on light backgrounds.

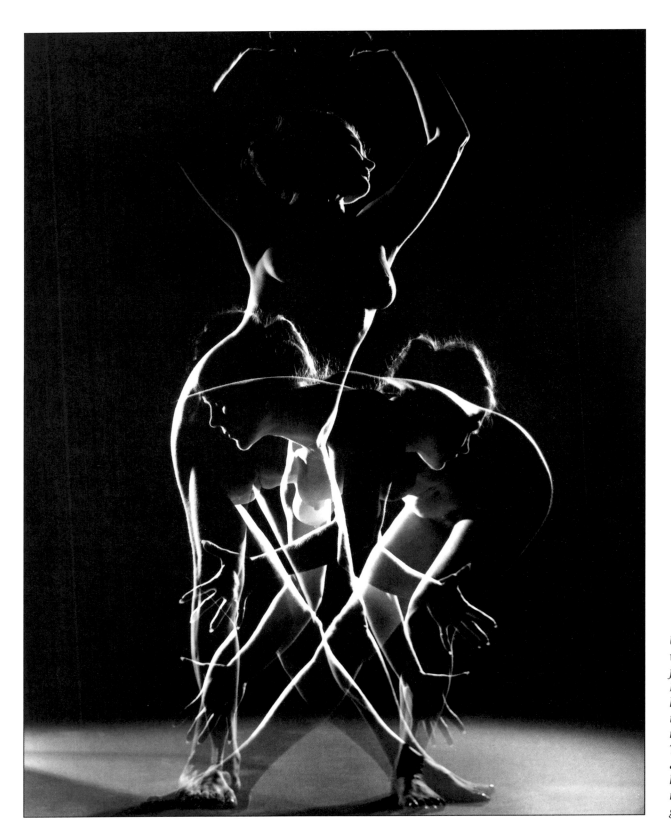

Using the rim light technique very creative possibilities arise from very simple means.
In this example a rim lit figure has been photographed several times, each exposure being made on the same frame.
The camera must be on a tripod and the model holds each pose briefly for the exposure to be made. See page 119 for a graphic version of this image.

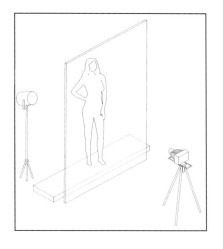

Another way to make a silhouette is to stand the model on a low stage behind a white cotton screen. Behind her, place one or more undiffused flood lights which will create the clean white background against which the black silhouette will work.

Where the model is moving over a reasonably large area, such as when walking or dancing, it is best to create a wrap around light. This is explained in the diagram. Such a light permits considerable movement, without danger of the model moving into any under-lit areas even if moderately wide angle lenses are being used.

Good photographers will work with a minimum of lighting units, if possible with only one, as this creates a cohesive mood and reminds us forcefully of the original light of the sun, but there are many occasions when the additional extra but subordinate lights will increase the feeling of solidity in a figure and suggest much more contour and dimension. These are called fill lights and accent lights.

The ratio of highlight to shadow can be controlled by these additional sources of light when they are carefully placed to open up shadow areas, but these extra lights must not create separate shadows or in any way interfere with the total dominance of the main key light. They are therefore, usually considerably diffused and are large in area.

Accent and rim lights are often introduced even to strong contour lighting plans which already separate the figure easily from the background, as these lights can skid across the skin wherever they strike the body to give an increased depth and tactile treatment. Wherever these accent lights are used, they should be in deep, well guarded reflectors, be close to the subject and the camera should carry a very effective lens hood.

DOMESTIC ENVIRONMENTS

Once studio lighting is mastered so the photographer can see light easily, it is possible to consider ambient lights, such as those found in domestic situations.

The nature of the subject often requires that pictures be taken under ordinary room lights and modern cameras and fast film have little difficulty with the comparatively low light levels to be found in this type of location. Shaded lamps throw very romantic lights and although by themselves do not usually give out enough light to cover the entire body, they can be very interesting for waist length pictures.

It is of course essential to use high speed film in this situation and this is generally a lot lower in contrast than film suitable for studio use, so this effectively counter-balances the high contrast found in domestically lit areas. A top light which washes the whole room can assist also in lowering this contrast, achieved by the use of bounce flash from an on-camera flash or by turning a strong floodlight in a large reflector upward and lifting it well above the eye line of the model.

If the scene outside a window is to be included and if daylight is still very strong, it will be necessary to augment the light inside the room until it is giving exposure times equal to that outside. This is best done by one or more powerful flash units or, in certain cases, a large but very bright tungsten halogen flood of 1000-2000 watts, which is bounced against a wall or reflector. Obviously, if colour film is being used, the daylight outside will be out of balance with the tungsten light inside and this must be corrected if perfect colour balance is required.

By learning to control environmental light as it enters the confines of a room, the photographer will begin to understand how to react to a light source which is fixed and yet one which can quickly vary in intensity. When moving to outside locations in daylight, away from buildings and interiors, or when working in an interior lit mostly by daylight, a great deal of observation before attempting any photography.

On overcast days the change in light intensity is not a great problem but on sunny days, with drifting cloud, it will need good anticipation and patience to make the alterations needed on camera to compensate for the changing lighting conditions. Observation over a lengthy period of any particular room which is to be used for a background for the nude will inform the photographer about the time of day when the light looks best for the concept decided upon.

Sunset and sunrise can give the most dramatic light to a figure in a room, but there are literally only minutes before the light is lost or changed so radically in position that the photograph has no longer the same force and character. It will be seen that the sun, moving through its daily arc in the sky, changes its position quite rapidly in relation to a fixed object like a house

and working on this type of assignment the photographer will have to be very certain of the visual concept and photographic technique in order to keep pace with lighting conditions.

After considerable experience with this ambient light in enclosed space the photographer can begin to explore the natural environment and daylight alone as a source of light. Sunlight seems most appropriate as a means of lighting the nude and, although it is a fixed light source, it is easy to turn the model to obtain different lighting values, without greatly altering the interaction of background and figure.

OUTDOOR ENVIRONMENTS

The main lighting controls available to the outdoor photographer are large reflectors or battery operated flash units. These are used to alter the lighting ratios as needed.

A reflector for outside work should be a large 120cm (48in) square and two may be needed: a silver, foil-covered hard-board panel and a white card. For ease of carrying these could be made in two sections and hinged with an elastic strap as a stabiliser attached to the top.

The foil can be household alufoil, crinkled up, to diffuse the reflective qualities a little and then glued to a 2mm ($^1/_8$in) hardboard. This reflector can throw diffused but brilliant reflection into the dark shadows. The white card is a more subtle reflector and just opens the shadows delicately to increase the dimensional effect. The most comfortable fill light to use outside is the flash, which is used as a synchronised fill light. This must always be diffused when used for this purpose. One thickness of facial tissue over the flash head is probably enough.

The photographer who becomes fully aware of the fall of natural light and how to recreate it in the studio and therefore becomes fully proficient at lighting the nude in the studio with totally controllable artificial light sources, will possess the major ingredients in the mixture of skills needed to acquire the flawless photographic technique so essential to this particular subject. Such virtuosity is only to be obtained with a dedicated and informed practical application of the theory of photographic lighting, undertaken over a lengthy period in very different locations and conditions.

CHAPTER FIVE

Finding the Model

Choosing the right model for nude photography is not particularly easy and it is virtually impossible to obtain your ideal. This deviation from the perfect was noticed first by the Greek and Roman artists 2,000 years ago when, in their diligent search for the earthy expression of immortal beauty, they chose to use the naked figure as the symbol. The female form, particularly, became the lode star in a quest they could not win. The partial solution to their problem was found in using many models, each with a claim to one ideal attribute and a composite work of art was constructed from these.

It is not open to photographers to follow this example, nor should they. The use of the camera to record the nude figure has, of course, a greater affinity to reality than does painting, but with this advantage comes also the special privilege of automatically endowing the figure with its own individuality and personality even if the face is not identifiable. So the strength of the photographic nude seems to lie in capitalising on this lack of perfection to be found in all models, rather than suppressing it, and to present the naked lady as she really is.

This acceptance of individuality in the figure has come a long way since Victorian times when the nude was mostly photographed as a reference for painters or as a subject of risqué postcards. Figure styles have changed, models have become more athletic and poses more naturalistic and frank. Draping the figure, shrouding it in shadows or destroying the optical definition have largely disappeared along with false modesty and sinister Victorian prudery.

This change in society's acceptance of the nude photograph has meant it is now far easier to find suitable models who will work with the photographer on such a subject. The photographer, while noting this relaxation of moral barriers and the return to naturalness, must also continue to take more than a passing interest in those artists of the past who faced the insoluble problem of idealising the image of female beauty.

The photographic nude model should be well proportioned and athletic, not necessarily tall and, in most cases, not big busted or with large hips or thighs. The camera adds considerable apparent weight to the naked figure, particularly when long

Models should be chosen for those attributes required for the work planned. They should have good features, good hands and feet, preferably have some dance training and not be shy of posing nude for the camera. This model is made up in character for an editorial assignment on ancient Egypt.

lenses are used and any tendency to fleshiness in the model will be much exaggerated. She should have good features with hair, hands and feet all well kept as these extremities gain enormous importance in the nude photograph. If she has any dance or athletic training, this is advantageous, but there is no real age limit which need be imposed.

Albrecht Dürer, the famous medieval artist, brilliantly featured some very sour examples of advanced womanhood in some of his less appetising engravings, but the modern photographer will have to respect the awesome fidelity of his camera machine and choose models who display their femininity, whatever their age, with some expression and personality, while avoiding those models with any tendency to freakishness or who have excessive physical problems such as poor skin conditions, large moles or too well defined body hair.

Skin colour is immaterial but in both black and white and colour photography, black or brown skinned models are particularly suited to the technical needs of photography. My own preference for a model has always been for one with a lightly tanned body (with no bikini marks) or a non-Caucasian with light brown skin. The source for such models may be near at hand among friends, wives or lovers or may be found via advertisements in the classified section of the local paper or perhaps they can be located at a modern dance school, exercise centre or from selected professional model agencies. A prolific source of possible models exists in colleges and universities. A request placed on the notice board may bring many hopeful models because, usually, they do not object to such work and badly need the fees which are available.

It is possible that someone seen in a public place appeals as a potential model and usually a restrained approach with a clear statement from the photographer about the nature of the work anticipated, will at least bring a hearing of the proposal. A surprising number will undertake an assignment, but to avoid being misunderstood in respect of motives, it may not be advisable to approach girls who are unaccompanied.

Wherever they come from, they must be suitably motivated and orientated towards the work in mind. It is not enough that they should be nice ladies with nice manners who do not object to taking off their clothes. As Göethe remarked, exactly a decade before photography was born, the man uncovered is only then the man. Nakedness is not always a satisfactory ingredient of the totally artistic image and a deeper commitment than that is essentially required from both the model and the photographer.

The word 'nude' itself, traditionally implies that artistic and aesthetic properties are paramount, whereas 'naked' does not. If the model is primarily motivated by earning a good fee for sitting, this is usually a good thing. It tends to overcome shyness and any fears of personal involvement and puts the whole project on a business basis from the start. Then in executing the work itself the model will often display a great and real interest in the whole assignment, contributing inventive effort and many ideas as the photography takes place, wanting it to be successful.

MODEL RELEASES & FEES

All nude models will ask for certain essential information. This will include the fee for the session, the use to which the pictures are to be put, the type of model release to be signed and if she may edit certain pictures out before submitting final prints to the client. Some models may ask that their identity he hidden, or that they appear only topless or that no pubic hairs be shown, particularly if the face of the model is clearly recognisable. All these matters should be discussed frankly before the session can begin and a clear understanding must be reached between the parties concerned.

Fees, of course, vary. Amateur models will not usually have an accurate idea of what fee is proper and the photographer must guide them in this matter, basing the fee on the extent to which the photographer will profit. Amateurs are usually untrained in this work, often self-conscious and the photography will be produced more slowly. The naïvety of such models is often very appealing, however, and well worth the effort to achieve good results. Hourly fees, of course, would be far less than those made to an experienced photographic model. Dancers, especially those trained in modern jazz or Martha Graham methods usually make excellent and graceful models and their fees must be higher than that paid for painters' models or amateurs.

The highest paid models will be trained photographic models. The photographer will deal with the model's agency and often some very hard bargaining will take place. Apart from the basic hourly rate which is doubled for entirely nude work, a poster fee is charged for any session which is designed to produce a poster and this is often many times the hourly rate. Calendar assignments will also bring a special fee. Lower rates are applied for editorial work or for topless work, but the savings are usually also tied to a restricted model release.

A photographic model from the agencies (for some reason often listed as 'glamour' models), will tend to work faster, be easier to direct and be less inhibited about her working environment, consequently a lot more usable work will result from the session. However, such work can also sometimes suffer from having little poetic depth and a tendency toward clichés, banality or commercial eroticism.

The photographer will usually have to satisfy the model on the usage of the pictures, who owns the final copyright, where and how the pictures will reach the public and if there is any residual fee to be paid if the pictures are used outside the stated first purpose. Most models will also wish to see the pictures before they are submitted to outsiders and this is a reasonable request. It should not be that a model has the right of veto on the photographer's pictures, but it is a fair compromise to agree that nothing distasteful or harmful to the model will be sold to the client.

For both model and photographer, the model release is a most important document. It defines copyright usage, fees for that usage, exceptions and any continuing interest the model may have in such pictures. The model release should be worked out by a competent lawyer and be written in clearly understandable language, setting out the exact details of the contract.

Each model must sign the release for every session and this should be done immediately the photography is completed. No payment should be given by the photographer to the model or her representative before such a release is received. Nude pictures, however tasteful, can be a target for 'invasion of privacy' actions in court should the model have second thoughts about her verbal agreement. No photographer should begin a session of nude photography without making the model aware of the exact nature of the assignment and its usage and the fees involved and no session should end without a signed agreement which confirms these terms.

Do not photograph under-age models, even with parental approval. The age of consent as an adult will vary in different communities, but the photographer who flouts this convention risks criminal prosecution.

When working with unknown models, the photographer is advised to book each for a preliminary session for a minimum of one hour and a maximum of two hours. This will give the model and photographer a chance to see if the session goes well. If good work results from it, further sessions can take place.

MODEL RELEASE

NAME OF THE PHOTOGRAPHER

....

NAME OF THE MODEL

....

WORK DATE ....

USAGE OF PHOTOGRAPHS

....

FEES .... ☐ PER HOUR ☐ PER DAY

TERRITORIAL RIGHTS GRANTED ....

EXCLUSIONS ....

EXTRA FEES OR RESIDUAL FEES AGREED

....

AGREEMENT

IN CONSIDERATION OF THE SUM OF .... WHICH MAY BECOME DUE TO ME OR MY AGENT IN ACCORDANCE WITH THE MUTUALLY AGREED FEES DETAILED ABOVE FOR POSING FOR PHOTOGRAPH(S) REFERRED TO ABOVE

I PERMIT ....

OF (ADDRESS) ....

....

OR THEIR ASSIGNEES OR LICENSEES TO USE ANY OR ALL THE PHOTOGRAPHS ARISING FROM TODAY'S WORK EITHER COMPLETE OR IN PART OR RETOUCHED IN ANY MANNER WHATSOEVER FOR THE PURPOSE STATED ABOVE. I UNDERSTAND THAT I DO NOT OWN OR SHARE IN THE COPYRIGHT OF THESE PHOTOGRAPHS IN ANY WAY. I AM OVER 18 YEARS OF AGE. UNLESS OTHERWISE AGREED THE PHOTOGRAPH(S) OR ANY ADAPTATIONS OF THEM WILL BE DEEMED TO BE OF AN IMAGINARY PERSON.

MODEL NAME ....

SIGNATURE ....

DATE ....

OF (ADDRESS)..

....

WITNESSED BY ....

SIGNATURE ....

Every model should sign a model release such as the one above for every session of photography. The wording of the release can be similar but photographers are advised to ask a legal adviser to approve the final printed agreement.

During the first session with a novice model, she should be encouraged to adopt any discreet pose she prefers. The photographer should use a telephoto lens so as not to intrude in her personal space.

Once the model has adapted to the studio space, a good beginning could be a simple silhouette. The model gains confidence from the darkness which shrouds her body and with encouragement and positive direction from the photographer, serious and successful work can begin.

WORKING WITH THE MODEL

Very often, even if a girl has a noticeable body defect this can be hidden by clever lighting or good directing from the photographer. These test sessions must always be paid for at normal rates but it soon becomes evident which girls will produce the kind of work most suited to the photographer's needs and these can be booked for future sessions.

Models should be warned not to wear tight clothes or belts or even underwear or carry heavy bags on shoulder straps as these marks take a long time to disappear from the body and the photographer should state whether bikini tanning marks could be a problem or not. Finger and toe nails should be manicured and perhaps given a light red varnish to add extra elegance to the hands and feet. Rings, necklaces or bracelets may be useful and very often the wearing of very high heel shoes may help the line of the thighs and buttocks if the shot is for a fashion or glamour subject needing added touches of eroticism.

Choosing models for the art or exhibition field may be safely left to the photographer, but in advertising or editorial work the eventual client will have considerable interest in who the model is to be. It should be noted that while fashion and editorial clients will often require lean and athletic models, most calendar clients, especially if they are publishing in the industrial field, will ask for much more buxom subjects.

Here the photographer must step neatly between the problems of too much eroticism and too much vulgarity and, if in doubt, take test shots of each girl. On many calendar assignments, work is done on location in tropical situations and the professional photographer will be responsible for bringing home the most useful photographs possible from what is often a very expensive operation. Photographers are also frequently responsible for maintaining a strict professional etiquette between models and other members of the team and failure to do so can sometimes bring calamitous failure to the assignment.

Whether working in the studio, on location nearby or in far away countries, the model must feel safe and confident in relation to her environment and the conditions within which she works. Many models require a closed studio or absolute minimum crew members, often none at all. Some refuse to permit even the client or art director to be on the set and it is the photographer's job to see that these conditions are obtained and that considerable diplomacy be exercised in dealing with other parties to the assignment.

Obviously on such closed sets the photographer effectively becomes art director, studio assistant and total arbiter of taste and design and while this asks much more of the photographer than usual, models often produce much better work, even if the session, of necessity, moves at a slower pace.

After some workouts, direct the model to adopt poses of exaggerated relaxation.

Working and stretching on the floor, with her back to camera will help the novice model gain confidence.

Directing nude models is best done by a continuous stream of conversation, aimed at getting the body attitude in its correct aspect to camera and light. Most girls will also benefit from a non-technical explanation of the lighting plan, the concepts sought and an opportunity to study any Polaroids made.

In studio work a musical background is advantageous, as nude subjects are greatly concerned with mood and this can be projected more easily by models when they feel comfortable with their working environment. The studio area may need extra heat as a smooth skin loses its appeal if it looks too cold.

Professional model fees are expensive and especially those of nude subjects. This means that the studio or place of work must be prepared in advance for the projects in mind, all props within easy reach, any backgrounds, colours or small room sets completed, lights tested and overall lighting positions established. The photographer must be ready to begin work the moment the model arrives.

Because it is often necessary to work without studio help on these sessions, close attention needs to be paid to preparing photographic equipment, setting up lighting plans and so on. One item of considerable use in a studio is a large mirror placed near the camera so the model can see herself in almost any way in which the camera does. It will be found that models are much

more relaxed and more inventive when they are re-assured by controlling their poses this way.

If the photographer seriously intends to study the nude as a subject in depth, it may be advisable to begin by purchasing a shop mannequin with articulated limbs. Although these can be expensive, they can be used extensively for lighting and processing trials, obviating the cost of long hours of model time while practical matters are tested and studied. See Chapter 4 on Lighting Plans.

Technical fluency may then be acquired in the special areas such as contour lighting, edge separation, skin texture and so on at considerably reduced cost. Once these techniques are understood and can rapidly be applied to the lifeless mannequin, the real model can be brought in to implement the total concept. Before any major session the photographer, however experienced, can use the same shop dummy to help prepare lighting set-ups and the background to the picture, permitting almost total preparedness before the model arrives. She will be relieved of the tedious wait while technical matters are sorted out and will be more effective and relaxed for the actual job.

An essential part of any indoor area which is being set aside for nude photography, whether it is a temporary or permanent arrangement, is a changing room. Here the model can have complete privacy while she prepares for the session. A full length mirror, a small table, chair and good lighting should be included and a simple gown or loose wrap of some sort is often useful, as many models feel a need of a covering garment to put on between actual photography and it is surprising how many forget to bring anything suitable.

The question of body hair is a delicate one, to be discussed between photographer and model prior to the session. Mostly it can be left to the femininity of the model to dictate the way she prepares her body for photography and most would prefer to be shown without defined hair on legs or under arms, especially if it is a glamour or fashion picture which is being made.

Documentary or fine art photography may have other guidelines, but it is important that the model is given a choice in the matter. Pubic hair is a different matter. Today, most models will not be particularly sensitive about a frank and natural representation of the body and the pubic hair can be included in the picture. Others would prefer it to be lightly shaved to leave a neat triangle (usually the preference of professional models), still others will insist that this area of the body must be excluded from the shot, or shrouded in shadow.

Strangely, this request for exclusion of pubic hair is particularly true of the models from the professional photographic agencies who appear totally nude in many commercial publications such as calendars, some of which are deliberately very erotic indeed. Such models will not sign a release if pubic hair is shown in any picture where the model is easily identified.

Careful lighting and direction from the photographer can overcome the problem or photography can be confined to the area from the waist up or a drape may be used. This can be a factor which inhibits good work during the session and, as any suggestion of coyness is detrimental to the final result, the photographer should try to persuade the model to drop this condition for the session, but allow her to review the proofs to edit out any problem images before the client sees them.

The novice model, however confident she may appear, is often very nervous of the first session and the photographer can do much to ease her tension. First the studio, or place of work, must be ready, equipment checked and cameras loaded. The photographer should be clear as to the exact programme of the first session which should not be longer than two hours and be certain of the picture concept and what the model is to do. When all is ready, the model can walk in front of the camera and immediately should be given simple, clear and confident direction by the photographer.

It is easy to devise a small repertoire of poses which are requested from any new model, especially nervous ones and this will also assist the photographer in assessing the qualities of the model. These early exercises should possibly be treated as silhouettes with a strong back light which shrouds the body in shadow and gives extra confidence to the new model.

A psychological point worth remembering: all humans (and animals) surround themselves with an invisible 'bubble' of space, within which they feel comfortable and secure. Strangers who violate or intrude into this space, trigger the 'flight or fight' response. The bubble expands or contracts according to the personality and experience of the person. A new or nervous model will set the outer limits of this space very close to her body and this can often create effects of embarrassment or even of resentment which will be seen in the photograph.

One solution is to use a long focal length lens – this places the photographer outside the critical distance, but the image is unaffected by the increased distance from the model. If it is judged that the novice model seems to be lacking in confidence, use longer lenses in the early part of the session, at least three times normal focal length. This minimises any feeling of intrusion which may arise in the beginning of a session, but it will alter the optical shape of the image.

When outdoor photography is required, it is necessary to use very experienced and uninhibited models, particularly if the location has any public access such as may happen with beach scenes. The model should wear a loose wrap after changing near to the chosen location and keep it on until the photographer has set up the picture, selected backgrounds and studied the lighting problems. At the last moment the wrap can be dropped near the model but out of camera view and work can begin.

The logistical problems of outdoor nude photography call for even more technical expertise from the photographer than nude photography in the studio and some preliminary research of the location site beforehand is essential. Use the camera viewfinder to select possible standpoints, check the time of day with respect to lightfall and so on.

It will be found then, in general, that the nude model needs to be treated differently than perhaps the average female subject for the camera. To the usual human concern that the photograph should express the sitter's own idea and image of themselves, is added shyness, nervousness, eroticism and perhaps, in the final analysis, reluctance. The photographer will only obtain interesting photographs of the female nude if all these aspects can be handled with tact and skill.

As the session develops, walk the model around a limbo background in bright open light. Ask for many different poses and finesse these by constant direction. Make many photographs of this event and later, review these with the model.

CHAPTER SIX

Indoor Environments and the Nude

Existing light in indoor situations creates special opportunities for the photographer of the nude but also certain problems. For those who do not have a studio situation or who do not wish to use outdoor locations, it is reasonably easy to make a beginning in this field using normal rooms and every day interiors. But once the photographer has command of the technical difficulties encountered when working in indoor environments and wishes to extend the possibilities of such work, it will be seen that the deeper commitment also brings further difficulties.

Compared to outdoors, conditions of working are much more controlled. All that is needed is a room which has a large window preferably one not overlooked by neighbours and one which faces unobstructed sky light. Such a window should be masked with a diffusing material such as Roscofrost, architectural tracing paper or large sheets of white tissue paper. This creates privacy and also provides a diffused fall of light within the interior or, alternatively, a 'burn-out' screen for the model to work against for simple design shapes.

If sheer curtaining material is used instead of other diffusing material, it should be slightly off-white to counter the excessive blue cast coming from some of these materials. Remember also, from the point of view of privacy, that while sheer curtains do create an impenetrable screen for the indoors, this is only in daylight and then only if no strong floodlights or room lights are turned on within the room. At night opaque blinds must be used for privacy.

INTERIOR SPACES

The room chosen for nude photography should be private, warm and contain many rich textures to act as a suitable tactile contrast to the smooth contours of the body. Any special ambience in furnishing, colours, or structural details will make work for the photographer easier and more rewarding.

When choosing any one room for a photographic background or when the whole house is to be considered as a location, it is important to observe with care and considerable understanding,

the light fall in each part of the room during the entire day. As with exterior locations when using day light, the light source is fixed to some extent and will impose restrictions when working and undoubtedly make certain camera angles desirable and others impossible.

Lengthy studies of these interior spaces without camera or model will pay considerable dividends when it comes to actual work. Best times of day and any possible augmentation of the light for each part of the day should be noted in the photographer's log-book if much work is contemplated in the same interior situation.

LIGHTING & LENSES

For work with existing daylight or tungsten light indoors, the photographer should consider some modifications to equipment and technical methods. During early observation of the room selected, it will be noted that the light appears very contrasty, that there is surprisingly little light and that the sun travels at considerable speed in relationship to fixed objects such as door frames and windows. Changing light also changes exposures rapidly, at the same time radically altering shadows and the ambience of the room, sometimes within minutes, so that the photographer who cannot work quickly may lose the most memorable pictures.

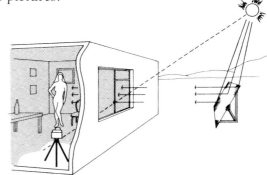

This is a diagram of a simple arrangement for beaming sunlight into a room. Remember that the sun will move and the mirror will need constant re-adjustment. Very quick work is required but the results can be so dramatic, the technique is well worth attempting

The best camera for this work is undoubtedly a 35mm, preferably a single lens reflex type, fitted with very fast lenses, both normal and wide angle, even ultra-wide. Suitable focal lengths would be 80mm, 50mm, 30mm, and 28mm, all with maximum apertures of f2 or faster. A compact tripod, equipped with a ball and socket universal camera mount and a geared centre post, plus a long cable release, would complete the basic equipment.

For augmenting any existing light, an electronic flash with fast re-cycling and bounce capability is useful, as well as at least one, but preferably three, 500 watt floodlights fitted with tungsten halogen photographic lamps and barn doors. A variety of reflectors will be needed to help modify the heavy shadows always encountered. These would include the 100 x 120cm (40 x 48in) acrylic mirror suggested for outdoor use, a 100 x 200cm (40 x 78in) white board designed to be free standing and a large white double bed sheet with a means of hanging on a movable stand, such as a lighting boom stand.

Large size reflectors although more difficult to manipulate in small interiors will be found to give much improved contrast ratios, especially when working with colour film. Apart from being used as an intensified source of reflected light to fill in shadows, the mirror can be used to turn sunlight into the interior from considerable distances away. Catching the direct light of the sun and redirecting it into whatever area of the interior it is required, gives the photographer a powerful source of extra light and extends the length of time in which photography may take place. The mirror must be able to stand outside and have sufficient means of angling it. In windy conditions some method of counter weighting may be needed to keep it in place.

The use of wide angle lenses has a special place in working indoors with the nude and it is only in this kind of figure photography that the optics of such a lens may easily be exploited, as it is rarely used otherwise. The main problem with such lenses is that as soon as the camera is angled up or down, verticals begin to converge either at the top or bottom of the room.

Use simple props and natural feminine activities.

63

*Daylight from an open door
can flood the model with a very
textural light. Here the model
is posed against a white paper
fall. This type of controlled
daylight can increase contrast
substantially.*

The need often arises especially in some editorial shots, for a more comprehensive view of the interior than that which can be obtained by normal lenses. The correct way to do this is first to locate the camera (with the wide angle lens in place) on a tripod, making it precisely level by the use of a spirit level if possible. This levelling must be in both directions, horizontal and vertical, and the camera is then locked into position. Looking through the view finder, it will be seen that verticals and horizontal are now geometrically correct. The tripod is more effective in this work if it has a geared centre post so that the camera may be raised or lowered in complete parallel to the verticals seen in the viewfinder.

The model is then, and only then asked to move in front of the camera to a pre-determined position. If the camera is centred on the model's body and this is done only by racking it up and down on the centre post, no distortion of model or room will take place. Of course if the model moves her body or limbs directly toward or away from the lens axis, distortion will be seen.

Even ultra wide angle lenses may be used this way and these considerably intensify the dramatic scale of the figure as it relates to the interior or, in small rooms they increase the apparent spatial dimensions and give added aerial perspective behind the figure.

Long lenses, longer than three times the normal focal length, are rarely used when working with the nude indoors because with their narrow field of view, they tend to eliminate most of the interior and there is also usually insufficient physical space to use them effectively.

FILM

For black and white photography, much can be done to assist the control of lighting contrast. First by choosing high speed film such as Agfa APX Professional 400. Such film will aid the photographer enormously by giving increased sensitivity to low light, but these films are also inherently lower in contrast when compared to medium or fine-grain emulsion. This lower contrast and higher speed also brings with it a slight increase in grain which is usually found aesthetically and artistically complementary to the moody, documentary style of image which often arises when working with existing light.

Processing in black and white also permits considerable control of contrast, particularly if a fine-grain compensating developer is used such as Patterson Aculux diluted 1:15 or Agfa Rodinal. These developers permit an uprating of film speed, ranging between two-thirds and two f stops. For maximum contrast control for such developers it is wise to over expose the film by 30 to 50 per cent, using the uprated film speeds which the manufacturer recommends and underdevelop by 15 to 30 per cent. Tests are advisable when first working with these processing techniques to reduce contrast. When faced with difficult or abnormally high contrast lighting situations include several frames on each film for a clip test.

Always when working in difficult conditions, where shadow or highlight details may need compromises of exposure or processing to render them correctly, it is advisable to bracket exposures. The Contax RX has an auto setting to do this, which is very useful.

Bracketing is a much used professional technique both in colour and black and white, whereby three frames are exposed in rapid succession, one under-exposed, one normal and one overexposed. In black and white, the bracket is usually shot with one stop differences, with colour it is usual to make half-stop changes. Under certain conditions ultra high speed film may be needed and one of the easiest to use is Polaroid. A positive black and white film with an ISO rating of 3000, this is low contrast, has a pleasing grain structure and is easily copied on to conventional negative material for further enlargement.

Ultra-high speed in 135 films in black and white material is available when using Kodak 2475 recording film. This is a very high contrast material which, under some circumstances, can be rated up to 10,000 ISO. It is usually better not used at these extremes, but at 4000 ISO, it is extremely effective. Some developers produce chemical fog with this film and manufacturers' data sheets should always be followed. Shadow detail will tend to drop out and tonally the image will be rather coarse.

COLOUR INDOORS

When colour film is used under available light conditions, contrast will very often become a major problem. If 'push-processing' is used to increase shadow detail, highlights will tend to burn out and contrast is greatly increased. This may of course create a special effect which enhances the picture, but such increases in processing times are only effective with transparency (reversal) material. Negative colour films do not respond satisfactorily to push-processing, but new films are being rated as high as 1600 ISO by some manufacturers. A possible alternative would be to shoot the picture on a digital camera and manipulate contrasts on the computer in Photoshop.

The only truly effective way to lower contrast when working with colour materials is to augment the existing light by using reflectors or diffused flash to add light into the shadows and thus reduce the highlight to shadow ratio.

When working with colour in these indoor existing light situations, colour temperature is another additional problem, often requiring testing beforehand. When no sun is present in the room, reflected light from the sky will often be excessively cold and, on the nude figure may not be attractive.

This can be altered quite precisely by the use of the Kodak Wratten CC (colour compensating) filters which are fitted over the camera lens. To warm up cold, northern light, light from

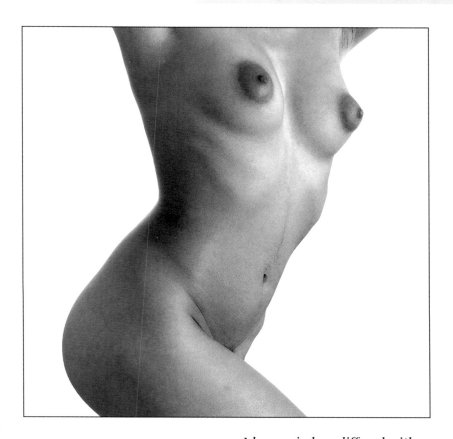

A large window, diffused with gauze curtaining can provide a useful back light. To maintain the mood of such pictures, process film to retain good shadow detail.

overcast skies or reflected light from blue skies, use the 81 series of filters. Where double glazing, skylight glazing or any thick plate glass is in the window areas, light from these sources can often carry excessive green casts from the glass itself and this can be modified by using a magenta CC Filter, usually at least of a density of 0.10 or 0.20.

Other light which may be in the picture and which may also have different colour temperature includes fluorescent lighting, which can be modified by commercially available FLD filters (for daylight film) or FLB (for tungsten Type B film). Normal household electric fittings exposed to daylight film will appear to be warmer than is natural, but this may be an advantage. When the nude figure is lit by daylight and correct colour balance is obtained, those domestic lamps and shades which are kept on, are rendered in warm gold tones and may provide added pictorial charm.

Conversely, when Type B film is loaded (balanced for 3200 Kelvin), these lamp fittings will be seen in their natural yellow-white colours, while the model's body and all areas touched by daylight will be rendered in a rich blue. By adding a heavy 81 filter, say the 81EF, the blue areas will shift to a cool grey and the artificial light will be restored to deep gold. Candlelight may also be used, even as a sole illuminant and on high speed 400 ISO colour film, exposures may be between four and ten seconds at f4. A tripod is needed and a cable release must be used.

COMPOSITION & DESIGN

When faced with photography of the nude indoors for the first time, the photographer should not be too ambitious. After close observation of the light fall in the room and any processing or colour tests the character of the room can be assessed and, with an understanding of this, it may then be used to complement the essential qualities and actions of the model. No other props may be needed at this time especially once lighting contrast is under control.

The skin colour of the model is also a factor to consider. For example, if a dark skinned model is used and reflectors are added to improve the value of shadows on her body, black and white film can be considerably overexposed. Highlights in the environment around the model will then be overexposed and tend to burn out, but the body will be in perfect lighting contrast and shadow detail will be seen throughout the room.

Another situation for those beginning work with the model indoors can be to pose her in front of suitably large windows so that they may act as a white screen, giving a somewhat studio effect to the picture. By opening up two f stops to capture shadow details in the body the window will burn out and be rendered white. Where privacy is of concern the windows must of course be screened with diffusion material, but where there is no problem about privacy windows may be left uncurtained and the sky used as a background.

Sunlight falling through distinctly patterned, but sheer curtain fabric can produce interesting lacy patterns on the model's body, breaking up contours and introducing visual ambiguity in the image. The model can be directed into various poses which will alter the pattern and this may be watched carefully in the camera. The more natural the model appears in these indoor situations the better, as any artificiality or theatricality may not suit such pictures.

Shadows endow the picture with mystery and theatrical overtones.

USING SHADOWS

From using light as the only 'prop' in the picture, the photographer can move into the more difficult assignment of using the darkness of the room. Someone has said, 'the dark is light enough' and anyone who has studied the rich, charcoal or crayon drawings of Seurat will see the significance of this. Tying together small areas of relative highlights by the use of deep but translucent shadows teaches the photographer to work with negative spaces and requires considerable processing and enlarging skill to bring it off successfully.

Shadows endow the figure with luminosity, a sense of mystery and a degree of concealment, while at the same time acting to simplify and unify the whole design. Skin colour of the model is again a factor and some detail should always be found even in the richest blacks. Over-exposure and under-development are the most usual techniques for this kind of subject when using black and white film, but additional light, for example bounced from the ceiling, may be needed. Such use of shadowy blacks can be successfully used with colour film but it is particularly dramatic with high speed black and white film processed to exaggerate grain structure.

Openings in the room are potential sources of light. Any overhead skylights or fan lights high above the door can be used in the picture to produce a somewhat narrative mood to the image. Dust or smoke can be used to make the light beam visible from windows; doorways may be flung open, or alternatively, half closed, to admit nothing but a little light or to allow glimpses of rooms or landscapes beyond. The mystique produced by admitting controlled amounts of light into the room is one of the most attractive features of photography of the nude indoors. It exaggerates the feeling of privacy and concealment which are both natural attributes of such pictures.

Mirrors are also very often used, frequently to the extent of becoming uninspired clichés, but mirrors are symbols of windows; they suggest overtones of narcissism and hint at metaphysical worlds beneath the surface of our minds, so they are simple but powerful props to use with the nude. When using mirrors where the image is to be sharp, always focus on the image not the mirror.

Simple actions suggestive of femininity, can also create mild eroticism if the character or the interior is suitably subjective. The model dressing, the figure partially draped, the model washing, bathing or showering are all natural and simple actions. In existing light conditions and if there is no hint of artificiality in either lighting or the pose of the subject, the model can display both dignity and sexuality at the same time. Richly tactile compositions are always possible with wet skin but, again it should be stressed that any augmentation of the light source to fill shadows should not overcome the dominance of the natural existing light, because this is the principal ingredient of the beauty to be found in such images.

Models who have sufficiently long hair can provide good visual interest, especially for the full length figure, when they are seen washing or brushing their hair. These scenes are further dramatised if there is a chance to back light the action to some degree. Wherever possible, look for these opportunities to photograph the model indoors, without any props, using only the beauty of the light and the naturalness of the situation to draw the picture together.

Changing the camera viewpoint is another way to add dynamic interest to nude photography indoors and the high viewpoint with perhaps the model on the floor or the bed, is a situation likely to produce most effective images. The bed, naturally

Backlighting a model's hair can dramatise a pose.

enough, is often used to stimulate erotic fantasies in the viewer, especially in pinup photography, but in a deeper sense, it does offer many opportunities to be used as a symbol or as an environment for the female form. The bed is a natural enough place on which to pose the nude and waking, sleeping, sitting up, reading are all good points to begin natural actions which make well designed images. A high camera viewpoint can take advantages of a strong cross light on the body, as beds are frequently placed near windows or doors.

***Using ambient light and high
speed film can assist in
generating mood***

SURREALISTIC IMAGES

Indoor photography of the nude offers considerable scope for sequential images so that a number of linked actions can be seen in a grouped collection of pictures or a portfolio essay. Very careful thought must be given to the interiors which are to be used as these will be a powerful, influential symbol of the whole work. In this kind of assignment, surrealism is very often present and paradoxical, comic or threatening visual concepts may be built into the visual story.

Many photographers are excited by the work of the surrealist painter Rene Magritte in this respect and certainly he should be studied. To successfully emulate this kind of painter or use techniques of interesting juxtaposition of image fragments, the photographer must master such things as montage, overlay and mutually exclusively masking and this is discussed more fully in the chapter Digital Workshop. In thinking about any sequential or surrealistic photography, a story-line must be invented and the whole sequence planned in detail in advance.

MOOD

Of course in any photograph of an interior, but especially if it includes a nude figure, mood will be paramount. Photography creates mood easily and with the strongly directional light fall which comes from doors or windows, mood is considerably enhanced. The enclosure of a room gives security and intimacy to the figure and the observer of this type of image is encouraged to take the role of voyeur, particularly if the figure appears to be somewhat shrouded by shadows.

This naturally heightens any sense of eroticism but also, as the naked figure is never more private than when found within the sanctuary of a room, there is a sense of invasion of that sanctuary, bringing to the picture a degree of aggression. These concepts create unconscious responses in all viewers and the photographer who understands these subjective factors in the composition of the image, may produce very memorable images, provided enough initial thought is given to the assignment before beginning actual photography.

Once all the preliminary research has been done, notes having been made, props assembled, and model and photographer are finally at the location, it is best to be guided by intuition. A controlled situation is needed right up to the moment at which photography begins, but the interaction of model, photographer, environment and light will appear more spontaneous and interesting if it is all impulsively and instinctively captured by the camera as events happen.

DOCUMENTARY STYLE

Apart from situations already discussed, the nude indoors may be photographed in documentary, cinema verité style. Here the photography tends to be lived rather than planned and it may be that images are accumulated slowly over quite a lengthy period of time. The photographer may not wish to impose any additional lighting on the existing condition, even to augment shadows, and may not wish even to use reflectors for fear of disturbing the intimacy and ambience of the moment, but if this is the preferred method of working, extreme skill will then he needed in processing and contrast control, in order to make satisfactory and reproducible images.

To carry this live documentary value further and attempt to acquire a socially meaningful role for the photographs is extremely difficult, for such photographs must be presented as an unyielding witness to unrehearsed events and the nature of nude photography is that it generally requires co-operation and rehearsal by both photographer and model, while the nude body cannot help but provoke unconscious symbolism in the mind of any viewer, far outweighing any social message. Some pictures by Brassai of night-time Paris in the 1930s do succeed in bringing these complex ambiguities together, but it is a rare gift.

WINDOWS

The window of a room by itself can be a very effective prop. The model can create considerable action around it, such as looking out, working with curtains, sitting on the window ledge and so on. If the view outside the window is an important part of the story or of added design value, it will have to be correctly exposed to fit within whatever tonal scale the film will accept. In black and white it is largely a matter of building up the lighting values within the room until they are suitably in proportion to the highlight from outside. This will generally be done by the use of flash or floodlight as reflectors alone may not be sufficiently strong.

If the photograph is in colour, however, further complications arise. First, colour film is less able to handle the contrast than is the case of black and white and there is almost no processing control possible; secondly, the colour temperature of outside should match that of the interior. A diffused flash fill in, using electronic flash, is the most successful, perhaps bounced off a white reflector near the model. If tungsten floodlights must be used, they will have to be given blue correction filters to match the daylight colour temperature or the entire window will have to be covered by a corrective filter or aerosol spray (obtainable

An abundance of natural light on a bright day, entering a room from a large window, will provide the photographer with a soft but strong light.

at a professional photography suppliers) which is sufficiently orange to lower the daylight colour temperature entering in through the window, by about 2000-2500 Kelvin.

Such is the interest and symbolism surrounding the window that it is well worthwhile spending some considerable time in exploration of this particular prop and its technical problems. As with all other aspects of serious photography, a study of past work and living masters will assist the photographer. Of course it would not serve much purpose to copy such pictures. Photographers who have successfully used the nude in environmental interiors include Brassai, Bill Brandt, Helmut Newton, Jean-Loup Sieff, Larry Fink, Duane Michaels, Harry Callahan and Emmett Gowin. A close examination of their work by those wishing to know more of this specialised field will be found to be most beneficial.

CHAPTER SEVEN

Under the Sun

T he natural affinity between the naked body and the sun provides the photographer with many opportunities for composing pictures of great beauty. Once the photographer learns to see the change of intensity as clouds pass by, the colour of late sunlight, the freshness of the morning sun and the graphic potential when using brilliant noon day sunlight, then he or she will be able to visualise many new images which are not obtainable in studio situations.

To develop an awareness of the light fall in nature requires that the photographer spends time in deliberate contemplation of the light out of doors. This should be done preferably without a camera and certainly for a complete day - sunrise to sunset. If it is also possible to look at the same landscapes in different seasons, this is an excellent extra benefit. For those who wish to make any serious photographs of the nude out of doors, this preliminary investigation into the behaviour of sunlight as it reveals form in the landscape or seascape is essential.

For those whose interests are not of this depth but who still wish to use natural light out of doors to illuminate the nude, such close study of natural elements and lighting can bring nothing but benefit, with improved work and perhaps surprise, at the rich quality with which sunlight endows the subject. It will be necessary to rise early enough before dawn to visit the planned location in time for sunrise, but this observation of light could also easily take place immediately outside the living room window if it is near to natural surroundings.

If the day is overcast, go back to sleep, as overcast light is only usefully observed when it reaches its greatest strength toward midday. A small mapping compass is helpful to get a true orientation of the direction of the light and if the dawn light is obstructed by trees, it is wise to move to another location. If possible try to be in a position to see the actual sunrise, as it comes over the horizon. For the rest of the day, time the position of progressive lightfalls and make notes.

Sunrise has always been a magical moment for mankind and has long been enfolded into religious and mystical beliefs. For modern man it is no less magical.

When photographing the nude in strong sunlight, expose for highlights and process the film in a compensating developer for a 20-25% longer development than normal.

WATER

The light, particularly if it is back light from the disappearing sun, will have an enormous effect on the way the whole image of the nude and water will appear photographically. Even after sunset, when the sky is still lit but the landscape is not, reflected sky light can produce a beautiful mood on water. When working in colour, blue haze in the light can be used to great effect to increase the mystique of the female body. If Type B film is loaded in the camera, balanced as it is for a 3200K colour temperature, the blue effect is greatly increased. If nearby objects are lit with tungsten floods (and this includes nearby water surfaces) very interesting colour mixes result. Battery operated video floods are very useful in this situation.

After sufficient contemplation of the role of natural light in outdoor life, it will become clear that there are many differences in the way a photographer should use that light and the environment of his model, when compared with that of the studio. First, the sun is a single source of light, but not a static one and it moves along a predetermined course, yet can, under certain circumstances, change its intensity dramatically.

This then is a basic problem: the photographer can no longer easily control either the lighting or the conditions under which work is done. Only sharp observation and pre-planning, can bring anything like success. The lessons of the studio, detailed in earlier chapters, and the classification of lighting positions for the key light, the use of fill light and reflected light, are not wasted when it comes to working outdoors, as these have all been based on original observations of the sun in natural surroundings before transposing them into studio terms. The photographer and model now become subject to natural forces and must adapt to conditions rather than impose them.

The observant photographer will still see how to use back lights or off-axis back light and cross lights to produce effects, but will have the added assistance of natural textures of rocks and trees, shadows and light patterns through leaves, wind blown hair or garments, and so on, increasing the interaction of the natural location with the female body. But it cannot be stressed too strongly that apart from pre-knowledge of the behaviour of natural light, the most important element of working with the nude out of doors is planning.

First, research the possible locations, making Polaroid or conventional photographic reference and note the times of day when certain areas look their best. Use various lenses. Keep all

Sunset provides a rich and often romantic background, even in black and white. The figure will be in comparative shadow and either a large reflector or diffuse flash may be used to restore detail. In this picture a diffused flash was used.

71

this material on file even if it is not used immediately. Always obtain permission from any owner of the location if it is on private property, paying any necessary fee. Be aware of the law if working in an unfamiliar country, because each community has its own rules about any public display of the nude and, in some, penalties for a display of the female nude are severe.

LOCATIONS

Suitable locations should not be too inaccessible, since travel time, at least with professional models, must still be paid for and it is not sensible to go long distances to a location where all arrive exhausted before even beginning work. Each day of the location should give opportunities for four or five major pictures and there should be backup situations envisaged, in case bad weather stops shooting as planned. This could include the use of barns, stairways, interiors and so on which are near the major location.

Nudist clubs and specially designated nude bathing beaches are possible locations, but it is essential to obtain the club's permission before taking any photograph and also to reassure chosen subjects about any intentions to publish. Although such places do provide almost unlimited models, it is not always certain that they are capable of, or enjoy being, in front of a camera for the serious business of photography. It is usually far better to find experienced models elsewhere and to take them to locations of personal choice.

Once a location is chosen, select the model to fit with the location and the concept. Certain girls will suggest beachscapes, others natural textures of trees and rocks while others will be more suited to water or buildings. The compatibility of models with their surroundings always makes the photographer's work much easier and the model more relaxed and inventive. If the location is in an exotic country, perhaps a girl should be chosen to contrast with her surroundings.

For this type of picture, distinctly glamourous models are preferred and it adds to the impact of the pin-up if these girls are to be found in rural or native landscapes. Be sure that the model chosen for outdoor work is comfortable in the type of location to be used. The girl who works with great imagination and effort in the controlled situation of a studio or an indoor setting may feel different if working in a natural environment.

If there is a sporting context in the visual concept, make sure the model can perform the actions envisaged. If water is being used in a pool or beach shots, make sure all the models chosen can swim well and are thoroughly at home in a watery

Selecting a good location is paramount to successful nude photography out of doors. The example here suggests bright light, water, a screen of trees, terracotta tiles, white walls and privacy. These are all desirable attributes for a productive location.

location. If horses or other animals are necessary to the photograph, be sure that the models are able to work closely with them and produce relaxed and unconcerned poses and expressions. It is sometimes part of commercially inspired photographs of the nude to work outdoors with exotic or wild animals and if the location is far away, as perhaps a safari concept may be, be sure to question closely prospective models on their ability to work in these conditions.

OUTDOOR LIGHTING

Apart from the normal logistics of getting to a location and working for the expected time without interruption the photographer will need to add extra technical items to the baggage, particularly those which control light. A large white card reflector about 120cm (48in) square, for soft fill lighting, a

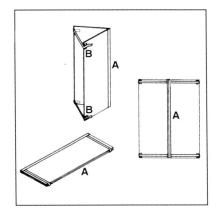

An outdoor reflector is an essential piece of equipment and can be easily made by the photographer. (A) is a hinge of strong cloth tape. (B) is a strap of Velcro tape top and bottom of the folded reflector. The reflector folds flat or can be freestanding. One side should be matt silver and one side white.

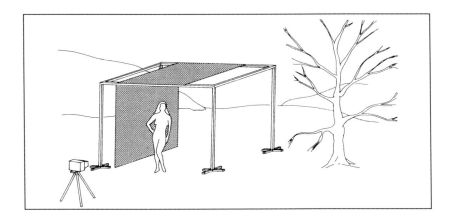

similar sized aluminium foil reflector, for a slightly more brilliant fill light and a 100 x 120cm (40 x 48in) acrylic mirror.

This mirror would be used by models sometimes to correct poses and to check make-up, but its main reason is for re-directing the sun with almost its original brilliance into dark shadowy areas or into archways or gloomy interiors which may form the background to the figure.

For example, if the model is standing in deep shade, a strong beam of sunlight may be picked up from far outside the photography area and beamed back as a main key light, to strike the body and highlight contours, or to light the background for increased graphic effect. Such mirrors need a simple stand and a method of weighting so that gusty winds will not be a problem. If the budget permits, a visit to a professional movie supply shop will provide very versatile and portable reflectors of many different types for outdoor work.

Where outdoor lighting differs remarkably from indoor and studio lighting is that whereas the studio is an environment which requires additive lighting plans, outdoor lighting is largely subtractive in nature. There is such a super-abundance of light available outside, that it becomes a matter of controlling it by taking it away from the picture.

This may be done by interposing large diffusing scrims between sun and subject to create a soft yet directional light, or by working in the diffused light which comes from white walls, or by the use of minus 'reflectors' which block out or absorb light. Very portable black light-absorbers are made by Larson Enterprises. They are comparatively inexpensive and do give excellent control in bright conditions.

Although form will be most boldly drawn when photographing in full sunlight, the misty diffusion of overcast days, especially around noon, can be of great interest. The cloud covered sky

The greatest problem when working outdoors with the nude, is the abundance of light. The hard edges of sunlight can dissipate the mood which is often an essential element in a successful picture. To create a softer light even on very bright days, a diffusing tent can be constructed as shown in this diagram. Alternatively, translucent, opalised nylon, parachute silk, or smoke can be used to reduce hard shadows.

acts as a giant diffuser, reducing texture, hiding skin blemishes and reducing the prominence of backgrounds. When colour photography is undertaken in these conditions it is advisable to use a brownish, warming filter of the Wratten 80 series in order to reduce the blue, cold atmosphere in the light.

For the camera, really effective lens hoods are needed outdoors and possibly two small flash guns with diffusers over the reflectors. The flash equipment is used in situations where deep shadows are creating too much contrast in the lighting ratios and the technique known as 'syncro-sunlight' photography is used. Syncro-sunlight is simply a method of opening up shadows by the use of flash while, at the same time, using the light from the sun as the main key light.

First a meter reading is taken of the sunlit areas of the model and the shutter and f stop combination is set which does not permit the shutter speed to exceed that recommended for flash synchronisation. On professional leaf shutters, such as those used in Hasselblad cameras, this covers all shutter speeds, but any focal plane shutter, particularly those of 35mm single lens reflex cameras, may not permit high synchronisation speeds. The objective is to expose the subject to daylight, using the shutter speed and f stop and record the flash by f stop alone.

This means that the photographer may have to limit the model's movement if totally sharp pictures are needed but, for example, on beach shots the blurring of wave action or of wind

This picture, made on 35mm Kodachrome with a 500mm lens, has been posed beneath trees which act as a natural diffuser. Delicate shadows on a white wall suggest sunlight, although no direct sunlight is falling on the model.

blown hair may give an added naturalness. Once the f stop for the daylight exposure is known, this number is divided into the flash guide number (GN) to produce a number which indicates how many feet or metres from the subject that the fill-in flash must be placed. Distances should be measured accurately with a tape measure.

To find the GN beforehand, place the diffused flash 3m (10ft) from a subject, use the x setting or correct synchronising shutter speed and make a series of test exposures using only f stop variations to alter the exposure. Start at f5.6 and make exposures at f8, f11, f16 and f22. Process these results and choose the best exposure and then multiply the f stop so chosen, by the distance which the flash was placed from the subject. This becomes the Guide Number. For example at 3m (10ft) with a selected best exposure of f11 the GN is 33. If 10m is the chosen measure, 110 is the GN.

Thereafter, whenever the same film speed is loaded into the camera, the GN can be used for accurate flash exposure. For location interiors where shutter speed is probably not important, divide the GN by the measured metric (or equivalent) distance between flash and subject. This number so produced, will be the f stop needed for correct exposure by flash alone.

With syncro-sunlight and outdoor situations where the shutter and aperture must be fixed to also record daylight, divide the GN by the f stop number chosen and the resulting number will indicate the distance from the subject at which the flash must be placed. In outdoor work avoid having the supplementary flash too bright, or an artificial look results. The flash head can be diffused by using a paper handkerchief or tissues over the reflector, each half thickness of a tissue reducing the light by about half a stop.

OUTDOOR FILTERS

For outdoor work certain filters are useful. Black and white photography with panchromatic film will generally benefit from the use of a yellow or a yellow-green filter to give a more natural rendering of skies or, perhaps, an orange filter to dramatise blue sky and white clouds so that very pronounced cloud forms are seen against a dark sky and figure, the body being rendered paler than usual. Red filters will render the body even lighter and the sky even darker and this is useful for highly designed graphic images which are to be very theatrical.

Rock forms are often reproduced with increased texture and tone when a red filter is used. A general rule of black and white filtration is if a colour is to be lighter in the finished print, choose a filter of the same colour; whereas if it is to be darker in the final result, choose a filter which is directly complementary in colour to the subject. Thus a red dress will photograph lighter when a red filter is used, but will be darker if a green (which is red's complementary colour) filter is used.

When using black and white film, do not forget that when using a colour filter to produce a certain effect on any chosen colour or individual object in the frame will also modify all other tones. The red filter will darken the sky, lighten the body, darken green foliage and so on, increasing image contrast.

For outdoor colour photography the first essential is to fit the camera with an ultra violet (uv) absorbing filter, sometimes called a skylight filter. UV filters do not generally increase exposure even when they are at their heaviest density and it is a wise precaution to screw a good quality UV filter into every lens. This protects the expensive lens under most circumstances and gives warmer and more saturated colours in the final result. It is far easier to clean a glass filter than a lens. Corrective and conversion filters will often be needed and the tables can be found in the chapter on colour photography.

LENSES

Lenses for outdoor photography will tend to be either distinctly longer or distinctly shorter than those used in studio work. When indoors, a normal lens is particularly necessary, but outside it tends to minimise the landscape without dramatising the figure. Wide angle lenses, although not especially popular with some respected photographers of the nude, can be used to increase the sweep of landscape behind a figure or to diminish the figure in the environmental scale.

If even ultra-wide angle lenses are used, the figure does not necessarily have to be distorted, provided the camera is located at the model's waist level and it is not too close to her.

One special aspect of outdoor photography is always best photographed with these ultra-wide lenses and that is where the brilliant image of the sun itself is to be included in the picture. The very short lens produces a tiny image of the sun and its rays and, with care, the camera maybe pointed directly at the sun with the nude figure also in the frame.

Watch for flare from the lens aperture or shutter blades in this set up and it maybe necessary to use a hand or a card to shade the lens itself from the direct rays of the sun. Only attempt this type of picture with an SLR so that the effect can be judged

The use of a telephoto lens isolates the model from her background, simplifying the *photograph and creating more dynamic compositions.*

A very powerful telephoto was used (1000mm on 35mm format), to isolate the model. *Such a lens creates halation in the brightest highlights, without the use of effects filters.*

precisely. The figure may need augmented lighting, flash or reflector cards, as this is an extreme back lighting situation and there is no doubt that it will be necessary to open up approximately two stops from a normal meter reading in order to gain detail in the body if augmented lighting is not used.

Much more useful are the longer lenses such as 150, 200 and 500mm for 6 x 6cm cameras or 135, 200, 250, 500 and 1000mm for 35mm formats. These lenses tend to compress the background, increasing the effects of mist, haze or fog if they are present and they produce more dynamics in the image structure. Long lenses are particularly useful in sunset conditions where the sun itself is to be part of the composition. Under these circumstances the longest lenses possible are used, at least 500mm or longer, in order to photograph the sun as large as possible in proportion to the figure.

By reason of their shallow depth of field, the really long lenses will permit a general softening of background focus, increasing mood and reducing visual noise from the image area around the figure. Such lenses also isolate the subject in a very narrow field of view, making it possible to use small parts of the environment easily while permitting the placement of lighting units or reflectors very close indeed to the subject, yet out of range of the camera.

One problem in outdoor situations when using long focal length lenses is one of communication between photographer and model, because of the distance between the camera and the subject. This can be done by pre-briefing the model and having a run through of any actions needed, or the model can be left to invent her own actions. The preferred way is to use very small low power, two-way radios one out of sight near the model, one fixed to the camera. Licences may be needed to run such equipment, but many countries permit these very low powered units without any restrictions.

In all cases when using the model outside, make sure she can work in the degree of privacy which is most comfortable for her, find some secure place for holding valuables, clothes or props and make sure that each model has a suitable wrap which can be worn if necessary during setting up a shot or even up until the very last moment, when it can be quickly removed and thrown out of camera range. Some wraps can be used in the shot itself especially if they are plain and of fairly sheer material. When the wind blows such a garment away from the figure or pulls it tightly around the figure, very dramatic images can be made.

PERSPECTIVE

Placing the model in an outdoor environment needs a lot of care and design considerations. Apart from obvious needs, such as separating the form from any excessively contrasty background which may confuse the eye and positioning her in the best light, the proportion of background compared to the image size of the figure must be watched most carefully.

The use of traditional lines of perspective and vanishing points can greatly enhance apparent depth.

This scaling of the figure is often very important. Apart from using just the right proportion of background to produce a dynamic image composition, well known or recognisable objects can be included in the photograph to give a sense of scale to the body. Clouds can be used to scale, as can trees or even the shadow of the human form but on sand, snow or sometimes on rocks, scaling will have to be produced by other objects such as hats, clothing, parasols etc.

All observers of an image of the human form are unconsciously interested in the size of that form as it compares to their own and when the model is given some means of indicating this, more interest will be found by the viewer in that particular picture. Scaling can also be produced by posing the model in door frames and windows, the photographer standing well away and aiming at the outside of the building while including some of the terrain which surrounds it.

Bird's-eye viewpoints and shots from above, particularly where they include buildings or trees, help to create a sense of scale, but they also produce a further psychological effect, particularly if the model appears as only a relatively small part of the design. These pictures increase the voyeuristic effect on the viewer, tending to suggest the viewer is hiding in some

When posing a nude in a rocky landscape the natural elements can be visually intimidating. In this picture the model is overpowered by the massive rock forms. By using a long lens (180 - 250mm on a 35mm camera), a selection of the scene can be made and the picture considerably strengthened.

In this photograph an open gate has been used to create an imaginary vanishing point.

vantage point, watching undetected. This is a legitimate means of increasing viewer involvement and therefore communication.

The use of exaggerated or increased perspective can be another means of attracting attention to the figure in outdoor situations. In this type of image, long objects with parallel lines or naturally occurring topographical features are positioned so that their vanishing points are well behind the model or even out of the picture while the model is placed so that the eye is led

into the picture and to the model by such lines. Certain low camera angles used with these more obvious perspectives can create considerable added drama.

The wide sweep of landscape behind the model in an outdoor situation can be of increased interest if flowers or definite patterns can be found in the picture. The photographer looking for locations should always be delighted when it is possible to pose the model in fields of flowers or, perhaps, in a crop of ripening grass or wheat. Fascinating rhythmic patterns may be found in all such green backgrounds when light glints on wind blown sections of the crop, while flowers give many opportunities for romantic themes.

Many clichés may also be taken under these conditions, because they are well known and well worn themes for the outdoor nude, but a good photographer does not disdain necessarily the use of clichés, as they are a very strong means of communication in certain markets. If the photographer is particularly inventive with such hackneyed themes, perhaps he or she may even create a new cliché, as the industry of pinups often plagiarises good visual concepts to a point of reducing the image to triviality.

One particular element on location, that of water, is always found attractive by photographers of the female nude, perhaps because this theme often inspired major classical paintings in past times and the female body has always been associated with the amphora shapes of antique pots which inevitably contain liquids. Water is a volatile and magnetic addition to the nude figure whether it is a restricted pool-side environment or the wide open space of an isolated sea beach. Light reflects off water in very interesting patterns, catching the body in strange, glistening nets of highlights, or the model can be placed so that her contours are better rendered in such reflected light, creating new dimensions in the whole composition.

The model may be seen entering the water, be found underneath it, be coming out of it or else be totally involved in it. Montage with water is also very successful with the model being photographed in the studio on a black or white background and the water action photographed separately and then blended in during enlarging or by computer.

The nude body emerging from the water, beaded with water droplets is another great theme, perhaps with a fairly revealing garment clinging to the naked body contours. This kind of subject needs a rich dramatic cross lighting and dark background. When working with beach subjects, do not forget the increased textural qualities possible if the skin is partially covered by sand or is found close to heavy textures such as those seen in ropes and nets.

When water is considered as a background, boats are a natural choice, not only those drawn up on beaches or in port, but those at sea and in action. Here far away from land, the boat, particularly the sailing boat, provides a private and very natural environment for the nude. Be sure when undertaking

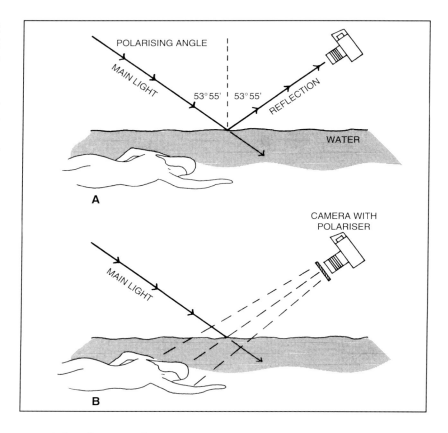

(A) High reflectance from water will obscure a swimming model beneath the surface.

(B) To penetrate the glare and allow the figure to be photographed clearly, a polarising filter is fitted to the lens and rotated until the surface reflection is minimised.

An SLR camera is needed to allow this filter to be used with confidence.

such photography that no excessive risks are caused by posing the model in any insecure or dangerous attitudes or situations.

There is such an abundance of reflected light from the surface of the sea that automatic metering in the camera may under-expose by as much as two stops, so extra care is needed when calculating such exposures. Neutral density filters or polarisers may also be needed. Polarisers are, of course, of considerable use in other outdoor situations as well, because they alter colour densities and therefore hue saturation without altering colour balance. The rotating type polariser is best, especially if the handle is a locking one, as it can be turned to increase the polarising effect which may then be watched through the viewfinder of an SLR.

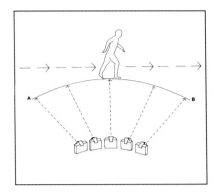

Working with a model outdoors permits the use of 'pan' shots. The model dashes past the camera and the camera is swung to follow the moving figure. This is the pan shot and if a shutter speed of $^1/_{30}$ sec is used the background will blur while the figure remains sharp.

This is an unusual camera support, available from professional stores or camera repair shops. The camera is quickly released for hand held shots and the clamp can be attached to solid supports for slow exposures.

Sky light is polarised only at specific angles to the sun and, of course, the polarised effect in the sky will change according to the time of day. With black and white photography rotating polarisers may be used as a variable neutral density filter because the filter factor alters according to the degree of polarising obtained. This allows for shallower depth of field to be created where due to a heavy filter density the aperture must be opened up, sometimes as much as four f stops, thereby reducing the zone of sharp focus to a very narrow band close to the figure. Unwanted backgrounds can become hazy patches or perhaps gentle reminders of everyday objects – symbols which effectively enhance the visual concept.

OUTDOOR PROPS

Props and accessories for the nude figure outside need careful planning and usually should not be excessively large. Certainly any prop which may need both hands for display or use could cause problems because the arms are forced to conceal much of the torso, often at the same time creating patches of shadow on the rest of the body. Simple articles of clothing are always useful, particularly hats, parasols, towels, swimsuits and so on.

Larger props such as chairs, swings and other outdoor furniture are natural to the figure and help with scaling. Where the sun is shining in the model's eyes, sunglasses are a natural prop but also helpful in order to shield the eyes from excessive glare and to prevent squinting. Even when used in other conditions they add a certain sense of mystique to an otherwise naked body.

Larger props such as cars, motor cycles, bicycles, aeroplanes and so on are certainly useful but expensive additions to any picture involving the nude. Conditions are usually most ideal during late afternoon and sunset for this type of shot. The nude is often only an incidental in such photographs so the major part of the photographer's efforts are directed to getting these objects to look their best and then adding the model.

When a prop is found to be working effectively it is as well to do several variations of the arrangement, particularly if the prop is an expensive one. This gives added opportunity to sell to wider markets at very little increased origination costs. Other props could be more ephemeral than any of the above and include man-made smoke and fog, wind or rain or vapour from dry ice. Obviously safety is a major consideration when working with these props on such an assignment, both for the model and the photographer, but also for the environment itself. Dry ice vapour can be used partially to mask backgrounds, but small theatrical smoke bombs or movie smoke generators are more controllable and produce better effects.

Whenever working in wooded country with such smoke effects, especially if it is summer, be careful to clear the whole operation with the fire guard or local fire department. Smoke and vapour are best back lit and therefore the photographer should choose a time when the sun is very low, in early morning or particularly in late evening. Point the camera into the sun, positioning the model to mask the sun itself and so prevent the rays from shining into the camera and creating flare.

If the lens is opened very wide and a diffuser is used with a blue filter, very convincing misty effects may be produced in colour or in black and white. These are especially attractive if the models are very young and naiveté and innocence are the themes. Do not use fill light or syncro-sunlight flash effects but open the aperture to increase exposure and gain detail in the figure, as the misty background areas also will be over-exposed and this adds greatly to the foggy atmosphere.

EVENING LIGHT

When sunset has passed the light has considerable power and is generally rapidly shifting to a heavy blue bias. In such conditions it is possible to use battery operated tungsten floodlights or heavy duty flash lights driven by portable

A location which has mixed and abundant foliage offers many interesting possibilities. Strong sunlight casts fascinating shadows to complement the smooth contours of the model.

generators to provide a spectacular light on the nude figure while still recording the mysterious details of the environment in the diminishing daylight. The sea or beach is of particular interest in this respect as the watery background gives plenty of separation for the body, yet generally contains many highlights of great visual interest.

Both photographer and model should be in position and ready to shoot this very atmospheric type of picture well before the sun sets and then work rapidly as soon as it does. As the light weakens constant meter readings will be needed, along with continual camera adjustments to alter exposure in order to follow up these estimates. However, the supplementary lighting will remain a constant factor, exposure being unchanged as long as the distance between model and the artificial light source does not alter.

When the best compromise is reached in having sufficient natural light, workable shutter speeds and the correct aperture

to record the right exposure for the artificial light, then the actual work can begin. The camera is usually best fixed to a lightweight tripod when making this type of photograph so late in the day, in order to prevent camera movement at some of the slow shutter speeds which will be necessary. A semi-automatic camera which changes shutter speeds (aperture priority system) in falling light, while the photographer selects the lens opening, plus a powerful electronic flash, is probably the best system. The flash should not be fixed to the camera.

Working outdoors with the nude imposes considerable extra challenges on both the photographer and the model, but by understanding the sun and becoming aware of its lighting qualities and by learning to 'see' the differences in natural or organic form under such conditions, very memorable pictures will be made. It must never be forgotten, however, that outdoor location work will only be successful if minute attention to detail and intensive pre-planning are part of the normal working habits.

CHAPTER EIGHT

Studio Assignments

Photographers who decide to do a large amount of work with the female nude in a formal studio situation must consider a number of essentials. The space itself should ideally permit a paper fall of at least 3m (10ft) to allow sufficient ceiling height when photographing a tall girl with her hands stretched above her head or a dancer who is jumping. The width of the studio should 3m as a minimum plus one metre on either side, 5m in all.

This would accommodate the standard photographic paper backgrounds of rolled paper which are made in 3m or 2.8m (108in) widths plus a narrow zone outside this area for placing lights and walking. If at all possible, the studio would have at least 2m (78in) on each side of the paper background, as the extra space for lighting units is most desirable. These indicated measurements are the absolute minimum for full length photography of one or two models, if they are to have any freedom of movement.

For those who do not wish to allocate a permanent space to studio use, but do have a large room which can be cleared of furniture for each session, the same basic space will be needed. To use the normal photographic background paper efficiently, various devices are made to get the roll up to ceiling height, but the most useful is probably the type of telescopic pole which is spring loaded and carries rubber buffers on either end, to fasten it securely but temporarily between ceiling and floor. Multiblitz of West Germany make such an item, as do Polecat in the USA.

The featureless or 'limbo' background produced by the long paper fall is one of the most interesting and attractive environments for the female nude; certainly it formalises the style to some extent and perhaps identifies the image a little too closely with the artificiality of the photographer's studio, but it does give an easily changed tonal screen on which the figure may work and does not in any way classify the picture in any historical or social point of time.

It would be usual for black and white photographers to use three main colours of paper: black, white and medium grey or medium blue. Colour photographers would use a blue and the

A typical small studio, showing a white background paper in place, a small flash in a diffusion umbrella, a heater (on the extreme bottom left) and a stand for the model to work from.

other neutrals, but would also need various colours and perhaps some shiny vinyls in varying colours as additional backgrounds.

The studio area may be without any natural light at all, but this is a distinct handicap for nude photography. There are many times when totally dark studios would be needed, but the advantages of a strong light falling from a large window on to the full length figure cannot be denied. Whether working in a formal studio or temporary room space, some means must be provided to black out totally the shooting area whenever it is considered necessary.

Most models will be more confident in their work if a full length mirror can be placed near the camera so that they may see themselves more or less as the camera will. The mirror should be approximately 2m (78in) in height and about 1m (40in) wide and should be on wheels. For safety reasons, such mirrors are usually made of acrylic material or mirror foil stretched on frames. The model will be much more inventive when given this opportunity to work towards a mirror, especially if she is a dancer.

To save costly fees and to avoid nervous waiting by the model, all photographic matters should be settled before the session begins. Equipment must be checked for mechanical problems, cameras should be checked for synchronisation if flash is to be used, film laid out neatly and all props and backgrounds or other accessories must be in place.

The photographer must be very clear about the concepts to be illustrated and also have a written schedule which lists these or sketches them. Even very experienced nude models are nervous at the beginning of each session and it helps them considerably if the photographer is highly organised and ready to begin at the time agreed. Photographers are themselves often nervous at this time and this preparation and structuring of the session helps to clear the mind and calm the nerves.

BEGINNING THE SESSION

The close organisation of such a photographic session does not in any way diminish or inhibit creativity, rather the reverse in fact, for once the studio is prepared, the whole time can then be freely given to creating and waiting for the inevitable interaction of the model with her environment.

If dancers are to be used as a subject, much more care is needed in organising the space in which they will work. Lighting units must be safely placed, overhead gear secured firmly, all cables put out of the working area and a minimum number of obstructions left near the camera. If the dancers are providing any choreographed movement, it is certain they will need increased space in which to work compared with that needed for standing poses.

Models who have never previously worked nude before the camera will be understandably shy and nervous and as long as their shyness does not ever become coy, their innocence and charm can be of great additional value to the visual concept. Such models can be best put at their ease by a relaxed studio atmosphere and a crisp professionalism on the part of the photographer and should never be kept waiting for the session

Using a mirror beside the camera is very helpful for the model so she may see variations of poses as they are directed by the photographer. In this picture an acrylic mirror has been flexed so that the model can work out some humorous poses and distortions. The mirror has been photographed, not the model.

The studio should have complete privacy, a high level of heating, and sufficient electric power to accommodate six separate lighting units, each burning at least 500 watts. Apart from the shooting area, there should be a place for the model to change, preferably a small room with a table and chair, a full length mirror and a power point, plus good lighting. If there is access to a shower, so much the better. The studio often benefits by having a background of suitable music and a small tape deck can help create the relaxed mood desirable for this type of work.

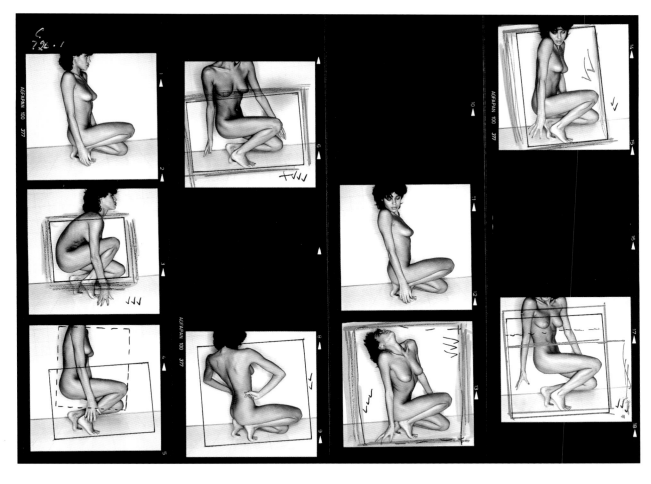

A typical contact sheet from one roll of a long session photographing a model with dance experience.

to begin. They should change into a loose wrap immediately they arrive and perhaps begin to walk about the shooting area. An explanation of the intended schedule of work is helpful and possibly a non-technical chat about lighting and conceptual matters would also assist their confidence and involve them more directly in the session.

It is as well for the photographer to have a repertoire of simple poses involving the full length figure for the use of any novice model or for those who have not been to the studio before. This allows the photographer to look through the camera at the model in various poses and permits a swift and unobtrusive survey of possible faults in her body or any special attributes. It also gets the session off to a relaxed start.

SHY MODELS

For very nervous or shy models, begin working with a simple prop, for example a hat. Start with waist length pictures of the

back, with face fully profiled. Work at first with long lenses so that there is no abrasive intrusion of the model's personal space and direct the model with a clear stream of verbal instructions about each of the successive moves which she must make.

Perhaps then use a loose piece of fabric as a prop, or the model's own wrap keeping the whole figure in camera, take photographs from all sides of the body. Set up a rich contrasting light from the side with very little fill light and this will assist in restoring confidence, shrouding the figure in a moody light, which the model can wear as a concealing garment.

During this build-up, before the main work begins for any new model, many photographers work without film in the camera but this must be a calculated risk, as the occasional successful piece of direction and posing could be missed. When working without film in the camera tell the model. There is undoubtedly a lot of wasted film material from these early sessions, thereby increasing processing work unnecessarily. A work-out with an empty camera makes sense at this point.

DIRECTING THE MODEL

Once the model has become used to the studio and the photographer's style of direction, it is time to begin working on a light background with a full length figure and no props whatsoever. Have the model walk past the camera from right to left, then vice-versa, then ask her to walk diagonally away from the camera and then return. Photograph her in each new situation. Call for a static pose and give clear direction as to how it is to be achieved.

For example, have the model stand diagonally to camera, so that the back and shoulder line may be seen, then turn the head to full profile while in this position and so forth. Ask for a three quarter turn to the front, all the weight on one leg, both knees slightly bent to take the tension out of the legs. Ask for this pose, but on the toes with hands stretched away from the body. The hands are so important in all nude photography and really good models will always have especially attractive hands.

Then have the model sit in front of the camera her back to the lens and work with this pose for some time. Next have her turn to the camera, concealing much of her body with hands and arms and folded legs. Mastery of this graceful pose is very often useful in photographs of the nude, as it is often used widely in editorial pages where total nudity is the key to the concept but absolute decency must be maintained.

Have the model stand and work through a series of closer shots of the body, with the model being directed constantly and quietly into every position that gives optical interest. The camera is usually aimed diagonally across the planes of the body, so twists and turns around the hips will be needed. The hips in fact impose major control on body movement and it is from this part of the body that good posing begins. The abdominal line can be improved by pulling in the bottom; the knees are always better if they are never pointing straight at camera, but across the frame, at a diagonal. Legs are also better not photographed from the back or front but look more attractive if turned slightly to the side and, again, form diagonals in the frame.

Feet are important, almost as much as hands and should, in any full length shot, be watched carefully in camera. If the instep can be arched slightly towards the lens at the moment of shooting, a better shape and line will be made. Nails should be manicured and varnished. It should be remembered during this work, especially when the model is sitting or leaning on something, the pressure of the body on the floor or against any hard edged prop will probably leave a very visible mark which

Shy models or novice models can begin working against a backlit screen to produce interesting silhouettes.
See page 188 of The Masterclass for an example of what can be done with such a simple set-up.

may even mean cancellation of the session half way through if it can be seen in subsequent shots.

CORRECTING FAULTS

While all this active photography is going on, the photographer will become aware of the strengths and weaknesses of the model, both physical and psychological. The camera can help correct some physical problems and the photographer can, with skilful direction, assist in masking any personality problems.

An absolutely simple full length pose of the model on plain paper and with no props. This could be an elegant editorial photograph for a mass circulation magazine.

Correction is needed optically if, for example, the model's hips are somewhat large, in which case the model can be turned across camera; if perhaps one breast is noticeably smaller than the other, place the smaller one nearer to the camera and use normal focal length lenses rather than long lenses. Wide angle lenses can be used to elongate the body slightly, only this should not be excessive. The exaggerated distortion of perspective arising from ultra wide lenses has to be most expertly used indeed for successful images of the human figure, unless caricature is wanted.

WHITE BACKGROUNDS

Working on plain white paper or limbo backgrounds is a peculiarly photographic style and only seems to have arisen since the 1950s, after Irving Penn was so successful with this technique in some of his early editorial photographs. Painters avoid this transitional tonal or featureless background, probably because of the arduous effort needed to render it well, but photographically it is easy to achieve, provided lighting and processing are up to high standards.

This pose is produced by twisting the torso toward camera and stretching the head back to produce tension on the neck muscles.

Hands (and feet) are important and should be given thorough preparation before the session.

Working on a white background for a high key result.
A wraparound light was used.

White backgrounds, of course, give an infinity of space behind the figure, sometimes too stark, but they do draw attention to the skeleton and infrastructure of the body which, although invisible, is always suggested by photographs of the nude. Exploring this hidden structure while maintaining interest in the surface texture of the body has remained the hallmark of masters of nude photography and although it imposes considerable technical and conceptual skills on the photographer, it should be thoroughly exploited.

Large expanses of white background, if evenly lit, diminish the personality of the model to a considerable degree, particularly if she is photographed full length, but this anonymity of background can be used as a compositional tool to create psychological tension. Where blurred body movement is an important part of the concept, using slow shutter speeds to produce unsharp images will be better if done on white backgrounds, because this increases the transparency of the blurred edges of the form and makes it easier to 'feel' the action of moving through space.

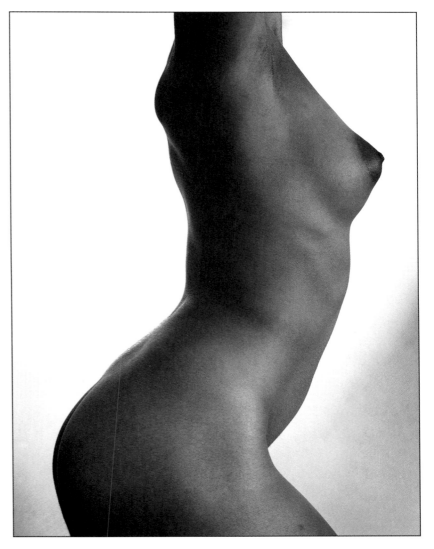

The body lit by diffuse and direct light reveals full texture and tone, even when posed on a white limbo background.

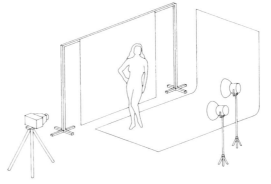

The lighting plan for the above.

For this image, an unevenly lit white background was used and bars of light projected on to the figure from a powerful projector. The resulting shadows create very mysterious and visually dynamic effects.

White backgrounds, especially in small studio spaces, tend to bounce a lot of light into the figure, particularly if white walls are nearby. If this is thought to be undesirable, black minus reflectors can be placed between walls and the subject or brought very close to the model's body. This has the effect of raising contrast in the figure by removing any reflection from nearby walls and, of course, it does not interfere with the tonality of the white background. It is often very important to work in this manner with colour film, if really deep shadows are needed and only a white studio environment is available.

Where the white background is not strongly lit, or is unevenly lit, a beautiful transition of pale greys may be built up behind the model, greatly enhancing mood and aerial perspective. Shadows which fall on the white paper can also be an attractive addition to the whole composition. White paper becomes easily marked and this is much less of a problem in black and white than it is with colour. A little careful control in enlarging can

easily remove the problem in black and white prints, but in colour it can ruin an otherwise flawless picture unless expensively retouched.

USING COLOUR ON LIMBO BACKGROUNDS

Do not continue working on damaged or marked paper if working in colour. Roll down a few metres more of new paper, as any savings at this point in the session will be found to be false economy. When photographing in colour, white very easily picks up a distinct colour cast, making backgrounds unpleasantly blue, magenta or green. This could be due to faulty film, lighting which is not perfectly balanced in colour temperature for the film type, or bad processing.

It is advisable to test a roll of film with all the final studio arrangements to be used if the assignment is to be a critical one. Colour compensating filters will easily remove unwanted colour shifts. White backgrounds, strongly and evenly lit, will be an essential part of any colour sandwich or overlaying montages and these backgrounds, of course, should be entirely neutral. High-key pictures, both in black and white and colour, demand a white background and this can come either from a large back lit screen or the conventional front lit paper fall, with the body strongly and evenly lit, without heavy shadows. Working on white, even for airy high-key effects, requires that definite modelling of the form is still present, with a key light which is easily discernible. Exposure of the film must be very precise.

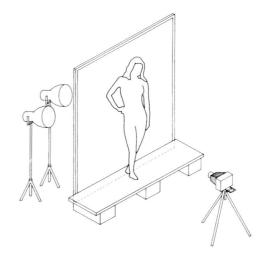

For high key pictures it may be necessary to burn out the background to absolute white. This is done by strong back lighting of a translucent screen behind the model. The figure is then lit from the front by bright diffuse flood lights.

88

Coloured Backgrounds

When the photographer works with a background of an entirely contrasting tone to that of white, many differences will be noticed. Absolutely black background paper is almost never found, but with careful lighting and correct exposure, it will be possible to render a final print in rich black. Absolutely black backgrounds, such as those needed for advanced colour montage, can only come from black velvet or similarly light-absorbent fabric.

Movement which depends on blur is much less successful on black, but movement which is to be shown as sharp, repetitive or stroboscopic, will be vastly improved by black or dark backgrounds. Many graphic forms which are later to be treated with tone separation or a solarising technique will also benefit by being shot on black. Back lighting, or off-axis lighting, comes into its own on black backgrounds, particularly when it becomes necessary to separate artificially the figure from the background. Lighting for black backgrounds often tends to be of higher contrast and richer, producing low-key images with brilliant highlights and deep shadows.

For special effects, it is also interesting to devise an image which is originated on black, but is then reversed during processing to form a negative on a white background. This is simply done by enlarging the negative on to an ortho graphic arts film such as Kodalith (made by Kodak Ltd), giving it a full exposure and shortened development in a standard paper developer and then using this resulting positive image as the new 'negative' from which enlargements of the final print are made.

If the tonal quality visualised for the figure has many subtle nuances of lighting which are to be maintained, it would be advisable to use Kodak's excellent Gravure Positive sheet film to make the reversed image, developing this in DK50 or Ilford PQ - Universal, diluted 1:1. This film gives a long scale of intermediate tones and with a little extra care and testing, contrast gain can be kept to a minimum.

White Silhouettes

Those who have developed an interest in conventional black silhouettes may like to try working also with white 'silhouettes' where the model is strongly lit from the front, along the lens axis and the film is slightly over-exposed to produce an even, white toned form against a black background. The image then concentrates the attention of the viewer into matters concerning area as well as edge, making it more complex than the standard

By over exposing a figure on a black background a 'white silhouette' is made, with no detail in the body. Black cloth must be used, not black paper as a background.

By combination printing the two figures can be doubled or trebled for graphic effect.

black form on white ground silhouette. This technique works better when the model is posed against black velvet rather than paper, as the over-exposure required for the figure tends to produce a grey tone in normal black photographic paper.

Alternatively, the first image can be taken against the normal black paper and then reversed by enlarging on to line or ortho film, processing in a vigorous paper developer or a lith developer. Then a new negative is made from which the final prints are taken, the progressive steps between original and duplicate negative having effectively increased contrast to give an intensely black background, while the white figure loses all form and texture.

BLACK BACKGROUNDS

Working with a totally black background, the model can be given strips of black velvet to cover parts of the body. This can be in preparation for graphic applications or merely to eliminate sections of the body not wanted in the final design.

On totally black backgrounds, when using a pale skinned model, projection of patterns on the body becomes an intriguing possibility. Man Ray was probably the first to use this technique of pattern projection on the female nude, but it has now become almost a cliché in the repertoire of studio photographic techniques. Even so, it is a legitimate area of experiment, particularly for graphic photo-artists and, with a little thought, can be much more than an average solution either in colour or black and white.

The best projector to use in this kind of lighting arrangement is one equipped with a 500 watt lamp and close focusing capabilities. Some means of attaching it most securely to a sturdy stand also will be found useful. Again, it is advisable to use a background of totally black light-absorbent material such as velvet, so that only the body receives a discernible pattern. Circular, spiral, target or moiré patterns are excellent to try as a beginning, but real photo images also can be used in the projector to create very surrealistic effects.

Black backgrounds shroud the figure, enhancing its mystery and eliminating time or historical clues to its identity and can suggest added sensuality in the female nude. Black has symbolic sexual meanings in both the masculine and feminine sense, setting up an alternating ambiguity which can never be quite resolved. It therefore is of considerable use to those photographers who prefer or are confined to studio environments for the nude figure. The only essential is that it must be rendered in

the photograph as a deep, featureless and unquestionably black tone, if it is to perform its proper task in the design.

TONAL BACKGROUNDS

Using a plain paper fall of either black or white sets up direct contrasts with the figure at the extremities of tone. But photography is also greatly concerned with the medium tones of silver and grey and when the nude figure is photographed on a tonal background of grey, whether it is to be for black and white or colour photography, several important differences arise. Firstly, the contrast in the entire image is always altered, lowering the separation threshold if it is of a dark skinned model, raising it if it is of a pale blonde. Also, when such backgrounds are subtly lit to give a transition of tone behind the model, suggestions of spatial depth are greatly increased.

When an image in black and white is printed to its full richness on this kind of background, a sense of theatre and mood is easily produced, emphasising the body and its sensuality without the absolutes that accumulate when either stark white or dead black backgrounds are used.

In colour the grey background is a very effective foil to the skin tones, acting as a screen so that the dynamics of the body may more easily be seen. With no technical effort the neutrality of grey can easily be shifted into cool or warm areas of the spectrum, the cooler bluish greys creating a receding space, the warmer, friendlier greys pulling the background up closely behind the figure.

Of all colours grey should not be presented as a flat even tone. Greys demand a transitional tonal scale. This transitional tone, produced by careful lighting, can also be specially prepared by hand painting or by spraying the background in large patches of grey of differing intensity or area. A further variation from this tonally grey background is to add texture using such materials as hessian, upholstery cloth, or canvas, and introducing hand painted grey tones on these, probably with a spray gun or airbrush.

COLOURED BACKGROUNDS

When the photographer moves on to use an actual coloured backdrop of paper probably the one most needed will be blue. Blue assumes an attractive mid-tone when used with black and white film and can easily be altered by filtration to a deeper grey (dark yellow filter) or to a pale grey (bluish filter). These filters will subtly alter the skin tone also, so tests are advisable. If the photographer is working in colour this blue background paper may be lit with lamps covered in blue gel filters to produce a transition to a dark blue at the top and with a yellow or magenta gel filter at the bottom to give a sunlit horizon effect. A very credible sky background can be produced in the studio this way.

Many different backgrounds can be found for the studio, especially for use in colour photography. They would include mirror and colour foils, coloured vinyls and felts, tissue paper, translucent or semi-transparent or frosted materials, packaging materials, carpets and so on. Most of these are obtainable in widths of 2m (78in) and usually come in a variety of colours.

Here a plain paper fall of white and rich lighting from a side left trench light with a ring flash fill light along the camera axis, has produced a silver grey tonal result.

91

SETS & PROPS

Once some experience has been gained with a model working on a plain limbo background or with a variable tone background to alter spatial values, it may be interesting to scale the figure in some way. On the limbo backgrounds, particularly white, no reference point is available to help the viewer to compare the subject with known real life dimensions and, of course, this is one of the primary reasons for using the limbo background in the first place.

When scaling is important it can be done with simple objects, usually those which are naturally to be expected in close contact with the figure. Chairs, ladders, wall textures all suggest normal environmental scale. Hats, scarves, towels and other items of clothing also indicate scale and reference points. Of course, once the model is associated with a definable prop or reference object, the valuable anonymity of the nude as an unaccompanied figure and the classic timelessness which this suggests will be lost.

Therefore, whenever using any object with a model who is posed on a limbo or plain tonal background, make sure that the prop will contribute correctly and significantly to the desired concept. Bizarre or unnatural props can be used equally well as scale reference, but will usually provoke surrealistic readings of the image. Where a narrative is important but no props are to be included, the model will have to be chosen for her expressive visual qualities and her sense of mime. The hands become vital in this type of photograph: they must look good and photograph well, yet be totally expressive. It is usually far better to use a trained dancer for this type of assignment.

Because of the need for privacy or because of seasonal or budget limitations to photographing in an outside location, it is often necessary, at least in professional photography, to achieve a believable natural impression of a location, often a tropical one, in the studio. These location 'sets' must be carefully built and augmented with actual objects belonging to the environment which is being suggested. Plants, flowers, textiles, household objects all must be carefully researched to fit, particularly if it is in any way an ethnic location which is to be featured.

If it is remembered that the long focus lens is very selective and accepts quite a narrow angle of view, it will be seen that the set does not have to be enormous. Consider carefully the whole picture, the shape of the format, where the figure will be and so on. Pre-visualise the permutations of the concept decided upon and, if possible, make a rudimentary layout sketch. This planning will mean a reduction in the amount of set building needed, saving time, space and money in the studio and it will produce more certainty and style in the final image.

In studio sets, first seek to use natural textures, as these look good with the body. Use plants which have small leaves, long fronds or spiny shapes and avoid large, flat leaves of irregular shape as they often command too much attention. Use rough textiles: grass weave mats, textured white walls, mock stone or brick, wherever they may be legitimately applied as these create interesting contrasts and tactile values when compared with the smooth contours of the body.

Old wood rather than new is better near the naked figure and fabrics should have definitive, but large patterns where possible. Flowers should be large and few, rather than many and small. Avoid textiles or floor coverings with intense, small patterns. Only really small areas of props need be associated with the figure, if well known objects are used. The eye is extremely capable of completing partial patterns and forms and will unconsciously assume the rest of the object suggested, provided it is a familiar one.

If the set is cleverly built, the entire room and its styling with its placement in social history can be recalled by a mere fragment of such a room which need occupy only a tiny corner in the studio. One most useful part of the set and, in fact, one which almost by itself alone can make the shot look like an interior, is a window.

This can be set up with a small surround and some 'flats' of compressed board which may be wallpapered or textured to reinforce the impression of a normal room. Light can be cast through the window and the curtaining, to create a main source of light, while the 'interior' can have a dark and moody fill light. This creates a mysterious feeling of security around the figure or sometimes one of restraint and a lot can be done with such a set.

By using a strong fan and very light material, the curtains may be set blowing, billowing into the room which will produce effects that give a good model considerable help in striking interesting poses and will assist the photographer with many opportunities to make memorable pictures.

If the studio is large enough, several of these small sets may be built for one day's shooting and the photographer and model can progress around these without waiting for long periods between shots, while sets are dressed and finished. These highly planned days of very active work can bring substantial savings in model fees and increase studio productivity considerably.

Where the concept of the image does not demand an elaborate set or the work is being done on an amateur basis, very abbreviated sets will suffice and yet still be believable. A piece of tile board as a background, another on the floor, can suggest a bathroom, shower or gymnasium. A wooden pine partition suitably aged, could give the impression of an old house and so on. Another budget saving approach can sometimes be found by building surrealistic sets, where this mismatching of objects creates juxtaposition of concepts, producing ambiguity and surprise. Those who do not have large budgets for backgrounds can often make very witty and successful pictures with the female nude in such surroundings.

It is well to remember that the figure will often look better for being placed at the junction of two walls rather than be found standing against a continuous single wall. If even a hint can be seen of a return wall towards camera, it is much easier for the viewer to associate the set with a real room. Even two white walls and a white floor which form an enclosing corner for the figure are enough to suggest an environment which continues outside the camera view point.

LARGE FORMAT WORK

Professional photographers and fine art photographers may be faced with the need or desire to use a large format camera in the studio and this is a particularly difficult technique to master with the nude. The design and concept of pictures of the nude depends almost entirely on the line of the body, its contours and its parts. Certain poses which produce ideal shapes may be seen on the ground glass screen of the view camera, but may be so transient that while the cumbersome technique of stopping down, priming the shutter and settling the double dark slide into the camera back is all being done, however fast, the model breaks the pose and loses concentration.

One answer is to use a 9 x 12cm (4 x 5in) camera which is faster to use than larger formats yet still gives extraordinary detail. The use of the 9 x 12cm (4 x 5in) camera gives almost as much quality control as larger sheet film cameras, especially for black and white, with the added advantages of cost cutting and easier processing techniques. Be prepared to use considerable amounts of film, however, but by taking plenty of time in rehearsing each shot and with careful thinking through of all visual concepts and lighting needs beforehand, this high throughput of film could be reduced somewhat.

An interesting alternative camera for large format work in the studio, but one which offers no perspective or depth of focus

An essential item is a strong tilt head and tripod.

This is a typical large format studio view camera.

control, is the large format press camera, such as the Speed Graphic, a press camera from the 1950s. Although out of fashion for press work today, they are ideal for studio nude photography, which does not usually need camera movement.

Equipped with two shutters, wire frame sights and usually an optical viewfinder, a rangefinder, plus a ground glass focusing screen, the Speed Graphic may be aligned like a view camera through the back, ready for exposure and then all action can be seen and directed through the wire finder. Focus can be refined at the last minute with the rangefinder. This camera can be used off the tripod and is an excellent, very rugged location camera.

Studio work with the nude leads to strong and expressive pictures, with the model usually happy and confident to work in the privacy of such a place. It offers the photographer total control over lighting or backgrounds and the opportunity to devise interesting experimental graphic solutions for the final image. However, it does tend to de-personalise the model by putting her more into the category of an object and there is often a tendency for the images made in a studio to appeal more directly to the intellect than perhaps is the case of the pin-up made on locations. Once these pitfalls and strengths are realised, very fine photographs indeed may be obtained, particularly in the fine art sense.

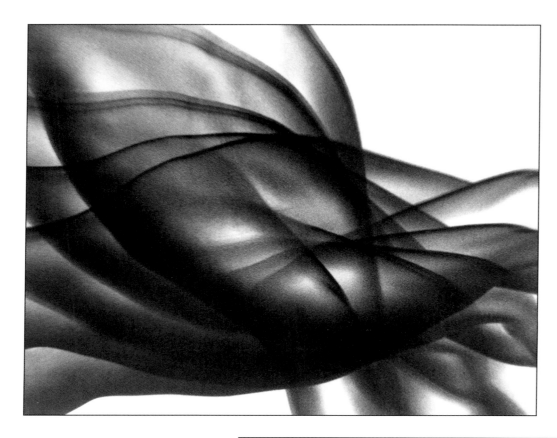

By double exposing together with movement of the camera, very interesting images can be made. The example here has been reversed into negative on lith film. This type of image cannot be made with a camera which has double exposure prevention with no override.

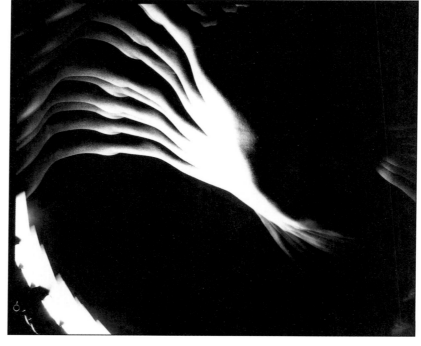

A variation to camera movement can be made with a view camera fitted with a sliding lens panel or film back. In this example, after each exposure, the sliding panel is moved a few millimetres and the film re-exposed.
These effects are useful for later use in darkroom special effects.

The model is posed on black with strong side lighting and no fill light. Successive exposures are made on the same piece of film. As each exposure is made, the camera is moved slightly by tilting the tripod head. The model remains absolutely still.

CHAPTER NINE

Special Effects

For various reasons, the image of the female nude lends itself to those photographic techniques which mask the identity of the model, by destroying the optical clarity of the straight camera image. Purely for aesthetic reasons, the photographer may want to reduce recognition of the model as an individual and build up the essential femininity within the image, until it is a representation of the female in general.

Very often within the area of commercial communications, in advertising for example, where the nude figure is made more socially acceptable by low level recognition values, the photographer will be asked to produce a special effect to achieve this. Photographer-artists also understand that to particularise on one model and to make too much of her identity may introduce alien elements into the visual and mental concepts of an important image.

Many editorial pages where a female nude is essential to the illustration of accompanying text and where circulation to family readers is anticipated, the editor will also want to avoid overt sexuality or close identity of an individual model, while models themselves may also want to conceal their identity for various personal reasons. A special effect which assists this concealment of the entire body is far better than close-cropping of a normal image to exclude the head or face.

The female nude is so strong as a symbol in almost all cultures that any destruction of the image, however severe, will leave sufficient visual clues for the viewer mentally to reconstruct the 'essence' of the figure-form and the visual concept which is intended. This destruction of the pure camera image, while lowering recognition thresholds in early stages of perception, vastly increases the interaction of those unconscious impulses (which lie deep within each viewer) with the image presented on the page.

Special photographic effects can be divided into two main categories of activity: those taking place during the original making of the image by the camera or manipulations made at the dark room stage or in a computer. Even at the most elementary level of camera manipulation, abstraction begins to occur. Black and white photography itself is already an abstraction of the natural colour values to be found in real life and often more dynamic because of that fact.

Special effect photography of the nude therefore should be considered as various steps towards abstraction. One word of warning on the subject of abstraction in modern photography: the final image, however much the optical structure is manipulated, should remain recognisably photographic in style and should not be pushed so far that only meaningless clues are left for the viewer to follow. Abstraction and all photographic special effects will be found to require controlled skills in a craft sense and refined value judgements in taste and design.

Special effects using computer manipulation are another and tempting path to abstraction but photographers must take care to retain the photographic structure of any such image, if the image is to retain credibility as a photograph.

SPECIAL EFFECTS WITH THE CAMERA

The camera is a machine and the image it provides is not reality or truth itself, but an image of that reality. However pure and geometric the results, such photographic images are already several stages removed from real life and the photographer can either gently or dramatically separate this image even further from the events of actual experience.

An elementary but basic ingredient in special effects may be achieved by using different film stock particularly in black and white photography. Infra-red, a film sensitive only to the invisible infra-red light in the spectrum is interesting, as it alters contrast and tonal scales according to time of day and the filter used, and is most useful in outdoor situations. In colour, very bizarre results may he obtained with infra-red film.

Special film, sensitive only to ultra-violet light, is also intriguing in colour, where the source of illumination is only invisible uv light, but this must be a studio set-up as complete darkness is needed to allow only uv light to affect the film. Special filters will be required over both the light source and the lens. Tests are essential.

The use of ortho or line film, for example Agfa Ortho 25, available in 35mm format, can also offer many interesting experimental possibilities. This type of film may be handled in a low intensity red safe light, so processing is particularly easy. Tonal scales are compressed according to whatever developers are used, until with lith developers, pure black and white effects will be seen with no intermediate tones. This making of a direct camera image in line or high contrast values is a most interesting creative area to explore.

Exaggeration of grain is another special effect that is easy to obtain, especially with a 35mm camera. Choose a fast film such as Fuji Neopan 1600, uprated to 3000, Ilford HP5 or Kodak Tri-x 400, over-expose it and process it in a high energy negative developer such as Kodak DK5O or a normal print developer. Transfer the resulting negative by enlargement to a 9 x 12cm (4 x 5in) sheet of high contrast film such as Kodalith, again over-exposing and using a print developer somewhat diluted to half strength. Underdevelop by as much as 50%.

This positive will acquire an increase in grain which will be further enhanced by making the necessary negative from which the final print is to be made. This negative is made by contact on Kodalith film again given over-exposure and then processed with print developer. The original camera image should be on low contrast high speed film, as the build-up of contrast during these various processes is quite considerable.

Working with high speed reversal colour film is also of interest to special effect photographers seeking grain enhancement and by under-exposing as much as three or four f stops and subsequent push-processing, low contrast images will be made, but with considerable increase of grain.

The simplest means the camera has to produce a controlled optical special effect, is to use the aperture to achieve a deeper or shallower zone of focus near the main subject. When working with the nude in studio situations it is wise to create the most depth possible in the zone of sharp focus but elsewhere, particularly outdoors, shallow focus may be desirable in order to soften detail in objects near the model so that their presence becomes less insistent and intrusive.

This is done by opening up the lens (letting in more light) and compensating with a higher shutter speed (see Chapter 2). This use of what is called 'differential focus', or selective focus, is particularly effective in colour, as colour forms will blend in soft edges and very beautiful and complementary visual effects will be seen.

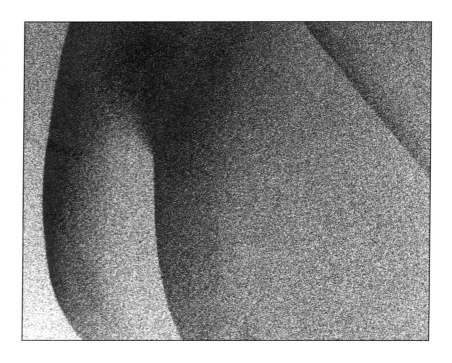

This is a section from an Ilford HP5 120 film, uprated by 100% and processed in print developer to produce exaggerated grain.

DIFFUSION

Apart from the use of selective focus, the sharp mirror image of the lens may be modified by the use of filters or other attachments. Diffusion is much sought after by nude photographers, especially for colour images and this can be obtained in several ways. A diffusing net screen can be stretched over the lens or lens hood itself (a black fine mesh stocking is ideal) or a special glass or plastic filter with the surface etched in a random pattern can be used.

Sometimes these filters will have the centre completely clear of etching, rendering the centre of the image optically unaffected, providing normal sharpness to that part of the image while the outside of this centre area is softly diffused. This is called a 'centre-sharp' diffuser.

To obtain similar effects many photographers will smear thin, petroleum jelly on to the clear uv filters normally attached to the lens, or they will use clear acetate film which has been crinkled and crushed. All these diffusing mediums show increased effect when wide apertures are used and when bright highlights are included in the scene. The skin itself, particularly if slightly oiled and then harshly lit by spotlight, will provide this brilliant highlight when diffusers are used.

Sometimes when working with colour film, not only is diffusion needed but also de-saturation, so that colour forms are not too insistent. Here a fog or de-saturation filter is used in front of the lens and if smoke or mist is present in the scene as well, very striking pictures may be made.

If the level of light is such that the camera must be stopped down so far that the diffusion effects are lost, a neutral density filter must be included in the filter pack. These ND filters are grey in colour and do not change colour temperatures. They come in various densities, one having an ND value of 0.50 for example, reduces the light entering the camera by about 70 per cent, requiring that the lens be opened two f stops in order to compensate for the loss of light.

These ND filters are extremely helpful when needing large apertures for selective focus effects in bright sunlight. The partial ND filter, which has a gradually increasing density over half the filter area and is clear otherwise, is a handy device. In an outdoor picture this would permit the top half of the format, for example, to have much less exposure, producing a darkened sky, while the model could also be brilliantly lit by flash to maintain normal tonal values on the figure itself. This technique is most successful with colour film.

EFFECTS FILTERS

Filter manufacturers such as Cokin (France) B&W (West Germany), Hoya (Japan) and Tiffen (USA) all make many special filters which may be attached to the lens for diverse optical effects. The star filter, a device which surrounds every sharp highlight with a four, six or eight point star is much used; a prism filter is another, where the filter is optically cut or moulded to give a faceted effect, producing several interlocking images with one exposure.

Chromatic effects can be created by diffraction-grating filters which endow bright highlights with rainbow halos and flaring traces of colour, while 'flow' filters will produce blended colour effects in normal scenes. Whenever filters or optical attachments are used, be aware of the artificial and uninspired images which can be the result of such techniques. However, when used with restraint and discretion they are most effective and easy to use.

EFFECTS WITH SHUTTER SPEEDS

While the lens collects light and its images can be modified by interfering with the purity of the optics, the shutter can also be used to alter the image merely by changing speeds. A camera is unique in providing a visual trace of time and if a very brief moment is recorded by a high speed shutter, an analysis of action is provided and the tiny moment is frozen and a sharp image is seen.

With slower shutter speeds, used when the model is moving, a blur of some or all the action ensues, suggesting the essence of motion itself, and this can be very creative in the hands of special effects photographers.

The model, of course, must be given a planned action to perform and it is vital that in any excessively blurred action the model herself is seen, at least in part, in extremely sharp focus.

Soft focus and softening of the image by the use of slow shutter speeds is usually far too abstract to maintain the viewer's interest, if carried too far, even with the nude figure. With slow shutter speeds the model may be moving, the camera may be moving or, in the case of the zoom lens, focus and field may be moving during exposure.

When using these techniques to produce blur, load with slow film and calculate an f stop which allows for a shutter speed of $\frac{1}{8}$, $\frac{1}{4}$ or $\frac{1}{2}$ second. Much slower shutter speeds are worth trying, between 1 and 10 seconds, but be sure that the model's actions are not too rapid at these speeds or the contrast too low in the surroundings, or the action will not record.

These ultra slow speeds are intriguing in colour, particularly if patches of bright colour are arranged behind the model. The figure will then fuse into these colours as the action blurs. With very slow shutter speeds 'panning' the camera to keep exactly parallel with the action is another creative area to explore. Use the smallest f stop possible on these occasions: f16 or f22 at least and a shutter speed of 1 second or slower.

In the studio other possibilities for blurred action exist, for example, when working on a white limbo background, slow shutter speeds and the action stopping attributes of electronic flash may be combined with good effect, producing images which have considerable blur, but which also have one attitude of the body which is completely sharp.

To make this technique work beautifully, light the figure and background with a bright tungsten halogen flood in such a way that areas of the body are left in dense shadow. Position the

This intriguing image has been made by lighting the figures with bright tungsten floods and also electronic flash. A slow shutter speed records blur from the tungsten lighting while the flash stops part of the action.

flash to light this deeply shadowed area only. Rehearse the model to perform an action suited to the chosen shutter speed and picture concept, then fire the flash while the shutter is tripped. The 'X' flash contact on the camera must be selected.

The correct exposure of the flash is controlled solely by the use of the aperture setting and guide number, while the tungsten exposure is achieved by combination of shutter and f stop. When working in colour these disparate light sources must be balanced to the colour temperature of the film if it is judged to be creatively desirable.

STROBOSCOPIC IMAGES

Stroboscopic images of the nude have always been of interest to professional photographers ever since the British photographer Eadweard Muybridge began his analytical photography of movement while in the USA during the 1880s. These multi-images appear together on one frame and can be achieved by several methods.

A rapidly flashing stroboscopic lamp (sometimes even a strong disco strobe can give enough light) is used to expose a planned action while the shutter is kept open. On cameras such as the Contax RX, which is equipped with facilities for an electronic rapid shutter release, the film frame is held in place, while a series of rapid exposures (one tenth of a second apart) are made of the action.

These techniques are more effective when the model is on a dark background and strongly back-lit or side-lit. Pseudo stroboscopic effects, using the lateral traverse on the back of a view camera are also most effective, but here the model is posed in each position while successive exposures are made on the one sheet of film. After each exposure the camera back is racked across in minute, pre-determined steps, producing a sequential effect as each image is made. Working on black velvet is almost always necessary with this method. All stroboscopic images make excellent departure points for originating graphic abstractions or for solarisation.

USING LIGHTS WITH COLOUR FILTERS

For use in montage or graphic effects, an easy but interesting result can be obtained by painting with light around the contour of the model. The model is posed in an easily maintained position against a black velvet backdrop, an assistant dressed in dark clothes traces the outline of the model using a very bright torch or small spotlight, aimed directly at the camera lens while the shutter is left open the whole time.

Other room lights must of course be turned off. After this trace is complete and before the model alters her position, a normal flash exposure is made on the same sheet of film. A 9 x 12cm (4 x 5in) view camera is probably the easiest to control when using this technique. By placing colour filters on the moving light, the trace outline can be given any desired colour.

Other very interesting colour graphic effects may be produced by the use of sharply focused spotlights, each with a strong colour filter. The model will need to oil her body somewhat in order to pick up highlights from the colour spots. As the spotlights are spaced out, so each highlight will separate, each being of a different colour. Positioning the model against a neutral grey is a good starting point for this type of picture.

A variation of this involves the use of a model standing behind a diffusing screen large enough to cover the whole format, the camera being on the other side. The coloured spots are also behind the screen and angled in such a way that they produce separate shadows. Each shadow will be a different colour with intriguing mixtures happening wherever shadows meet. See Masterclass, page 188 for an example of this technique.

If the model touches the screen with her body, this form will be rendered in a soft dark silhouette. The technique works just as well in black and white, giving multiple contours of the body and strong, slightly abstract forms. Changing the material of the screen gives further variables and front lighting of the screen with strong cross-lighting, will add texture and soften contrast. Bubble glass shower screens used this way give very interesting images.

Special effect photographers working outdoors will be largely limited to the use of camera attachments, but the studio photographer has unlimited possibilities. One colour method open to both location photographers and those who work indoors is a flash technique using a colour filter on the lens of the camera and a precise complementary colour filter on the flashhead. Where the flash strikes the model or background, colour is rendered as normal, but in other areas that are lit by means other than the flash the image will be in colours similar to that of the camera filter.

Making truly stroboscopic images directly on non-scientific cameras is not easily possible. This is shot at 10 frames a second on a Rollei SLX.

A motor drive 35mm such as a Contax RX, working at 5 frames a second, can produce creative results, although not to quite the same extent.

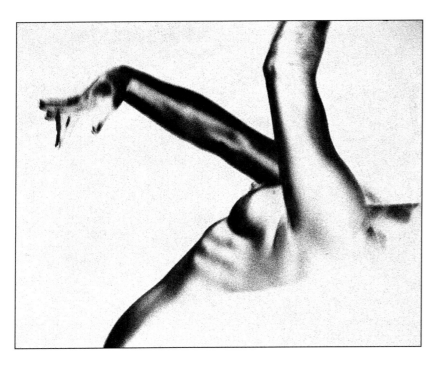

By placing a tissue or tracing paper over the negative in the enlarger, a simulation of a paper negative may be made.

IMAGE CONSTRUCTION IN THE DARKROOM

Nearly 180 years have passed since the miraculous phenomenon of photography was unveiled to the world, shocking those painters who had sought to imitate nature and who could not accept that an automatic machine could produce an image far closer to realism than they had reached in thousands of years of effort. The refuge and comfort of the wiser painters lay in the fact that they believed the camera must stop there: at the point of creating startling documentary and geometrically accurate images. This would allow painters the sole right to venture into the uncharted area of impression, abstraction, expression, minimal images, cubism and so on.

By now we know that the camera is capable of much more than merely witnessing an event and, in the hands of experienced photographers, may also enter many of the subjective realms once thought to be exclusively the property of easel artists. When not attempting to parody their painterly colleagues, photographers may also contribute to the stream of modern art images. As members of a recognised and vigorously influential group within more conventional photography, they identify themselves as being interested in 'constructed' photography.

Such images are usually made in the dark room, often from fragments of other images in an attempt to synthesise subjective and elusive concepts which the photographer wishes to express. Often these are private dreams made visible, yet far from being self-indulgent reverie these images often trigger intense, but equally intuitive responses in those who behold them. The female nude is a particularly favoured symbol in such work, being socially unclassified, and a subject with uncluttered form and line, while having a rich cultural meaning in most societies.

Those who construct images for special effects draw on a well documented reserve of technical evolution from the past and all the standard historical photographic chemistry of normal photography, which they have no hesitation in adapting for their own purposes. Photographers wishing to begin the practice of constructing photographs will need some basic equipment which others do not: a larger than normal darkroom, safe lights of red and amber, a large, efficient film drying cabinet, a professional enlarger taking at least 9 x 12cm (4 x 5in) format, a light table or light box, plus a registration board and register punch.

The other essential is often a healthy budget, because much work is done on expensive graphic arts materials. Because 18 x 24cm (8 x 10in) film is frequently used, large sinks may also be

Colour photographers also have a choice of easy montage effects using overlay techniques. The model is photographed on a clear white background with the figure slightly under-exposed. A second transparency, or a transparency from file, is then overlaid or sandwiched onto the original. Wherever white, clear background is found in the original transparency, the second image will he seen and where the denser image of the body is on the original, the secondary image will barely register.

There are many permutations of this technique. For example, if the secondary transparency also has clear white areas, a third overlay may be added, or a positive black and white film transparency may be included and so on.

necessary and washing and drying facilities for film must be able to support a rapid throughput of material.

SELECTIVE TONING

It is perhaps easiest to begin in this field of advanced darkroom work by working only on the print itself and several possibilities present themselves, once an interesting original negative has been made. For example, the finished print may simply be toned selectively. This is done by painting the dried prints with liquid mask in any areas to be left untoned. This masking fluid is available at professional graphic supplies stores and will prevent toner from reaching the print surface.

When toning is completed the mask is easily stripped or rubbed away, leaving normal image tone alongside the new colour tone. This protected area of the image could then be toned in a secondary operation with a different colour toner, giving a duo-tone colour effect. The same partial masking technique can be used selectively to protect the print before chemical reduction or bleaching is carried out on fairly dense black and white prints.

A partial print solarising technique is possible where tone is also produced. This may be achieved by making a normal print with rather full exposure, then only partially developing the image: quickly place it at this stage in a stop bath for one to three seconds (maximum) and for not more than five seconds in a weak fixer. At this point turn on a strong white light and the image will begin to reverse in some areas to give a negative effect, while at the same time picking up a distinct colour tone in other areas.

Another variation of print manipulation may be made by exposing a print normally and placing it in an empty dish, then applying developer selectively with a brush or cotton wool swab to whatever areas are desired. The image will only be visible in areas touched by the developer and very creative pictures may result. This technique can also be concluded with the solarising treatment discussed above.

STRIPPING FILM

The special attributes of stripping film, which is much used in graphic arts and printing trades, are very interesting. The emulsion of this film, after processing normally and while still wet, may be stripped easily from the base and given a new support, perhaps one which is heavily textured, or the image may be folded and draped on a plain piece of paper support, before being dried while in a flat position. Kodak and Agfa both supply such film. If the stripped and folded image is fixed to a

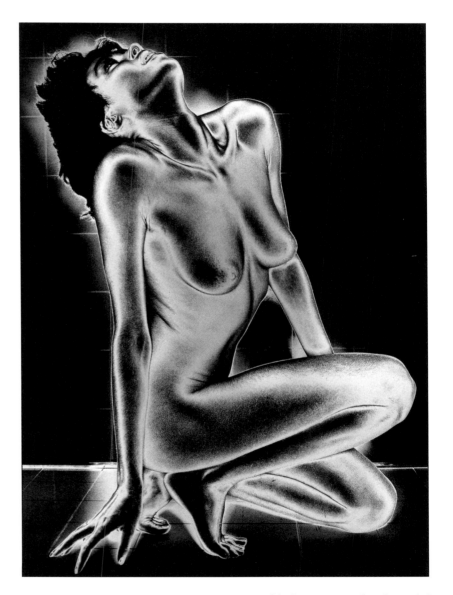

This is an example of partial print solarising with tone separation.

sheet of 9 x 12 cm (4 x 5in) cleared film, this can then be enlarged to magnify the effects of the manipulation.

SELF COATING PAPERS

One other print method that is growing in popularity is the use of self-coated papers. These are normally water colour papers of rough texture; emulsions may be commercial ones such as are obtainable from Rockland Colloid Company, USA, or Kentmere Ltd, Staveley, Cumbria UK or Silverprint Ltd, London UK. Silverprint is the best British source of unusual chemistry and fine photographic papers for special darkroom effects and they ship globally. Their website, http//www.silverprint.co.uk, is well worth visiting. Photo-resists from Kodak Limited or other graphic arts suppliers are also most useful, or resists may be mixed at home from antique formulas. A source of these is to be found in Wall and Jordan, Photographic Facts and Formulas, Amphoto, USA.

The photographer using liquid photo-emulsions will need to obtain heavy rag papers, usually with pronounced texture. The paper can be sized with gelatin first or the light sensitive emulsion can be applied directly to the surface. Coating can be with a broad soft brush or, in my experience, a better result comes from using a coarse sponge paint roller. The coated paper is left flat to dry. Of course, a red safelight must be the only illumination during coating, drying and enlarging. A very detailed source reference on these techniques can be found in the book *Silver Gelatin*, by Martin Reed and Sarah Jones, obtainable from Silverprint Ltd.

COLLAGE

Once experience is gained in these wet processes, it may be of interest to try manipulation of dry prints by collage. Careful planning is needed and the required number of images are made on separate single weight paper prints or laser prints. These images can then be cut and pasted or even stitched into place with a sewing machine, to provide a fascinating piece of construction. Collage has a most honourable history in modern art, particularly in the photography of the 1930s and 1940s and it is technically simple to achieve, but again it must be stressed that the whole final image should be planned meticulously before the various parts are photographed.

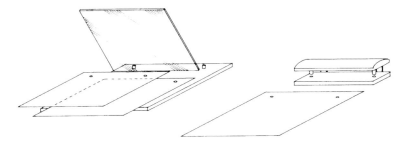

The Kodak Register Punch is a very precise and fairly expensive item, but essential to many advanced darkroom special effects. Separations, reverse negatives and mutually exclusive masks are made on lith film and punched for exact registration of multiple images.

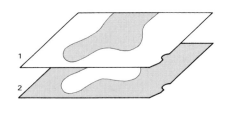

This is called a mutually exclusive mask. A positive is made of an image punched on the register board, then a negative of that image, again punched on the register board is made. The area shown in the diagram with tone, excludes its counterpart which is solid black. Partial exposures and solarisations can be made with these masks.

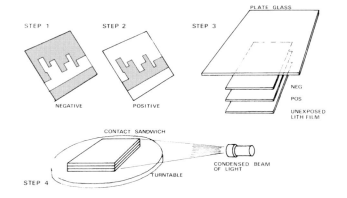

This diagram shows how to use mutually exclusive masks.

Step 1 and 2 show mutually exclusive masks which have been register punched.

Step 3 shows the sandwich of Neg/Pos lith films which are set up to expose on to lith film.

Step 4 shows a sandwich of masks placed on a turntable and spun during an exposure to an oblique light source. This produces a thicker line around the masks.

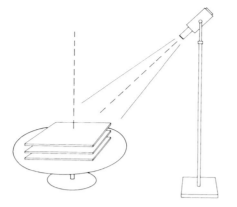

Exposing the film sandwich to oblique light gives great control over line thickness. By raising the exposing light, the line is thinner. By lowering the light source, the line becomes much thicker.

MONTAGE

The use of collage and multi-faceted images leads on to the true filmic montage. These are made in the darkroom, whereby each image fragment penetrates the borders of others within the format, creating an impression of shifting values of time and place, while offering a complexity in the visual concept not possible by straightforward photographs. The montage is made by holding back selected areas of the print during one exposure, either by dodging with the hands or the use of masks. These unexposed areas of the print are subsequently printed in the same way from other selected negatives. An example of filmic montage appears on page 169.

Multiple printing includes the possibility of printing repetitive images on to the same piece of paper, thereby giving a stroboscopic effect, or printing surrealistic backgrounds behind the figure by the use of masking techniques or by the use of normal photographic images coupled with photogram printing.

These various enlarging techniques will require that the final image is exactly planned and that each part of it is projected to scale beforehand, sketched on graph paper and painstakingly brought together with complete accuracy and registration. This may mean that the negative carrier in the enlarger will require a system of registering each successive image or mask or that the print easel will have this facility. Both are easily made by the use of register pins and register punches or home-made versions of them. The register board or easel is by far the most used and most useful piece of equipment in all special effects darkroom work. See diagram opposite.

TEXTURE SCREENS

Other fairly elementary tools for dark room manipulation, would include texture screens. These are commercially available, but are better if made by the photographer and chosen to fit the concept, using a particular screen only for a particular concept. They may be physically dimensional screens such as textured glass, loosely woven fabric or paper, open metal grids or random textures of translucent plastic or they may be photographic in character made by photographing any organic textures found to be attractive or suited to a particular need.

These screens may be large enough to be placed over the whole print area under the enlarger, in which case their texture is minimised, or they may be placed in contact with the negative itself in the enlarger where they become magnified along with the rest of the image. Tissue paper or lens tissue for example, placed on the negative carrier will produce a very broken texture when magnified eight to ten times.

Similarly, dot screens, obtainable from graphic supply stores will create exaggerated dot patterns if placed in contact with the negative to be enlarged and interesting screens may also be made by enlarging clean, sharp grain patterns from 35mm film and solarising these to enhance the effect, before transferring them finally to a lith film.

This is an example of overlay to create a montage. The model has been posed on a white studio paperfall and a very grainy black and white positive has been sandwiched together with it to create a simple but intriguing image.

Texture screens may be taped to the film channel inside the camera. This gives an unusual effect and some halation of highlights. Here a zoom effect has been used on slow film to produce blurring as well as the screen effects.

PHOTOGRAMS

The photogram is of considerable interest for itself alone, because it was taken up by a number of famous photo-artists of the 1920s and 1930s in Europe, notably Man Ray, Christian Schad and Moholy Nagy. This technique permits the photographer to produce fascinating and serious images without a camera by placing objects on the enlarging paper or on a glass stage slightly above the easel. A further extension of this technique involves the projection of an image from an enlarger on to such three dimensional objects. Because the photographer of the nude, who is looking for photogram effects, almost always chooses this image projection method, it may be as well to describe it in detail.

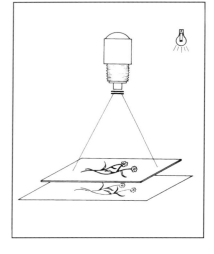

Photograms are a substantial source of creative images. The diagram above shows that these may be created without a lens or enlarger. Photo paper is placed on a darkroom work surface, and an arrangement of solid objects is placed directly on the paper and a brief exposure made.

A more complex photogram can be made under an enlarger. A previously made image can be projected on to photo paper, through an intermediate glass stage, upon which 3-dimensional objects have been arranged.

The positive or negative of the nude subject is chosen and will usually have been made on a black background to produce large areas of clear film in order to give a clear printing light for the photogram, over as much of the print area as possible. Objects are chosen which may relate in scale with the projected figure or in some way complement the entire concept. These are then laid on the enlarging paper in a pre-determined position, or on an elevated glass stage two centimetres above the paper. Some may even be placed in the negative carrier itself and so be magnified along with the image. It is one of the most flexible and satisfying of all the graphic techniques available to those who construct images.

An alternative method of making photographs of the nude involves a life size photogram of the figure. This requires that a weak exposing light is arranged above a chosen area in the studio, which must also be equipped with red darkroom safe lights and otherwise be totally dark. After turning on these safe lights, a large piece of unexposed mural paper is fixed to the floor with weights at each corner and the nude model is arranged on the paper, along with any other elements necessary to the finished design. These props could be life size, of course.

A complex photogram image has been made by using a broken wine glass on the photo paper plus a flower. The bubbles come from a plastic sheet which has been heated in a hot oven until it melts and bubbles. This is placed on the unexposed photo paper. The exposing negative, made on a black background, produces the two figures. After 50 % of its development, the print has been exposed for 5 seconds to a 15 watt lamp at 75 centimetres above the developing dish. This has resulted in a partial solarising in the mid-tones of the print.

*To make a makeshift developing
tank for mural size paper, first
make a frame about 2 metres
(72 inches) x 60 cm (24 ins) of
50 x50 cm (2 ins x 2 ins) wood.
Then apply very strong plastic
to the frame and staple it in
place. Large paper rolls can be
processed by first filling the
tank with water and rolling the
exposed print through the
water. When the paper is limp
and very wet, discard the water
and pour in print developer.*

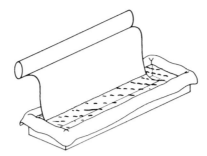

*Continue the usual steps of acid
stop and fixer. Follow this by
1 hour washing of the loosely
rolled print.*

For example, a bicycle has interesting forms which allow light
to penetrate. The exposure light is switched on for a brief
period, determined by previous testing and then the paper is
rolled up in a light-proof container and held for processing later.
Professional black and white labs can handle these large sizes or
photographers with large darkrooms can process the print
themselves, using a home-made tank. Very exciting fine art
images are possible, but the method is laborious and expensive.

CHEMICAL EFFECTS

The abuse of photographic emulsions, although it may offend
manufacturers and dedicated photographic chemists, produces
unusually satisfying results for photographer-artists. The
phenomenon of 'reticulation', a term used to describe the
breaking and crazing of the gelatin emulsion due to abnormal
extremes of temperature during processing, is such a case.

Reticulation can be deliberately caused by processing the
negative film in warm to hot developer, (considerable under-
exposure may be needed) and then dipping it quickly in ice
water before fixing. Different films react with more or less
success to this treatment and many modern emulsions will
stand much of this rough treatment with no effect at all, but
tests can be made with hottest solutions at 40°C (122°F) and
cubes of ice in the intermediate water bath.

SOLARISATION

Another abuse of the emulsion, not particularly liked by the
modern manufacturer, who takes great care to prevent such
things, is that of pseudo-solarisation. True solarisation was
noted in the original Daguerreotypes of 1839 and 1840 and was
caused by the power of the sun, the only exposing light possible

*Reticulation is caused by
rapid changes in developer
temperature and gives very
interesting graphic effects.*

for some of these early processes, which under certain
circumstances caused a partial reversal of the positive image
into a negative. This true solarisation by extreme over-exposure
is rarely possible with modern emulsions and it is considered
necessary to increase exposures by at least 1000 times to even
approach conditions likely to cause it.

In 1862 Armand Sabattier, a French scientist, described 'pseudo-
solarisation reversal', which he discovered while inadvertently
exposing a partially developed wet plate to white light. This is a
more accurate description for the reversal which is induced in
modern emulsions, by exposing them to white light at some

SOLARISING

Step 1   Step 2   Step 3   Step 4

Step 1: Rim lighting highlights the figure edge.

Step 2: A lith positive is made from the camera negative and after 45 seconds of development in ordinary print developer which has been warmed to 25°C., this film is exposed for two seconds to a 15 watt lamp which has been fixed 70cm (30in) above the developing dish. Immediately start vigorous agitation by flicking the hand to and fro in the developing dish. Solarising can be watched taking place. When at a suitable stage, rapidly transfer the film to a stop bath. Fix as normal.

Step 3: Make an unsolarised positive of the camera negative.

Step 4: Follow Step 2 procedure but develop fully. The Mackie Line will be more evident and contrast will have increased a great deal.

Step 5: After making a reverse of Step 4, make a new high contrast film of the result. This should be a true line image with no tone.

Step 6: This is a result of assembling one or more of the above steps and making a new lith film which is solarised.

Step 5   Step 6

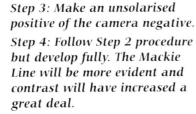 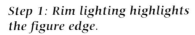

stage during development. Each emulsion and developer reacts differently to this treatment but certain essentials may make the results easier to achieve.

1. EXACTLY TIMED FIRST EXPOSURE;
2. EXACTLY TIMED PARTIAL FIRST DEVELOPMENT;
3. EXACTLY TIMED SECOND EXPOSURE;
4. VERY RAPID HAND AGITATION DURING SECOND DEVELOPMENT;
5. SUFFICIENT CONTRAST IN THE ORIGINAL TO BE SOLARISED.

Some workers insist on ageing the developer to be used some days ahead of time but this is not really necessary. Weak fresh developer will solarise when the first and second exposures are correct and made by a 15 watt lamp 1m (39in) above the developing tray. This must be determined by testing. Always make notes in the darkroom log book of these complex processes and it will then be easy to find references to past experience when needed. Solarisation of this kind is characterised by a fine line, called a Mackie line, between borders of extreme contrast. This tends to increase the apparent sharpness of the image.

Above: This is an example of a solarised print which has partially reversed the image.

Right: This is an example of a solarised lith negative.

Control in this process is exercised by altering exposure and development for the initial stage and altering the time of re-exposure to white light and the subsequent second stage development. All these variables may be changed to interact with each other but the more normal the processing of the first stage and the more complete it is before the white light exposure is given, the more it retains details of the original image. Originals should be reasonably high contrast for best results. Best results will be achieved by using high contrast lith film or grade 6 bromide paper, processed in a universal print developer such as Dektol, diluted 50% more than normal and at 24°C (75°F).

NOTE: Solarising requires warm developer, split second timing of each stage, timing of the reversal exposure, timing of the continued second development and very rapid agitation after the brief exposure. Lith film must be used with a print developer not a negative or process developer.

TONE SEPARATION

Tone separation and/or compression is a simple but useful technique in graphic special effects. It involves repetitive contact printing on lith film which frequently shows pinholing in the emulsion. These must be spotted or covered before further work can take place. Static electricity is another problem in darkrooms which handle large sheets of film because it attracts dust particles from the air and this can be alleviated somewhat by the use of an air ioniser or by the use of anti-static brushes on the film and glass surfaces.

Tone separation is a special effect often used in graphic arts photography by those who wish to illustrate the nude and the result is negatives or positives which display absolute black, pure white and a variety of grey tones in between, not usually more than three in number. A simple method to do this is as follows: using the register board and punch to ensure perfect register, expose a fairly crisp negative to lith film for 20 seconds and develop in a standard paper developer such as Kodak Dektol for three to five minutes. Make another positive at 40 seconds and another at 80 seconds all from the same negative, taking great care that they are exactly in register to the first.

Develop these for precisely the same time as the original short exposure. From these three positives a combined negative may be made: take the densest positive and a test strip of lith film and make a test exposure, then develop it in print developer diluted 50 per cent more than is usually needed for paper prints. If this is satisfactory, make test strips for each of the other positives and develop them for the same time, noting those exposures which give the preferred results.

When certain of the effects of the tests, return again to the densest positive and take a full sheet of lith film to make the first exposure according to test data. Then on the same sheet make successive exposures of each of the positives, until finally the lightest is exposed. Make certain each positive is perfectly registered each time. Process this multiple exposure in diluted print developer as above and a separated negative will result, with solid blacks (which print white), completely clear areas which print dense black in the final picture and as many flat, grey tones as there were separations to produce them. All other intermediate tones and therefore the modelling in the original, should have gone.

Tone and line is a further sophistication of these graphic abstractions using lith film. This method creates first, a negative lith film and then a positive lith from this, made by contact printing so that each is a perfect complementary to the

Tone separation is achieved by making three lith masks which are punched on a register board. One is processed as a negative and a positive is made. From this a mid-tone grey is made. All three are sequentially exposed on to the same piece of photo paper. The negative of this set has been solarised.

other, forming what is known as a mutually exclusive mask. When held to a strong light, if they are in perfect register, such a sandwich of negative and positive masks will appear to pass no light at all. However, if the eye is brought to a position 45 degrees from the surface, and viewed from the side, light may be seen through the edge of the sandwich.

An exposing light is angled at 45 degrees through the masks by using a turntable arrangement, or by exposing in sequence on all four sides of the printing frame. By placing clear or diffuse film spacers of various thicknesses between negative and positive or between sandwich and unexposed film, the lines maybe thickened and altered at will. By using the negative on top of the sandwich, a different effect is created than when the positive is on top, and so on.

Throughout this deeper involvement with darkroom processes which are needed to support the final assembly of constructed images, the photographer will be using various graphic arts films and developers. Film material will tend to be lith film such as that which Kodak, Agfa, or Fuji produce. This is basically a very high contrast film capable of being processed to offer only two tones: black or white. If processed in dilute print developer and slightly over-exposed however, such film can provide crisp mid-tones and continuous tones, very suitable for intermediate stages when using the Sabattier effect or in tone separation. My personal preference for suitable lith films are those manufactured by Fuji in 24 x 18cm (10 x 8in) size.

To get absolute contrast on such film it is necessary to process in a high energy caustic developer of the lith variety, obtainable normally in a two solution pack which must be mixed together just prior to working. Dektol or other print developer, used with almost no dilution, although not giving perfect line results, does give commendably dense blacks and clean highlights and is a single solution formula.

Almost all lith films will show evidence of pinholing or small emulsion defects and these must be spotted before further work can take place. This is done by the use of a red water soluble opaquing medium, obtainable at graphic arts stores. It is painted on the film emulsion side with a small brush.

POSTERISATION

Once a degree of darkroom skill has been acquired, the photographer can move on to posterisation, so called because it abstracts the natural photograph to the point where the structure of the image becomes quickly accessible, which is the usual result of well designed posters. The technique is similar to tone separation in that continuous tonal areas are condensed by transferring them to lith film masks and as many separations as needed can be made. These are then recombined, using a register board, in any way the photographer wishes, either in black and white or by being given arbitrary colour filters, to produce full colour prints. When working in colour both negative and positive masks may be used.

Some of the masks may be solarised. All darkroom posterisation is easier if done on 24 x 18cm (10 x 8in) film. When an interest in using these various darkroom techniques deepens and experience accumulates, the photographer will see many possibilities of combining them: texture screens Sabattier Effect, tone separation with texture screens, bas relief and so on. The imagination may be left to invent without restraint and often many file negatives of the nude, lying unwanted in storage, can be re-used to produce new and dramatically different images.

It should be stated once again that when making any photographic special effects, whether they are optically created in the camera and therefore acceptable to the photographic purists or whether they are in the more experimental field of constructed photographs using darkroom methods, the technique should never be the sole reason for the picture. Special effects, where the conventional geometry of the camera image is arbitrarily altered, requires that the visual concept be

Colour posterisation can be achieved by solarisation and tone separation techniques in the darkroom or by the use of tools to be found in Photoshop.

strong enough to carry its message to the viewer, despite the deliberate concealment of perceptual clues.

For an entirely different technique for obtaining special effects on images of the nude, see Chapter 12/13 on digital photography and image manipulation with a computer. These digital techniques will not emulate darkroom special effects and must be seen to be a different, but dynamically interesting effect in their own right.

CHAPTER TEN

Imagery & Imagination

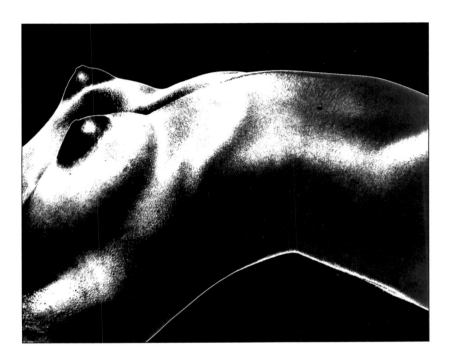

Using abstraction techniques such as solarisation, tone separation and tone compression, the nude can lose its eroticism and become less subjective. Here the first steps have been taken towards creating an image of the body as a landscape.

All photographers benefit by knowing beforehand what it is they wish to include in their pictures and how they wish to execute these ideas when it comes to technique. The most memorable of images are usually those which show the most style and those which disclose a preconception of the composition. This has become axiomatic in photography in general and for those interested in photographing the female nude, thoughtful visual and psychological concepts are even more important.

Obviously, a still life or a highly stylised interior and perhaps even a landscape can be planned minutely beforehand and, as very little movement is involved, unlimited permutations of major elements of composition do not arise. Action photographs and images of living things may be broadly planned, but the surprise or accidental re-arrangement of the subject plays an important part in the final design and therefore must be left open until the moment the shutter is fired.

Planning is vital to the success of any photography of a living thing and never more important than when the subject is the nude. Visual concept and the rationale behind the nude picture will vary enormously and before going further, the photographer must ask: '*Why am I making this photograph?*'

Nude photographs may be roughly classified into three main categories: intellectual, erotic or fine art. Technical methods vary somewhat in categories, models often must be very different, and concepts change enormously.

INTELLECTUALISING THE NUDE

The intellectual approach to the nude considers the female body as an aesthetic expression of beauty, drawing heavily perhaps on the 2000 years of philosophical opinion which has been built up behind the classical art image of the nude. The visual concept may be very graphic, using lighting and dark room graphics or colour control to flatten the body and emphasise the edges.

Alternatively, the photographer may rely on discreet poses, subtle lighting and restrictive choices of model to de-emphasise sensuality in order to make the photograph coolly objective in a way that tends to de-personalise the model in favour of generalising about the universal attributes of the female. It is not, of course, impossible that eroticism also becomes part of such a picture or that the intellectual picture does not enter into the territory of the fine art photograph, but intellectual concepts of photography of the nude lean heavily towards asceticism and classically academic images.

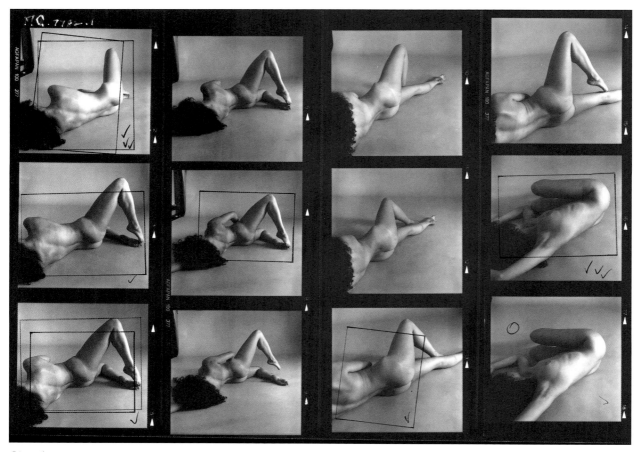

Step 1

An image of the nude may be intellectualised. The body can become a landscape.

Step 1: The contact print.

Step 2: A first work print

Step 3: A selected crop of Step 2.

Step 4: A second work print cropped to a vertical.

Step 5: A selection of an area of Step 4 and an increase in print contrast.

Step 6: The exhibition print.

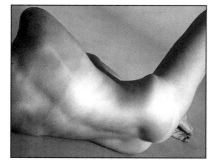

Step 2

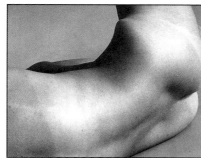

Step 3

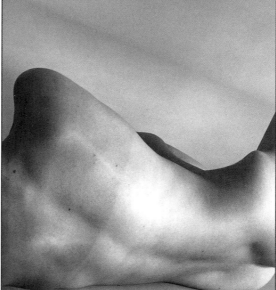

Step 4

Step 5

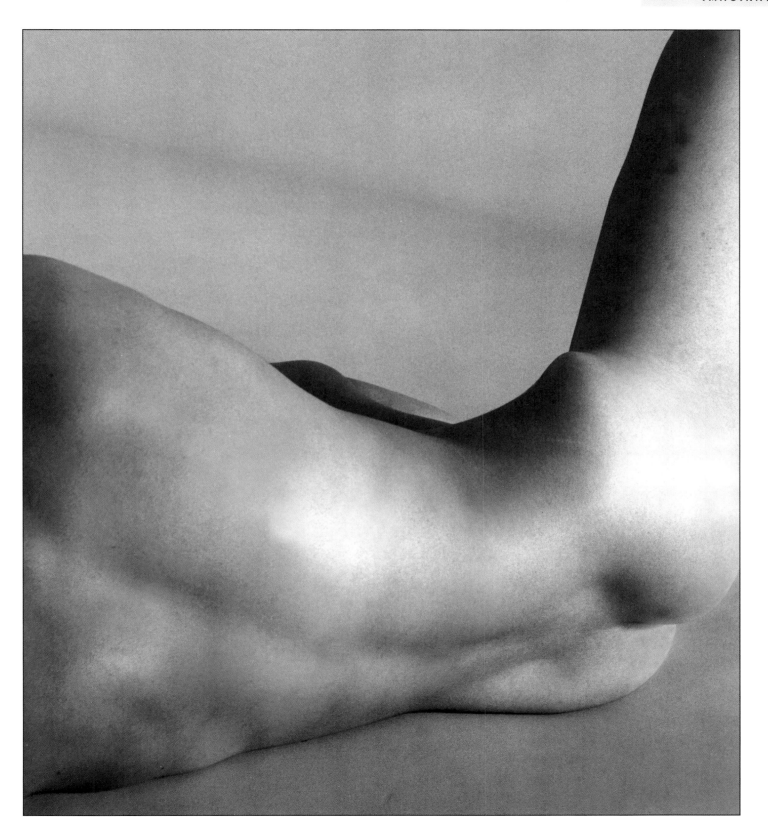

*An elegant and revealing image
with restrained eroticism*.

EROTIC NUDES

The consensus of public opinion about nude photography of the female will always be heavily weighted towards the opinion that such pictures are always erotic and nothing else and it is true that the majority of photographers and their viewers will seek to present or find this element above all others in such images. Even in the changing social climate of modern Western society where the public acceptance of nudity and nude imagery is much more enlightened or permissive than ever before, the photographer will do well to note certain areas where care should be exercised in respect of deliberately erotic pictures.

Contact sheets.

Each community guards itself with its own statutes in the matter of publicly displayed eroticism in any published work and transgression against these could bring the photographer some painful legal reminders that even today there are certain social taboos which cannot be disregarded if these images are to be shown in public.

The photograph, because of its optically pure image of reality, has always been a special target for suppression whenever the nude body is the subject. It is only three or four decades ago that the US post office would not accept photographs of the nude if there was the slightest trace of pubic hair showing. It is still an offense in many countries to post pictures which can be legally considered obscene.

Obscenity is not well defined by the law of any country but it can generally be taken to mean a corruption of public morals and that it includes pornographic imagery. Pornography is rather more narrowly fixed in legal terms by many legal systems and is considered to refer to material designed by its explicitness to appeal exclusively to a prurient interest in sex. The photographer therefore must step neatly between these two obstacles if eroticism is to be the theme of any nude photography considered for public exhibition or publishing.

PIN-UP PHOTOGRAPHY

The most innocuous of erotic concepts and the one which has reached cult proportions amongst males the world over is the pin-up. Everyone (or every man, perhaps) likes to look at beautiful women. If they are naked, or nearly so, this increases the interest and enhances the fantasy. With a watchful eye on the local obscenity laws and another on the prized markets which may be activated by such a strong medium of communication, many commercial enterprises support the pin-up in various forms such as posters, books, magazines and calendars. With the relaxed social attitudes to nudity and a degree of understanding of feminine desires, there is also a trade in publications where the male nude is featured.

The pin-up can be traced right back to the discreetly erotic post cards of late Victorian and Edwardian times, but the simple post card of those days has now become bolder, flashier, bigger and usually printed in full colour. For the modern pin-up, total nudity is usually not required. Sufficient sexual attraction comes from the partly clothed model.

This increases the sense of voyeurism, particularly if the girl is innocently found in natural surroundings, but looking at the camera. Ideal concepts for pin ups will be found around this

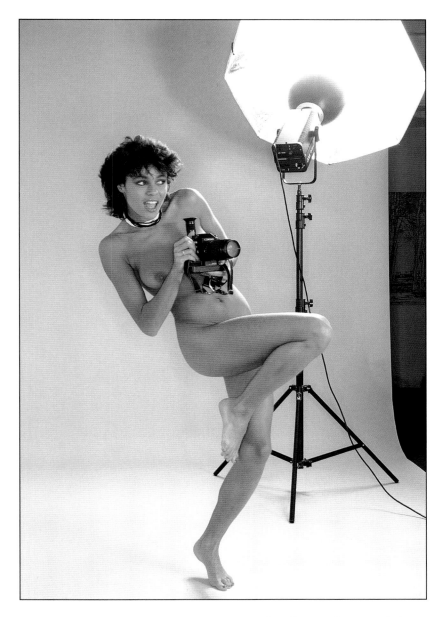

*The pin-up photograph is
usually an acceptable cliché.*

element of naturalness: dressing or undressing; sleeping or waking up; in the bath or shower; combing the hair; getting out of a bathing suit; dressed in the minimum of underwear or wearing partly unzipped or unbuttoned clothing.

The essential pre-requisite of these situations is that the clothing worn should be loose fitting and the environment of the model should enhance the activity being presented. The model contributes an enormous amount to this kind of photograph and should be selected with great care. Her features and expression, particularly if she is looking into the lens, will increase the mood of the picture and invite the viewer deeper into the fantasy of the image.

The best of these pictures use models who are not overtly sexual but appear simply as attainable and recognisable personalities with whom the viewer can identify. Many clichés are contrived in this kind of photograph but at this level of contact, clichés are one of the strongest forms of communication. Cane furniture, sumptuous beds, furs, silks, leathers and satins, wet T-shirts and so on, are often to be found as props in pin-ups, while colours tend towards strong saturation and complementary harmonies. Models chosen for this type of assignment, if it is commercially sponsored, tend to have fuller figures than those used for intellectual or fine art photographs.

For the successful pin-up picture the photographer must choose a particularly attractive girl and one who has a memorable face, good hands and feet and who can act expressively. The concept of comedy should be explored in this type of picture, as it is rarely attempted in any other area of nude photography and a really amusing nude photograph tends to be accepted by a much wider public than perhaps any other.

Beach environments are also particularly suitable for backgrounds to the pin-up with abundant light and entirely natural surroundings, establishing an easy rationale for the composition. Pin-up photography can never be classified as great art, but it is usually considered great fun for the viewer and not too difficult for the photographer or model to produce. It is certainly the easiest to sell as it has now been largely established that these images may be exhibited in most public places without too much complaint.

Fine Art Nudes

The female nude as fine art is a very different matter. First, a long and brilliant history of using the naked figure in art as a statement in its own right supports the fine art photographer in his efforts to do the same. Even among many of the most protective guardians of Western morality and culture, the nude, particularly the classic Venusian female nude, has come to mean 'Art' itself.

This, of course, both assists the photographer and ensnares him in an ancient and disagreeable battle about what is and what is not art. Provided the photographer is seen to be supporting sentiments approved by the critics and academics of the art

establishment, he proceeds with ease. Should he deviate from this path and seek originality, he may risk exclusion from exhibition prospects and constant opposition to his chosen point of view.

The fine art photographer must, of course, not compromise. His concepts must remain true to his considered philosophies and technical experience, whatever is said about them, but that task is greater perhaps than for photographers working in any other field of interest. Technique must remain flawless, choice of model must be impeccable and the execution of the assignment must touch some universality other than eroticism, if his work is to stand the test of time.

If the photographer-artist is working on a theme which has a strong narrative element within it, then this will indicate the nature of the girl chosen, how she styles her hair and even, to some extent, her pose. If the naked body is being used to express a private statement, the choice of model may be difficult, as could be the type of lighting used and perhaps the many technical matters leading up to the picture.

For example, the most difficult statement in art to communicate to others is one which depends solely upon a naked body against a plain background. The intellect is involved, but not exclusively, yet sexuality must not be the complete message. Somehow the photographer has to find and present for scrutiny something of the cosmic arabesque which has become attached to the woman through aeons of parallel, but very different, development with the male. The uniqueness of the female body has always characterised important and symbolic mysteries for artists since painting began and photography is perhaps better able to communicate this in the twentieth century than most other art forms.

The naked female standing against a plain background is totally unclassified. Except for evolutionary changes in body proportions, she could come from any era. Once she is even partly clothed, she may be identified precisely as to class, position and the exact point of time in which she dwells. If the artist is making a sufficiently deep and universal statement, this historical information may destroy it or diffuse it.

Models for artist-photographers need not be fashionable or overtly sexual, but they must be able to take the most exacting direction and to give long hours of attention to the assignment. For the photographer designing an image of the nude, the placement of the limbs, the tensile strength suggested by the body position, the activity and line of a pose, must all be related to the frame of reference, that is to say, the film format and camera viewfinder.

If the model stretches, the elongation of the figure may not improve its disposition within the shape of the rectangle of the finished print. If the figure is proportionally reduced to a small part of the format, with a very large area of background remaining, dynamic tension is introduced by virtue of the pressure of this void of space on the tiny figure. If the pose suggests insecurity, the effect of tension is heightened. Obviously, if we return to the examples discussed in the pin-up, the powerful ambiguity being introduced by the art photographer will be very much out of place and probably be most disturbing to the viewer of that type of material.

Many photographers following a fine art career will use the nude in very frank and natural ways, almost as a social document. Larry Fink of the USA is one modern photographer who became interested in this, another with a different concept is Emmett Gowin, also of the USA. Duane Michals (USA) introduces some very natural concepts into otherwise quite surrealistic pictures, while Leslie Krims (USA) may use the nude figure to express fiercely anti-social sentiments or cynicism.

Richly photographed eroticism, sometimes perhaps bordering on pornography, can be seen in the work of Helmut Newton, while there is a tenderness in the images of women as portrayed by Jean Loup Sieff. Bill Brandt, particularly his 1945-1960 work, exposed his subjects to hauntingly subjective environments while his camera invaded the voluptuous spaces of the body which presented themselves as the model moved.

Looking back at the silver elegance of Edward Weston, the body is seen as deep structure, covered with a fragile eroticism which, in the 1930s when he worked, no doubt shocked many viewers with its unaffected naturalism. But today his work seems to be the hallmark of the classic statement in nude photography.

The graphic nude form, bordering on the intellectual, may forever be represented by the originality of Man Ray and the rare examples found in the work of Moholy-Nagy, in their photographs during the 1930s. Whatever the present day concepts sought by the serious and fine art photographer of the nude, the past masters of the subject should be studied closely to see how they handled the problems and concepts.

CHARACTERISTICS WHICH CAN CLASSIFY THE PHOTOGRAPH AS ART

Certain characteristics may be found common to all works of art, others may be seen exclusively only in a given medium of expression. The following are attributes, all or some of which may be identified in photographs which perform as art objects:

SIMPLICITY
The art in art is the art of omission.

ASYMMETRY
Symmetry and perfection is complete, leaving nothing to be discovered; asymmetry is mutation at the peak of transition.

INNOCENCE
The artlessness of spring conceals the raw power of innocence, growth and naturalness.

PEACE
Inner stability is the dynamic partner of subjective communication and visual contentment.

ORIGINALITY
Unfamiliar, even uncomfortable, imagery which arises from unconscious experiences in the creator.

SURPRISE
A sense of wonder, revelation, awe. A presentation of unexpected things by familiar means.

MOOD
Volatility, a sense of theatre, tension, pathos or ecstasy. A cosmic ripple of emotion.

MATURITY
Timelessness, ripeness, incontrovertible truth and, ultimately, connection to cosmic man.

LATENCY
This is hidden energy and the incompleteness of potential growth, the dynamism of controlled flair, the vitality and force of an authoritative but subdued promise.

FREEDOM
To be original, to have none of these listed attributes. To be symmetrical, immature, aggressive, convoluted, extrovert or self-contained but, above all, to be new and to be original.

SEXUALITY
Man and the world in love, the world and the cosmos inextricably linked, man and woman unified, a voluptuous celebration of tactile virtues.

PARADOX
Duality and polarity, juxtaposition and surprise. Intuition and reason, the occident and orient interacting, female versus male.

RELEVANCE
Consistency and affinity to the present, coincident with space-time dimensions of past moments and memories.

FELICITY
Happiness, joy, contentment and harmony and an element of playfulness. Art for art's delightful sake.

CONCEPTS

For photographers of all categories of nude work, the environment which surrounds the body and the props nearby are important; nothing which is irrelevant should be left in the picture. The pose, background, mood and gesture should be as simple as possible yet be expressive of the concept desired.

Colour designs should be arranged so that harmony may be found for the figure. This, of course, does not mean that bright colours are forbidden but only that they should be used intelligently. It is usually preferred by most people who view the nude body in full colour that the skin takes on the slightest sheen and a lightly tanned appearance. This can be the result of light body lotion and the use of an 81A Wratten filter on the camera or a gold reflector behind the main light source.

After deciding the broad concept of the picture to be made, the photographer must then begin the search for the model. Concepts in nude photography are often tied very much to the girls who are chosen for the picture and sometimes must be changed if the model does not fit sympathetically into the visual arrangement first decided upon. The model chosen should be one who will work well in a given situation and who can add something of her own to the success of the assignment.

PRE-VISUALISATION

After a general discussion about the entire job with the model a date should be fixed for her to return for the actual work and then the photographer may begin to design the picture. In all nude photography, the visual concept must be clear in the photographer's mind well before work begins and the only successful way to do this is by the process known as 'pre-visualisation'.

Pre-visualisation of the actual image which will fit the concept can be attained by an activity similar to meditation. Sit in a comfortable and calm environment, breathing in deeply with the diaphragm and exhaling slowly. Soft music may help, lying full length or looking at a lightly textured but softly lit white wall may make it easier to visualise.

Clear the mind slowly of all the irrelevancies in the surface consciousness and begin to concentrate on the forthcoming picture. Visualise the shape and size of the format, try to see in the mind's eye the position the model will occupy and the actions she will take. Try to conjure up the same picture but with a longer lens, watch for the compaction of aerial space which this introduces, add colours and perhaps a few simple props. Continue the deep, relaxed breathing and maintain a calm body attitude and then let each image slowly fade away. Often a flash of imagination will enter the mind unbidden and an entirely new line of thought begins.

This is the uncontrolled feedback coming from memories and past experiences which are surfacing from the unconscious. Follow each new inspiration, test it mentally with actual photographic experience and conjure up possible permutations of equipment and lighting, plus new environments, all in the mind's eye. This is the imagination working but working under conscious control once the image surfaces, and those who learn this simple exercise of pre-visualisation need never be without visual concepts.

As this meditative search for visual ideas takes place, it is useful to have a notepad and felt tip pen nearby so that any prospective picture can be noted, either by a few words or by very quick structural sketches. This need not interrupt the meditative nature of the activity. Later when the session is over, these shorthand scribbles can be tidied up into possible layouts and worked over in detail.

LOGISTICS

Once the basic design of the picture is found and the background is known, a detailed list is made of all the props and logistics which relate to the session and this becomes the working schedule for the assignment. Once the mundane facts and basic concepts are fixed, the photographer will be free during the actual shoot to take advantage of the happenings in front of camera and any unplanned actions which may be caught in consequence. The pre-conceived planning in nude photography does not ever become an ironclad guide. The photography must reflect the interaction of model, mood, lighting, environment and the photographer... a very volatile mixture indeed.

Whatever is decided upon by the photographer or his client, certain compositional factors will make their presence felt, simply because the naked body is the subject before the camera. The fluidity of the body can express rhythm in a visual sense, the repetition of lines and forms. This can be achieved by using stroboscopic techniques or by finding and disclosing repetitive contours in the body.

The body can be posed to offer symmetry to the viewer, bringing peaceful weight to the picture. Tension can be expressed by the pose itself in which the body structure is apparently under tension, or dynamic psychological tension may be expressed by an image where the body relates to the voluminous space around it and indicates movement or insecurity. Where the body is placed away from the centre line of the format, movement will be suggested. If the body is facing out of picture and well past the centre line, it will indicate a passing movement; where it is facing in and approaching the centre line it will suggest future movement.

When the whole body is considered as the primary and entire subject, structural line will become more important. Line can be suggested as a hidden force beneath the flesh and may be seen in outstretched arms or legs and how these relate to the torso or head or it may he found as a vertical line through head and torso, which reacts with the horizontal flow of the limbs. The line present in the female nude will tend always to the arabesque, the continuous swirling of thin outlines of contour, creating considerable sensuality in its progress around the format. Line, of course, can be made an entirely visible entity rather than a deeply hidden structure, by the use of rim light to light only edges of form. Solarising such edge-lit forms further increases the attention to line only.

The fine art photograph of the nude must be a result of 'seeing' the image in the mind's eye. It can sometimes be found within earlier work which has not been properly evaluated. Refer to page 52 for the full image from which this has been taken . A Lith reversal has been made from the original negative and solarised.

Contact print of 6x7cm negative original.

The body, of course, is asymmetrical when it is carefully analysed. No two breasts on a model will be the same, legs will vary, the two sides of the face are remarkably different and an image of the body usually becomes stronger when this asymmetry is at least suggested in the finished picture. Balance in an image sense also often depends on asymmetrical poses but in this case visual weight of primary compositional elements must appear equal while the structure of the body appears asymmetrical.

TEXTURE

The nude image is obviously very much concerned with texture. Once the deep structure of the body is suggested by the pose, and after contour is disclosed by the attitude to the body in relation to the key light, the visually tactile areas of skin and hair, hands or feet may be the next most important. Texture of the body is emphasised by the quality of the light, rather than its direction, although, obviously, revelatory low-angle lights placed at 90 degrees to the lens axis are also needed.

Only correct processing will produce the rich detail of texture of the human body and there is usually a tendency for photographers of the nude to print these body textures too light. Do not over-expose or over-develop either negative or print if full tactile qualities are to be suggested.

By flattening the body contours (by use of either graphics or lighting, or both) the expected form and contour of the body, that feeling of flesh and reality, may be heavily suppressed. The image then concentrates on area and explores this area in terms of its size, visual weight, edge boundaries and how these elements interact with the space around the body and most importantly, how this changing space and the body edges interact with the frame of reference or, in other words, with the borders of the format of the finished print.

Edge itself may be explored if the body contours are eliminated, by suppressing the form entirely with advanced dark room graphics or by the use of careful rim lighting. The silhouette is an excellent example of the use of edge.

TONE

Tone is usually present in all photographs and control of it is exercised by processing and lighting. The monochrome silver of the black and white photograph is particularly interesting when it is used to illustrate the nude. Tone interacts constantly in a photograph and it will be found that interest is heightened from a visual point of view when patches of dark tone penetrate patches of light tone or vice versa. The volume, area and visual weight of tone should be controlled by this inter-penetration of tones in order to keep the eye moving in the direction which the photographer has decided upon.

The ratio of highlight (light tone) to dark tone (shadow) has considerable psychological impact on the viewer. Close ratios, 1:1, 1:2 or 1:3, where there is not a marked difference in the light and dark tones, tends to promote feelings of happiness, relaxation and a willingness to identify with glamour and femininity. Ratios which are further apart, 1:4, 1:8 or 1:16, where for example, the shadow is 16 times heavier than the highlight, will intensify the drama, heighten the darker side of sexuality and can increase the feeling of gritty reality.

PERSPECTIVE

Another element of managing the nude image will be found in the two kinds of perspective to be seen in photographs. Geometric perspective is naturally present in any camera image and this may be changed by altering camera positions and lens focal lengths. Photographers should remember that when different lenses are used, even when they are wide angle, geometric perspective does not change at all as long as the camera and subject remain in identical and fixed positions relative to each other. Where any change in these fixed elements is made, geometric perspective changes also.

Photographers of the nude are usually not interested in exploring perspective differences brought about by ultra short or very long lenses, as the distortion of the naked body is often accompanied by a down grading of communication with the viewer. Lenses longer than normal are, of course, necessary for the proper suggestion of actual body volumes but these lenses are generally only two to three times greater than normal.

AERIAL PERSPECTIVE

Aerial perspective may also change with the change in lenses, long lenses increasing its presence and short lenses decreasing it. Aerial perspective in nature manifests itself as mists of tone which alter density as distance recedes, identifying different planes of background. Leonardo da Vinci was probably the first to use the technique in painting and noted its helpful enhancement of depth and dimension in landscapes.

Aerial perspective can also be suggested by the photographer in the studio by the use of light alone, expanding the volume of space behind the model by providing modulation of tonal areas in the background to suggest depth, and by placing the model at a great distance from the background itself. Extremely long lenses, particularly if used in a busy environment, do create a compaction of aerial space and draw it tightly around the subject and with proper lighting this may make a dynamic difference to aerial perspective.

Outdoors, particularly in closely wooded locations, firing a smoke gun or smoke pellet or photographing during heavy mist can vastly increase the presence of aerial perspective,

Three versions of the use of the drape. The draped nude figure has become the coy cliché of the photographic and the painted nude but it need not be so.
Step 1: This is a discreet use of a minimal drape, used in an acceptable way.
Step 2: Here, the drape is used for concealment as before, but a new dynamism is to be found in this image due to the use of a zoom-blur and a slow shutter speed. The print has been made through a random grain screen placed on the photo paper.

Step 3: In this picture, the drape is floating chiffon, the torso is twisting and the hips are relatively still. A slow shutter speed allows the abstraction to reach a very advanced level, yet without fragmenting the image completely.
Totally a camera effect.

dramatically separating planes within the background and creating an intensity of mood which is particularly effective in colour. Using a desaturation (fog) filter or diffusion filter, or both results in mysterious and misty nude images result, suggesting idealisation and romanticism.

IMAGE MANAGEMENT

Image management in respect of the nude figure is not at all easy, particularly where no environment is present other than the plain paperfall of a limbo background. The entire design of the figure in the frame becomes paramount and the figure will be considered in its totality of height, including the hands stretched above the head while standing on tip-toe, or arms or legs outstretched in an apparent attempt to break into the format edge.

Conversely, the body may also be considered for its parts, sometimes for its identifiable and secret contours, alternatively perhaps, by ambiguous shapes which are so elemental and organic that they may not even appear human. The nude then has a close affinity to a landscape.

In coming to terms with good concepts and imaginative pictures, the photographer should not neglect the exploration of blurred movement. The body moves, walks, runs, spins and dances and when this takes place in front of the camera and the photographer forsakes totally sharp images and high shutter speeds, very poetic and beautiful photographs can result.

This blurring of actions by the model seems to identify the essence of femininity and tends to suggest the fragility of time, and therefore timelessness, in a very much more dramatic way than does entirely frozen action. Because the body moves through space, lives in and reacts to a particular environment and span of history, it is of interest to explore sequential pictures of the nude. These may be serial pictures involving an elaborate interaction of many slowly evolving images, usually small, which suggest a flowing and limitless image of many facets. The work of Duane Michals and Ray Metzker, both Americans, is a worthwhile example of these two different approaches to sequential photography.

Planned visual concepts should include the possibility of constructed images which use overlay, montage, solarisation, double exposure, photo-mosaics and photograms, and the techniques behind this type of image is more fully explained in Chapter 9.

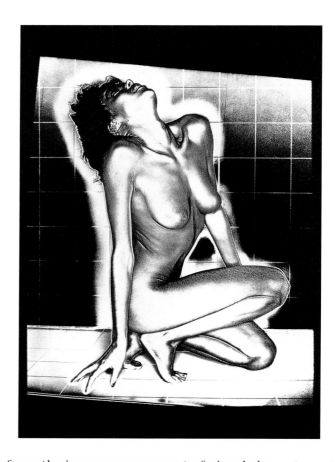

Apart from the image management of visual elements controlled by the photographer, there is a special emphasis on the psychological elements which are actively to be found in photographs of the nude, particularly the female nude. Symbolism will play a vital part. We all respond to symbols, usually unconsciously and these trigger both universal and individual reactions to images, particularly if those images are of the nude. The unconscious recognition of this deeply coded sub-structure of an image is part of the beholder's share in the image, an essential co-operation with the photo-artist, without which no image can become truly memorable.

Creating an image, particularly a modern photograph, is something of a two way street. There must be traffic both ways, between creator and viewer, and the unconscious of both plays very important roles. When this is recognised by the photographer who wishes to design an image to perform in a certain way deliberate clues can be placed in the composition to initiate certain responses. The cultural background and the personal events of the life and their individual psychology all modify the final reading of an image.

A darkroom adaptation of a studio image has resulted in a strong visual of the model.

Two thin reversals of this image have been made and sandwiched together, with one image flipped. The result has been copied on to colour transparency film for a very bizarre but arresting image. The photographer should be constantly aware of the potentiality of even quite mundane imagery which may be found in his own stock library.

MOOD

Photography is an adept medium when it comes to rendering mood, and perhaps no other form of visual language is so effective, except possibly the transient imagery of cinema and video. Mood may be altered or indicated by the richness of tone or texture in the skin, the fall of light on the body, hidden factors of symbolism, time and spatial dimension or colour harmony, ambiguous clues to the meaning of the image and so on. Mood may be defined as a frame of mind, a state of feelings, and when it is present in a photograph communication and response from any viewer of any age or culture will be greatly increased. It is an essential ingredient in the image of the nude.

The conscious management of the nude image can only come to the photographer after considerable photographic experience which raises photographic technique to an absolutely flawless level plus some knowledge of the psychological and philosophical mysteries involved. Research amongst the writings of Carl Jung, E. H. Gombrich, Rudolph Arnheim, Silvano Arieti, Anton Ehrenzweig and Faber Birren will pay dividends when it comes to understanding these hidden aspects of imagery and imagination.

FACTORS UPON WHICH VALUES ARE DEPENDENT

CORRECT OPTICAL VALUES
- CAMERA VIEWPOINT
- PERSPECTIVE • PROPORTION
- BALANCE • FORM • EDGE
- OVERLAPPING • PATTERN
- SPACE • TONE
- COLOUR • FORMAT

CORRECT PSYCHOLOGICAL VALUES
- RESEARCH • PRE-VISUALISATION
- QUALITY OF THE ENVIRONMENT
- EMOTION • DIFFERENCES
- MENTAL VIEWPOINT
- SYMBOLISM • JUXTAPOSITION

Mood is created by shadows and an expressive model.

CHAPTER ELEVEN

Images Immediately

The very nature of nude photography raises the question of privacy. The photographer, of course, will have set up the session so that strict privacy will be maintained. However, some models will be sensitive to the fact that after the photographs have been taken film will be sent to a professional processing laboratory for development. New or amateur models may be particularly affected by this issue.

The ideal arrangement for first time models would be to shoot early sessions on Polaroid film. This is now a very advanced technology, available in both colour and black and white, which would mean that all material from the session could be processed in the privacy of the studio and any awkward or embarrassing photographs simply torn up.

The model gains confidence and skill from this kind of instant imaging, giving as it does, a progressive record of the session as it evolves. The photographer also has much to gain from seeing in photographic terms, the lighting, pose and tonal values of the picture. The Polaroid can be considered as an intermediate proof before final commitment to film, at which point exposure can be checked, lighting plans refined and body attitudes considered.

Polaroid can also be used as the final artwork, particularly if it is being made on 10 x 12 cm (4 x 5 in) film. When using any of the films available in this format, creativity can be pushed to new levels of excellence and experiment, especially as the model can see and become involved far more than is the case when she has no knowledge of the image which has been taken on conventional film and must first be processed before editing

The first Polaroid camera went on sale at the Jordan Marsh Company store in Boston, USA in 1948. The technology began a revolution in photography which continues today, all over the world. For the modern professional who fully understands and exploits the system's amazing characteristics and chemistry there are enormous creative and practical benefits to be obtained, especially when applied to photography of the nude.

PRACTICAL POLAROIDS

The first use a professional photographer is likely to make of Polaroid materials is to check the behaviour of camera and lighting equipment and this is especially true of the photographer of the nude.

Nude photography is an end result of intensive planning and expensive production techniques and the more certain the photographer is that the final image is exactly to his or the client's brief, the better will be the photographer's reputation and continuing business. Equipment failure or a break down in lighting logistics is never an acceptable excuse for less than excellent results and such disasters can be avoided by preliminary checks using Polaroid in place of standard film.

Whether using 35mm formats or 120 film, special adaptor backs are available to take the 100 series of Polaroid film. For 9 x 12cm (4 x 5in) cameras, the 50 series provides a suitable range of emulsions and film speeds. For checking exposure, it is better to use Polaroid which has an identical speed to the film loaded in the camera. For checking colour exposures always use Polapan black and white film. It is more stable and tonally more accurate than the colour films. Colour Polaroids are very sensitive to temperature and to the time of development, and even slight variations can cause errors of judgement in assessing exposure and light balancing.

Once the final set up in the studio is complete, for all fee paying assignments, especially of the nude, I believe it is wise to make a Polaroid test before commencing the actual work with conventional film. Seeing the full picture, knowing also that all equipment is functional and that the model is close to final position, all just moments before exposure of the film, can most easily be done on Polaroid. This is essential if lighting with electronic flash. Routine testing as described, goes a long way to protect against failure in what is a very expensive exercise.

BLACK & WHITE PEEL APART FILMS

POLAPAN PRO 100

ISO 100/21° 30 SEC.
3¼ x 4¼ PACK 617537
4 x 5 SHEET 613271
4 x 5 PACK 613272
8 x 10 SHEET 613274

PROFESSIONAL PROOFING

- *wide tonal range* • *medium contrast*
- *no coating required*
- *studio/commercial photography*

Perfect complement to high quality transparency films. For informed judgements on exposure, composition and lighting or a quality print in its own right.

POLAPAN 400

ISO 400/21° 45 SEC.
4 x 5 SHEET 617603

SCIENTIFIC

- *wide tonal range* • *super detail*
- *medium contrast*
- *coaterless version of T52*

For light and electron microscopy applications where sharp, clear and bright images are required. Photographic characteristics similar but not identical to T52.

TYPE 51HC

ISO 320/26° FLASH
ISO 200/24° TUNGSTEN
30 SEC.
4 x 5 SHEET 619194

SCIENTIFIC

- *positive/negative*
- *high contrast*

For precisely rendered visual details in defect analysis; high contrast images of latent-fingerprints and line art with dense blacks, bright whites, no greys. Negative requires brief cleanng in sodium sulphite solution before use.

SEPIA FILM

ISO 200/24°
35 SEC.
4 x 5 SHEET 618965

PROFESSIONAL/ENTERTAINMENT

- *sepia tone* • *medium contrast*
- *no coating required*

For the production of 'old time' photographs taken at conventions, parties, historical sights, theme parks or outdoor special events.

COLOUR PEEL APART FILMS

POLACOLOR 579/679

ISO 100/21°
90 SEC.
3¼ x 4¼ PACK 621892
4 x 5 PACK 621895

PROFESSIONAL PROOFING

- *balanced for daylight & electronic flash*
- *studio/commercial photography*

Extremely accurate, true-to-life colours, whiter whites. Improved highlights and shadow detail. Sharp and vibrant. Highly recommended for the majority of Pro Photo applications. Not recommended for emulsion lifts. Ultimately replaces Polacolor Pro 100.

POLACOLOR PRO 100

ISO 100/21°
90 SEC.
4 x 5 SHEET 617833

PROFESSIONAL PROOFING

- *balanced for daylight & electronic flash*
- *studio/commercial photography*

Accurate, saturated, true-to-life colours; clean whites, deeper blacks. Extended shelf life. Highly recommended for the majority of Pro photo applications

POLACOLOR ER TYPE 669/59/559 88/809

ISO 80/20° 60 SEC.
3¼ x 4¼ PACK 605926
4 x 5 SHEET 604358
4 x 5 PACK 604780
3¼ x 3⅜ PACK 603140
8 x 10 SHEET 604929

PROFESSIONAL/SCIENTIFIC

- *extended (tonal) range*
- *ideal for proofing shadow or highlight details*
- *balanced for daylight & electronic flash*

For special applications such as 'Image Transfers' and 'Emulsion Lifts'. Type 88 is used with the Polaroid Pro Pack camera and other professional cameras with the appropriate pack film back.

POLACOLOR 64 TUNGSTEN

ISO 64/19°
90 SEC.
3¼ x 4¼ PACK 617150
4 x 5 SHEET 617149

PROFESSIONAL/SCIENTIFIC/MEDICAL

- *balanced for tungsten light*
- *requires little or no filtration*

Optimized for longer-duration exposures under tungsten, halogen or quartz lights. Ideal for macro-photography and microscopy applications, as well as professional proofing

LARGE FORMAT CAMERAS

The wide range of emulsion types in Polaroid 4 x 5 formats would appear to make the studio view camera a sensible choice for high resolution pictures of the nude, but in practice these cameras are quite difficult to manage in any photography involving live models. In particular, the nude model always needs last minute direction in the moments before the shutter is fired. My personal solution to this problem is to use a 4 x 5in Speed Graphic, equipped with a 454i Polaroid film holder. These are rangefinder cameras, with two shutters and flash sync, a ground glass focusing screen and both a wire sports viewfinder and an optical finder. Equipped with a 135mm Kodak Ektar lens, they deliver superb results in any live situation and are ideal for creating *final art* images on 4 x 5in Polaroid. Other lenses can be fitted, but then the rangefinder needs re-calibrating by a technician to accommodate the different focal length of lens.

Polaroid manufactures hundreds of products. This table identifies the most useful film types for photographers.

A Speed Graphic 4 x 5 inch Press Camera.

POLAROID COPYING

In the darkroom, with an enlarger, Polaroid further extends the photographer's capabilities. Quite acceptable colour proofs can be made, using the 4 x 5in 545i film holder mounted face up toward the lens on a firm and flat support, replacing the paper easel. By using colour correction filters from the Wratten series over the lens, considerable changes can be made to colour balance. Make sure that film and holder are stabilised in an environment of 24°C (75°F) temperature and use a stop watch or dark room timer to time development. Use T64T colour film for this work, as it is balanced to 3200 Kelvin, the colour of the enlarger lamp. Do not use Polaroid daylight emulsions.

Using a 4 x 5in camera on a copy stand, colour proofs can be made of transparencies provided that a trans-illuminated easel is used to hold the copy and that the light source is rated at 3200 Kelvin. This set up can also be used for 1:1 copying on to conventional filmstock of Polaroids made earlier, using T64T film for the camera and tungsten-halogen lamps, rated 3200 Kelvin, in the copy light holders. Be sure to time development to the second, and keep film temperature at 24°C (75°F). Otherwise accurate colours will not be possible. Have on hand appropriate Wratten c.c. (colour compensating) filters for the camera lens, so that further adjustments to colour balance can be made.

FILM TYPES

Polaroid is available in a variety of emulsion types and sizes, but the ones of most interest for photography of the nude are : Polacolor Pro 100, in sizes 669 for medium or 35mm formats. This is a colour emulsion rated at an ISO speed of 100. For 4 x 5in cameras Type 59 is used in the 545 film holder, also rated at 100 ISO and balanced for daylight at 5500 Kelvin. These films are best used for originating final art or for special effects. They do not respond well to emulsion lifts or transfers.

Polacolor ER is a slower colour emulsion with a different chemical specification. Its speed is 80 ISO. It is supplied only in 4 x 5in sheet sizes to fit the 4 x 5in holder. It is better suited to effects such as lifts or transfers than Polacolor Pro 100.

Polacolor T64T in sheet sizes for $3^1/_4$ x $4^1/_4$in and 4 x 5in film holders. This film is rated at a film speed of 64 ISO and is balanced for tungsten light at 3200 Kelvin. This film is used for colour proofing, colour copying, final art or for special effects such as lifts and transfers.

FILM TYPES

Polacolor 64 Tungsten

Polapan 100

Type 51 HC

Type 55 Pos/Neg

Sepia Film

Polapan Pro 100 Type 665 and Type 52, in sheet sizes to fit $3^1/_4$ x $4^1/_4$in and 4 x 5in holders. This is a superb black and white emulsion rated at 100 ISO and with a beautiful tonal scale. It is used for final camera and set-up checks and for very accurate exposure adjustments before shooting colour film in conventional cameras. Used often as final art. A 400 ISO speed emulsion is also available as Type 672 for medium format cameras and as Type Pro 400, 4 x 5, for the 4 x 5in holder.

Type 55 Pos/Neg is a film which comes as individual sheets for the 4 x 5in film holder and provides a black and white proof print as well as a beautiful quality negative. Film speed is 50 ISO and fine grain negatives with a rich tonal scale make excellent enlargements on conventional bromide papers.

Type 665 Pos/Neg has similar characteristics as Type 55 but is for the smaller medium format holder.

Type 55 and 665 negatives must be cleared in a Sodium Sulphite solution, then washed and dried. Prints must be coated for permanence.

Type 56 is a sepia print film often used for final art and is available to fit the 4 x 5in holder. Speed is nominally 200 ISO but may be rated at 250-400 for changes in density and/or colour. Testing speed changes in order to change tone, will be of great interest to the fine art photographer.

Type 51 is a Pos/Neg 4 x 5in film, a very high contrast black and white sheet film for prints and negatives. Film speed is 320 ISO and development time is 30 secs. It can be used for generating a high contrast negative, a final art print or special effects such as direct solarising. Negatives must be cleared in a Sodium Sulphite solution and prints coated for permanence.

SPECIAL TREATMENT FOR P/N FILMS

All P/N positives (prints) need coating for permanence. All negatives need clearing in a Sodium Sulphite bath,immediately after development to remove residual dyes and emulsion. Sodium Sulphite is a powder which is available from professional photographic suppliers or industrial chemists. The mixture is made up as follows:

Weigh 440g (16oz) of Sodium Sulphite (desiccated) and add slowly to 2 litres (70 fl oz) of warm water stirring continuously until powder is dissolved. Cool to 21°C (70°F) before using.

After clearing, wash briefly in running water, add a wetting agent to a final water bath and dry in a dust free place. The film is thinner than conventional negative film and can be more

The negative from P/N films such as Type 55, needs processing in a solution of Sodium Sulphite. Polaroid sell a processing bucket to perform this task, with a tank rack for 4x5 negatives. Together with the 545i Film Holder and a stopwatch a complete portable studio processing station can easily be carried, even to outdoor locations.

easily damaged. Exposing P/N film for a negative of good printing density, requires an increase in exposure of 15-20%. Therefore the print will be overexposed and should be discarded.

SPECIAL EFFECTS

DIRECT SOLARISING

Using Polaroid P/N films, the negative can be solarised, often with intriguing results, but it must be considered a random event governed by chance and results are not to be compared with those obtained by carefully structured solarising in the darkroom, using conventional films and chemistry. However, for photographers of the nude looking for new creative effects achieved with simple means, the Type 51 solarising technique is well worth investigating.

To begin the experiment, set up a 4 x 5in camera on a copy stand and focus on a black and white image of your choice. Load the camera with Type 55 P/N/ film, make a normal exposure and pull through the 454 holder. After eight seconds development peel the negative and print apart and discard the print. Expose the negative while held in a flat plane, to a flash held 60 cm above its surface. Place the flashed negative in a light-proof box for one minute. Inspect the result in subdued light and if satisfactorily solarised, clear the film in the usual sulphite bath, wash and dry. Experiment by altering first development and post-flash times and also by varying the strength of the flash exposure.

Almost the only technical problem which can arise with Polaroid is if the processing is inexpertly done. This example shows what happens if the pull through the rollers is not absolutely smooth.

This is the print correctly processed with a smooth, steady pull.

TRANSFER

Certain Polacolor emulsions can be processed and transferred to a new substrate support, thereby creating fascinating new textures and tints in the final image. The presentation of that final transferred image will need care and thought, because it is a comparatively small image which can easily be overwhelmed by its environment. Exceptionally deep box frames, much larger than the image, may be a starting point.

The most suitable Polacolor films for transfer are Polacolor ER, balanced for daylight and Polacolor T64T balanced for tungsten light. Both are 4 x 5 format for use in the 454 or 454i holder. When using a copystand and tungsten halogen lights, T64T emulsions are to be preferred. Existing images, either colour or black and white may be copied this way and form the basis for a transfer.

METHOD:

1. Prepare a receiving sheet such as 350gsm watercolour paper by pre-soaking, or use a dry sheet of similar weight matt art paper, both of which are white or cream. Pre-soaking seems to improve transfer techniques even when using silk or rice paper. The smoother, hard surfaces like glossy card make it more likely that parts of the transferred image will not stick to the new support.

2. Over-expose the film by one stop and pull the film through the holder.

3. Cut off the metal processing pod. Beware of caustic chemicals from the pod.

4. After 15 seconds, timed by stopwatch, peel films apart, discarding the print.

5. Immediately, place the negative face down on the receiving sheet. Delay in this action often means that dyes will dry out and not transfer.

6. Place a card on the back of the negative and apply strong finger pressure across the area, being careful not to move the transfer sandwich. A hard rubber print roller can then be used to apply further pressure.

*Make a copy on Tungsten 64
film of an existing image.*

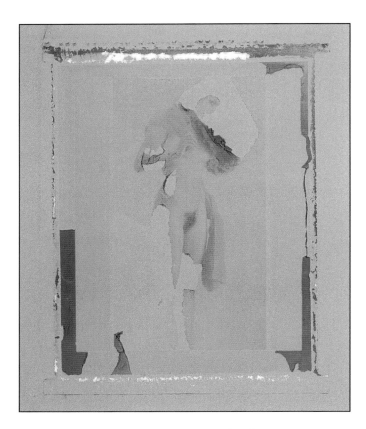

*Transfer the image to a
new substrate, as described
in the text.*

7. If transferring to a fairly absorbent substrate, begin gently lifting the negative at the edges after one minute (timed). If the emulsion is not transferring cleanly, separate it from the negative with the help of a fine blade or a palette knife, before pressing it back to the substrate with the fingers or the knife.

8. If the new support is not very absorbent begin peeling after two minutes, again by timer.

9. While still wet, the newly transferred image can be manipulated carefully to repair any damaged emulsion. Dense shadows in the image will be particularly vulnerable to fracture.

10. When the new image is absolutely dry, seal the surface with a clear acrylic varnish.

EMULSION LIFTS

Soaking certain Polacolor prints in very hot water will allow the emulsion to detach itself from its supporting base. It can then be lifted out of the hot water bath and placed on a new support, while at the same time being distorted, stretched or folded for creative effect. The best film types for this treatment are Polacolor ER and T64T, both 4 x 5 formats. Several different images can be treated this way, being placed sequentially on top of one another to form a montage image. If the base chosen is transparent film and the montage is then enlarged using a conventional bromide paper such as Ilford Galerie or Ilford MGFB Warmtone, very striking images can be made, particularly when the subject is the nude.

METHOD:

1. Process the print as normal and leave for two days for the emulsion to harden.

2. Use two small developing trays, one with very hot water, the other with warm water, blood heat.

3. Leave the print in the hot water for five to seven minutes until it begins to lift from its support. Use print tongs with padded tips or the fingers if the water is not too hot, to assist the separation. Lift the emulsion into the second tray of luke warm water.

4. Float the emulsion on the surface and examine it for debris, which can be removed gently with the fingers.

5. If the emulsion is to be fixed to a new support as final art, slide a new heavyweight (300 gsm) piece of paper or card into the water and raise it to capture the floating emulsion. Drain and dry flat. Varnish with a clear acrylic varnish when absolutely dry. A subtle image can be made by using polished metal instead of card as a final support.

6. If the image is to be enlarged or contact printed, slide a clear piece of film or acetate under the floating image in the warm tray. Gently lift it free from the water and re-arrange it on the clear supporting base in any shape that appeals, drain it and then let it dry flat. It can then be used as a

Above left: An example of an Emulsion Lift. The image has been floated off in boiling water and repositioned on a new substrate, in this case white lasercopy paper, 100 gsm.

Above right: This Emulsion Lift has been made on to a glossy coloured card of 150 gsm.

conventional negative. Further enhancement by solarising the enlargement can lead to very dynamic fine art images.

CAUTION

Some Polaroid films contain a small amount of caustic paste. If any paste appears on the film envelope or the rollers of the processors, avoid skin contact with any residue. Wipe equipment clean with a tissue and then wash your hands with plain water. If eye contact occurs flood the eye with cold water and see a doctor immediately. Keep these materials away from children and pets and dispose of them with care. Such residues will stain clothing or furniture.

ALTERNATIVES TO POLAROID

Both Fuji and Kodak have attempted to market peel-apart film technology, but Polaroid has remained the only global player to have successfully offered such instant film technology for almost half a century. Apart from Polaroid, one other very different approach is quickly becoming of use to studio photographers,especially if they are photographing the nude. Instant imaging is possible, excellent full colour 21 x 29cm (8 x 11in) prints can be made in seconds and total privacy is maintained. A product of sophisticated digital imaging technology, a digital camera (see Chapter 13) and a desktop colour printer are used in tandem to photograph and edit studio subjects, particularly live action.

EPSON STYLUS (PHOTO PRINTER)

There are many desktop printers capable of producing full colour and toners and paper substrates are improved constantly. Epson is one manufacturer which has become very involved in providing printers which go close to emulation of good quality photo prints made from conventional camera originals. The Epson Stylus Photo series require a minimum of technical input from the photographer in order to achieve excellent results. Epson uses a piezo-electric print head to minimise the dot size of the colour reproduction and different models print from medium to high resolution in terms of dpi. The professional photographer should choose the highest resolution and the A3 30 x 42cm (11 x 16in) size printer printing on special photo-tone paper.

Once the printer is set up and a digital camera connected to it, or a camera card is plugged in (via an adapter if necessary), photography can proceed either as an on-line activity or an editing summation of an earlier session with the camera alone. The concept from Epson is that photographers can be freed from the necessity of wet processing and film labs and can avail themselves of instant imaging. With an Epson Stylus Photo printer a computer is not needed to output a print and the results are superb.

THE DIGITAL CAMERA

A digital camera is needed to create the image and this must be of the 'mega-pixel' type, that is one which contains a chip with a display of 1.2 – 2 million pixels. These cameras must be considered as sub-professional in resolution terms but will produce acceptable prints up to about 18 x 24cm (8 x 10in). For any requirement above that size, higher resolution cameras may

The Epson Colour Stylus EX, a printer designed especially for photographers.

be needed and these can cost three to five times the price of a good optical camera.

Very good mega pixel cameras are made by (in alphabetical order) Agfa, Epson, Fuji, Kodak, Minolta, Nikon, Olympus and Polaroid. There is a very rapid development of this technology, largely driven by consumer and SOHO needs, rather than professional markets, but inevitably, this explosive growth will mean larger pixel arrays and higher resolution for less money,for all users. The concept remains the same: the making of a digital image and the immediate printing out of that image in full colour and at acceptable resolution.

IMAGE MANIPULATION

Unlike Polaroid, a digital camera image can be instantly available for computer enhancement and/or manipulation. With the Epson Stylus Photo printer connected, an immediate hard copy can be made of the screen image once it has been retouched, cropped and colour corrected. Low specification computers will satisfy sub-professional needs, but those who aspire to fine art, book illustration or editorial images should consider purchasing a high end system such as described in Chapter 12, under the heading The Photographer's Workstation.

CHAPTER TWELVE

The Zero Plus One Revolution

More than 90% of the world's computers are IBM compatible PCs. Almost all the rest are Apple Macintosh systems. In the beginning the PC was a business tool and Apple computers were visual tools, with an advanced yet transparent operating system and a superb Graphical User Interface (GUI). These were machines beloved by graphic artists and bureaus and still are.

Because business has become inseparably involved in visuals, that earlier demarcation between Mac and PC no longer exists. Photographers work in a dedicated field of processing two-dimensional flat images, not 3-D or multimedia graphics and should consider the very real benefits from using a highly specified PC, which will provide all the software available to Mac users and at less cost. For photographers of the nude, the revolution starts with a PC.

They will certainly find digital imaging an attractive option, but one which is so concerned with jargon and evolving technology, that it is easy to lose sight of the photographer's main objective - the making of a photographic image. It requires great discipline on the part of the photographer to avoid this technology trap and remain dedicated to an essentially optical image structure. What should be seen as a product of a photographer's skills and experience, should be a photograph, however much it may be digitally manipulated.

Discipline is not hostile to creativity... it is fundamental to it. Never has discipline been more desirable an attribute for the creative photographer, especially those who have chosen to specialise in the subject of the nude, than when they are faced with the maze of technology which is inherent in digital imaging. Digital manipulation is a tool for the creative photographer but should not be the only reason for the image.

Of course, highly motivated photographers will wish to make use of all possible improvements in imaging technology, particularly the vast potential to be found in the use of digital images. However, it should be remembered that a photographer who has acquired advanced levels of competence in making of memorable photographic images must work to very different

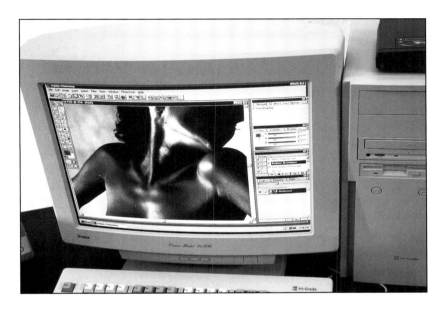

Probably the most important purchase will be a high quality monitor.

parameters than does the graphic artist when setting out to become part of the digital revolution.

A photograph is essentially a 2-D image constructed to create an illusion of reality. Usually the photographer will remain bound to the tools of photography, even when involved in digital image processing. These would include the use of optics, perspective, lighting, tone, movement and so on, all with a close affinity to reality. A graphic artist using digital means to produce art work is totally unbound by these rules of photographic imaging and can wander at will through all the magic fixes to be found in digital technology.

DIGITAL IMAGING

Instead of producing a latent image on film and then using wet chemistry to process it, as with conventional optical photography, a digital camera acquires the image on an electronic chip and stores it in the camera's memory, where it is instantly recoverable for output or manipulation.

For the photographer, the advantages of digital imaging include instant editing, retouching, cropping, rotating, colour balancing, sharpening and blurring. The main disadvantage is that to even approach the resolution which is commonplace in most mid-range optical cameras, a digital camera will be very expensive. In the next few years however, up to and past the approaching millennium, it is certain that the cost of highly specified digital cameras which can deliver professionally acceptable resolution, will be much less than at present.

Digital processing of words, numbers or pictures, uses a binary arrangement of electronic switching, symbolised by just two numbers: 0 or 1. These symbols denote that information processing is either on or off. From this seemingly ultra simple technology has come the immensely complex science of computing, including the processing of pictures. Before it is input any image, either artwork or photograph, must be digitised and turned into discrete but tiny lumps of visual information called pixels. This then is the revolution which now surrounds all imagemakers.

DIGITAL AND FINE ART

SILICON OR SILVER ?

This is the dilemma for the fine art photographer of the nude. It is easy to be caught up in this magical revolution but the photographer should not quickly abandon those skills which produce superb quality optical images on silver halide emulsions using conventional cameras and wet chemistry. Final presentation may eventually control the choice between digital or optical photography. Low resolution digital cameras can make postcard size prints, professional digital cameras at their best may produce an acceptable small poster. Optical cameras and conventional chemistry can scale up an image to life size and larger, while reproducing faultlessly in respect of tone, resolution and colour.

The fine art photographer of the nude must be especially aware of the pitfalls inherent in becoming too deeply involved in a love affair with this pixel revolution. Manipulation of the raw image is so easy on a computer that it is often tempting to play too long with these esoteric digital tools, resulting in an image which is weak in concept and content and technically indulgent, even if at first sight it appears magical. Too much technology between creator and viewer tends to produce a banal, stylistic image with impact but no resonance. Resonance is a hugely important attribute in any work of art, which if it is missing

from such work, brings it near to the threshold of failure, a brilliant image perhaps, but unenduring.

Many digital photographs that have been excessively manipulated on a computer end up simply as visual data, a product of this new binary technology and already an unresponsive abstraction of creative reality. At worst, such images are just visual gobbledegook, conceived by technicians to justify patronage or an art grant with a substantial price tag. At their best, they still compromise the photographer's experience, craft and creativity. Any photographer wholly ensconced in a digital world is in danger of becoming a digital hack.

Of course, it is wrong to suggest that digital photography can never become high art. But equally true, it cannot be classified as high art just because the image has been produced with the aid of expensive technology. There are wonderful artist-photographers, whose images are an end result of digital processing, but these photographers are certain to have acquired the discipline which conventional photography and a deep understanding of optically structured images brings.

ANALOGUE V. PIXELS

A photograph is an analogue image and as such is a continuous, seamless flow of tonal and visual data, symbolic of the reality which presented itself to the camera at the time. Such an image cannot be computer processed unless it is first converted into pixels, that is to say, digitised. This is either done directly 'on-line', using a digital camera, or by scanning the original camera image in a digital scanner which can accept either print or transparency.

A pixel is a finite picture element, a tiny point of light to be found in all digitised images. Each point of light may be further analysed to discover that they are made up of discrete areas of particular colours, either four or three in number. This colour space can be identified as either a mixture of Yellow (Y), Cyan (C), Magenta (M), and Black (K), or Red (R), Green (G), and Blue (B). In digital processing they are referred to as C,M,Y,K or R,G,B. To avoid confusion with Blue, Black is signified with the letter K.

Computer monitors re-constitute images using RGB colour space and hard copy such as ink jet prints or magazine pages use the subtractive primaries of CMYK. These discrete colours are all represented by numbers in the computer, and as such, can be altered and processed to produce changes in the original input. If a digitised image is enlarged beyond its appropriate size for the resolution employed, the pixels become visible and begin to fragment the image into pixellated patterns. A normal camera image does not display this unpleasant characteristic.

Basic Essentials

The photographer taking the first steps in digital imaging will need to have a fairly comprehensive understanding of the technology which is essential to acquiring a digital image and processing or manipulating this image. First read the glossary at the end of this chapter and then begin a wide reading of magazines which specifically cover the digital world. Magazines change features very rapidly to keep up with new releases of hardware and software, something which textbooks cannot do. Such is the speed of growth in digital imaging, that textbooks are usually out of date by the time they are published. Attending seminars such as Adobe sponsor, joining short courses at colleges and universities and attending trade fairs all broaden the newcomer's understanding of the subject.

Buying a Computer

The cost of a computer, software to run it and peripherals to extend its range of uses is a substantial one. It is not an investment in any sense because the hardware will depreciate 50% in less than six months. New and improved versions of software are very frequent, with lower prices generally being a feature of updated releases for the PC. This is especially true of all aspects of digital imaging, which will grow explosively over the next decade.

A wise buyer will start by talking to direct suppliers of high end systems, such as Compaq; Dan; Dell; Gateway; Hi-Grade and NEC. A chosen supplier should have a sound reputation, at least five years in business, be accessible with a local phone call and have generous open hours for telephone help lines. Once the direct suppliers are checked out, one-stop retail computer warehouses and showrooms may suggest competitive prices worth considering, but it is unlikely that these will offer the same interested support for custom designed systems which would be routine with direct suppliers.

Specifying a Computer

A computer for a photographer will probably have different specifications than those used by graphic artists and certainly much higher capacity than that needed for business or Internet use. First, the system needs to be based on a very fast CPU such as a Pentium II, running at a clockspeed of at least 300MHz,

have a fast graphics card optimised for 2-D images, a video card with at least 4 Megabytes of VRAM, and a highly specified motherboard with an inboard chipset appropriate to processing large image files.

A hard disk of between 4 and 8 Gigabytes should be fitted, preferably with a rapid access mode and SGRAM (random access memory), which is critical to speedy handling of large image files, should be as much as is affordable, but not less than 128 Megabytes. The machine should also have an inboard CD-Rom, a good sound card and, if access to the Internet is required, a fast modem, preferably external. A removable storage device such as the ZIP Plus, made by Iomega will also be essential.

Discuss these specifications with your chosen supplier, get comparative quotes from other sources before closing any deal. Bargains do exist in the dozens of computer magazines and warehouses, but the serious worker should stay with reputable, well established direct suppliers and their help lines.

For my own work, I have chosen The Photographer's Workstation, an IBM-compatible PC, specifically built by Hi-Grade Computers Plc, London, to handle large photographic files at useful speeds. The workstation is illustrated below and its specifications are also listed here.

The Monitor

The monitor is the key component in any computer system, designed expressly to process photographs. A professional type monitor is needed, not smaller than 17in, but ideally with a 19in or 21in display. Such a monitor must be generously specified, be flicker free and be capable of full calibration. My personal choice has always been an Iiyama who have a global reputation for advanced technology and value for money. They guarantee their monitors for three years. Others may prefer a Sony monitor which has a high standard of performance and is also good value.

Types of Monitor

Shadow Mask Images are formed on a monitor by electronically focusing three coloured electron beams on to three phosphor coatings of matching colours, within a cathode ray tube (CRT), producing red, green and blue light. So that each electron beam is constrained to strike the correct phosphor of the correct corresponding colour, a metal mask is fitted within the CRT. This type of monitor is designated a shadow mask monitor. They are generally cheaper, but can produce acceptable quality and accurate colour images.

TRINITRON is an aperture grill monitor made or licensed by the Sony Corporation of Japan. Instead of phosphor dots, these monitors use a system of colour stripes receives a tricolour electron beam from a single gun. There is no metal mask, and instead parallel wires direct the path of the beams to their matching colour stripes. The benefits from this system include brighter, sharper images with less contrast. Within the CRT there is a reduction of heat with this type of monitor.

DIAMONDTRON monotiors are built and licensed by Mitsubishi of Japan, these monitors are also of the aperture grill type, but use a dedicated three gun system to generate and focus the necessary three beams of RGB colours. This improves brilliance yet again and improves contrast and colour saturation. Iiyama is such a monitor.

QUALITY FACTORS FOR MONITORS

DOT PITCH Dot pitch refers to the space between phosphor dots and ultimately, defines monitor resolution. Dot pitch values in high performance monitors range from 25mm to 28mm, a smaller pitch usually being more desirable, especially in 17in monitors.

REFRESH RATE As the electron beams scan the CRT, a single image is formed from the digital data. On completion of that, it is replaced at once by a new image or refreshed. The speed of this image replacement is called the refresh rate. If this value is too low, the average person will see a flickering image on the screen. A minimum of 75 frames replaced per second (expressed as 75 Hz), is acceptable for 17in displays, but a higher rate is desirable for larger screens.

BANDWIDTH This refers to the ability of the monitor to turn a single pixel on or off and is proportional to the change in pixel status per second. The higher the monitor resolution and refresh rate, the greater the bandwidth required. Insufficient bandwidth shows up as poor detail and lower density and brightness values, particularly in vertical lines.

GEOMETRY A good monitor will allow extensive control of image geometry on screen, either by physical controls on a command module at the base of the monitor or by the use of software, or both. Faults such as pin cushion or barrel distortion, rectilinear distortion and non-linearity, or mis-alignment of the RGB electron beams (seen as unsharpness and colour fringing), ought to be correctable by the operator. Colour balancing needs to be available at least in elementary settings such as adjustment of colour temperature, overall colour balance and individual alignment of the RGB electron beams.

PERIPHERALS

THE COMPUTER has attachments to provide inputs, outputs or storage. They usually are plug-and-play devices which do not need technicians to install them. They could include: a colour printer producing photographic quality, a scanner, either flat-bed or drum type, for digitising prints or transparencies, or a digital camera such as those, available from Agfa, Epson, Fuji, Hasselblad, Kodak, Minolta, Nikon, Olympus, Polaroid, or Sinar.

THE PRINTER This is the machine used for outputting from the computer a selected image. It should be full colour and produce photo-real prints of high resolution. One such printer is made by Epson and is designated as an Epson Stylus EX Photo printer, available up to A3 size (30 x 40cm, 12 x 16in) and in resolutions up to 1400 dpi using a MicroPiezo print head and Super Microdot technology. This printer also has a watermarking capability which prints into the image to protect it from piracy while in transit.

The higher the dpi the slower the print-out but the better the result. Use Epson glossy Photo-Quality paper for a photographic emulation which is world class. Epson Photo printers are six colour printers, using light cyan and light magenta as well as the standard CMYK printing colours to give increased colour gamut for difficult subjects. Epson printers can take a direct input from a digital camera without a computer, so offering instant proofing as a most useful option.

There are many, many excellent printers available, some of the best coming from the low end of the price scale. Canon, Hewlett Packard, Lexmark all make fine desktop printers, but value and innovative photographic quality are epitomised by Epson, one of the world's most advanced inkjet systems.

THE SCANNER

This device turns the analogue camera image into a digital copy. It works for both prints or transparencies. Professional repro houses and bureaus will standardise on drum type scanners. These offer extremely high resolution and an extended density range for coping with rich shadow areas and thin highlights. For the very best reproduction of a photograph it will be necessary to use this type of equipment. Drum scanners are very expensive to buy but scanning bureaus offer their services at modest cost, and the photographer seeking digital image inputs with extremely high resolution and amplified tonal scale, must look at using such a service.

An optional but important peripheral for the Workstation is a scanner. A very suitable flat bed scanner for photographers is made by Linotype. This is the Linotype Ultra 2, a 42 bit colour scanner with a dynamic range of 3. 4D. It scans either print or transparencies up to 254mm x 216mm (10 x 8 ins.) in a single pass at an optical scanning resolution of 1200 x 2400 dpi. Included is Color Factory Pro software which is acknowledged as a world leader in automated scanner interfaces for professional results.

In recent years, flat-bed scanners have entered the market in volume and at low cost. Instead of wrapping the image on to a glass drum for scanning, the flat bed system places the image flat on what looks very like a desktop copier. The photograph is scanned by an array of CCD's (Charge Coupled Devices) which translate the image into pixels. The best of flatbed scanners are very close indeed to quality parameters found in most drum scanners, with the added advantages of low cost, sufficient speed and excellent and de-skilled software for colour balancing and correction.

The photographer is advised to choose a flat-bed scanner as a peripheral to a workstation and to choose one which has a capability for handling both print and transparency material

equally well. Such a scanner is made by AGFA under the name DuoScan. Transparencies are scanned without the need of a supporting glass plate, because the image is held by a glassless filmtray. This avoids Newton rings, dust and diffraction and speeds set-up time. The film holder accepts up to 18 x 24cm (8 x 10in) transparencies and there are dedicated holders for smaller sizes.

Agfa DuoScan scans reflective copy up to 203mm x 355mm (8 x 14in) at raw resolutions of 2000 ppi which can be interpolated to double that figure using supplied software. It is a single pass device which can produce previews in as little as 11 seconds employing 36 bit colour depth. Included in the purchase price is a professional level intelligent interface and a colour management system. Software supplied also allows easy control of selective colour, colour contrast and density correction. The software is also completely compatible with Adobe Photoshop.

STORAGE DEVICES

Most high resolution photographs intended for magazine or brochure use, will need about 30 Megabytes of hard disk space to contain them. Once image manipulation has been completed, such images can be cleared from the hard disk by storing them on a peripheral storage device, using tape or cartridge drives. Total back up of a library of images needs one of the drives which can accommodate 10-20 Gigabytes, but the photographer who frequently needs to show a client only a small number of finished photographs, will also need smaller storage capacities .

A suitable and extremely versatile drive is made by Iomega, designated the ZIP Plus. These are inexpensive and the cartridges are very low cost. They hold 100 Megabytes of images, which is a much more flexible format than the big multi-Gigabyte drives needed for total back-up. If an external drive is chosen from the ZIP Plus range, these may be carried to a client and plugged into either Mac or PC platforms to show progressive proofs or portfolios. The ZIP Plus will detect which platform is its host.

The whole unit and five cartridges weighs in at just 1 kilogram (38oz) providing possible storage space for at least 15-20 high resolution images. The market for storage devices is getting very busy and therefore very fragmented. Iomega has achieved such world market penetration with the ZIP technology, that it has become almost ubiquitous, therefore making it very likely that a photographer's clients will have the means of viewing ZIP disks in a very simple and secure way on their own computer. This is an aspect of presentation which any photographer of the nude will appreciate.

CHAPTER THIRTEEN

Digital Workshop

CAMERAS

MEGAPIXEL CAMERAS These cameras appear at the bottom end of the professional market and use a CCD or CMOS chip to capture the image on an array of between 1.2 and 2 million pixels (hence megapixels). They will cost about twice as much as a highly specified conventional camera with one lens, and will generally feature a zoom capability which covers wide angle to telephoto, with a macro facility as well. They work at speeds up to 1600 ISO and generally use a small LED screen on the camera to view the image. Some also have a conventional reflex viewfinder and will accept standard 35mm lenses.

For some small outputs such as magazines and brochures, resolution is sufficient for photographic reproduction up to 13 x 18cm (5 x 7in) and of course they plug directly into a computer for image processing and can provide direct files for page make-up. One extremely important technical problem can arise with these cameras – they run on AA batteries and in some models supply only enough battery capacity for very few exposures. Either re-chargeable cells will be needed (they need 4-5 hours to charge), or a better option for studio use is a camera with a mains converter.

Recently a Californian company has produced a cartridge which fits the film chamber of any conventional 35mm camera and which uses CMOS technology rather than CCD arrays to produce a digital image. For the photographer with a highly specified 35mm camera and a suite of fast lenses, this could be an ideal entry into digital photography at a cost not much more than that of a fast telephoto lens. The cartridge insert also covers the rechargeable power pack.

Despite the amazing growth of the megapixel technology, it is still aimed at the top of the consumer market rather than the serious professional. For final outputs of hardcopy up to a size of 50 x 60cm (20 x 24in), a much higher resolution camera will be needed from a professional photographic dealer. Expect to pay three to five times more for these cameras than the cost of the sub-professional megapixel cameras.

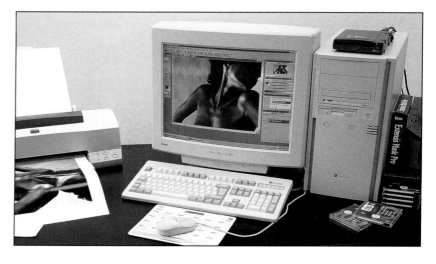

Photographers who wish to become involved with digital imagery, need to have the use of a suitable computer. They have two choices: those made by Apple (The Mac) which serves about 10% of the world market for computing and is much loved by graphic designers and those made by others and called IBM compatibles (The PC) which serve 90% of the world's need for computers. My personal choice is a PC, configured as a very fast Workstation which has been optimised for manipulating large 2-dimensional photographic files at high speed. It is built to my specification by Hi-Grade Computers Plc of London. The Workstation includes a 21 inch professional monitor from iiYAMA, a very fast CPU operating at 400 Mhz, an Intel motherboard specially suited for speedy handling of graphic files, a very fast graphics card from ATI, 8Mb of VRAM, 512Mb of SRAM, a fast CD-ROM, and a very fast access hard disk of 5 Gigabytes. The operating system is Microsoft's NT 4 Workstation, which has an exceptionally good interface for graphics and is very intuitive to use, especially for those with little technical skill in computing. The Workstation is also loaded with Adobe Photoshop 5.0, a world leader in photo-manipulation software and MaskPro, from Extensis which I have found an excellent plug-in for Photoshop and which is dedicated to the task of mask making. It is very much quicker and easier for photographers who are creating special effects for their work.

Images larger than 50 x 60 mm are better derived from conventional cameras loaded with silver halide emulsion film. If these images require digital manipulation, they can be scanned as prints or transparencies and then transferred to a computer as high resolution files. Once these are enhanced or altered using digital software, they can be output to large ink jet printers, turned into transparencies for conventional enlargement or printed to giant scale directly on to artist canvas and other textiles, by giant electronic airbrush machines such as are used by Maxx Aerosonic Ltd in London.

SOFTWARE

THE OPERATING SYSTEM The software which drives all the applications in a photographer's PC must be selected to permit the fastest possible manipulation of large 2-D images of high resolution. My personal choice has been Microsoft's NT 4 Workstation. For graphic processing at high speed and reliability, plus compatibility with a very wide range of graphic and special effects packages, NT 4 is to be preferred above some of the operating systems designed particularly for home and office use.

ADOBE PHOTOSHOP This software resides in the computer of every serious photographer or advanced graphic artist, digital artist or digital photographer, because it is so highly specified and because it has become the standard package for sophisticated image manipulation by which all others are judged. Using Photoshop opens up entirely new horizons for the photographer of the nude, and although the learning curve for proficiency is both steep and long, it is very well worth the effort. In the beginning a creative photographer would do well to hire a Photoshop specialist to assist.

Compared to other image manipulation software, Photoshop requires massive resources of memory (RAM), particularly if high resolution image processing such as montage making is to be attempted. At least 128 Megabytes of RAM would be a basic need, but two or three times as much would be more useful for a photographer involved with complex images.

The Iomega ZIP Plus External Drive. There are many devices on the market for holding image data and transmitting it. The ZIP Plus holds 100 Mbytes of data on an inexpensive disk and will auto-detect its host machine, whether Mac or PC. This has obvious advantages for photographers who wish to show progressive proofs or their portfolios to clients in their own offices.

The Epson Stylus Photo -EX A3 Colour Printer. Photographers who manipulate or retouch their work on computer will need to output proofs on a high quality colour printer. Epson make an exceptional and inexpensive printer, dedicated to printing out professional level colour photographs, up to A3 (297mm x 420mm / 11.75 x 23.20in).

Of course, there are other software packages for image processing, mostly with considerably lower RAM overheads, but these are usually more of interest to graphic artists than to photographers. x-Res is very well specified, as is Wright Design from Wright Technologies, a brilliant and innovative image handling package for graphic designers. For the photographer, however, who wishes to process and manipulate digital photographs, Adobe's Photoshop is essential.

A highly specified C.P.U. with at least 256Mb of RAM is essential, together with software such as NT Workstation, Adobe Photoshop and Extensis Mask Pro.

KAI'S PHOTO SOAP from Metatools Inc is a very fast and very accessible image enhancement package which is a stand-alone application for dealing with a modest range of photo-image processing needs at sub-professional level. Simple selections of buttons on screen start very complex operations without need for operator expertise. These cover such activities as correction of red-eye, wrinkles, poor colour balance, damaged or faded photographs, together with some elementary special effects. Although aimed at the consumer market and lacking the vast facilities of Photoshop, this software can swiftly solve basic retouching even for professional photographers.

ADOBE PHOTO DELUXE is a simpler specification of Photoshop and may be suitable to begin digital manipulation on a restricted scale. It cannot replace the full version for serious work. It often comes bundled with scanners and printers.

MASK PRO from Extensis Corporation is an edge detection software package which plugs into Photoshop, but uses an entirely different method to establish selected image outlines, areas for correction and colour balancing and complex mask outlines. Although it is memory (RAM) intensive, especially when opened through Photoshop, it is of great use to those seeking very fast solutions to professional special effects when dealing with the nude.

K5 PHOTO from Keybase Systems Ltd in Bristol UK is an image management data base of considerable sophistication. It enables search parameters to be established by individual photographers for their entire image library, together with captions and marketing data and image tracking information. Of course every image must be scanned first before input can take place. Keybase can be contacted on their website http://www.keybase.co.uk.

NORTON ANTIVIRUS from Symantec is for those needing a virus guard. This is one of the best for speedy and accurate detection and removal of all known viruses. It also comes with a lifetime of updates which successfully deal with emerging viruses. It is not expensive. For photographers using dedicated 2-D image processing stations such as featured here, it may be advisable not to use a virus guard because it may substantially increase processing times for big files.

It is better for the photographer not to import files on to the main computer, unless they are absolutely known to be virus-free. If using the Internet, the wise photographer will use a second inexpensive computer, just for handling Internet traffic and on that, install the virus guard, leaving the Workstation to function as a stand alone facility with optimised image handling speed and no chance of unauthorised access. This is particularly vital for photographers of the nude.

THE INTERNET

The Internet has become an integral part of the lives of most people who possess even elementary computer literacy, but for the photographer of the nude it probably should be avoided, except for research. If the Internet is used, no nude photographs should ever be placed on a website, or transmitted over the Internet. It is still a very insecure system and a photographer could easily lose control of images routed through the global network. This raises all sorts of possible problems especially those concerning copyright and model releases. Different communities also have different views on obscenity and the role of the nude photograph as an artwork in its own right.

AFRICA GIRL

This image is a composite which was started in the darkroom, using conventional wet chemistry and then scanned into Photoshop for further, but fairly elementary manipulation. The entire job could no doubt have been completed in either mode, but I felt it may interest the reader to see the result of a hybrid technique. The contribution of conventional photography is absolutely critical to either method.

THE MODEL AND A LARGE OSTRICH EGG (PAINTED MATT BLACK), WERE PHOTOGRAPHED IN THE STUDIO AGAINST A WHITE PAPER FALL.

A SECOND MODEL, AN EXPERIENCED DANCER, WAS ALSO PHOTOGRAPHED ON A WHITE STUDIO BACKGROUND, AND DIRECTED TO CONDENSE HER BODY MASS AS MUCH AS POSSIBLE SO SHE COULD LATER BE FITTED INSIDE THE EGG. PAINTING THE EGG BLACK MADE THIS MONTAGE A SIMPLE ENLARGER STEP AND NO MASK WAS USED.

A FILM POSITIVE WAS MADE FROM THE CAMERA NEGATIVE OF THE GIRL WITH THE EGG.

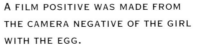

AFRICA GIRL

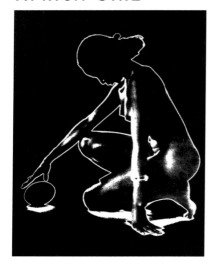

A REVERSAL CONTACT FILM WAS MADE FROM THIS AND SOLARISED TO PRODUCE THE CHARACTERISTIC. MACKIE LINE AROUND FIGURE AND EGG.

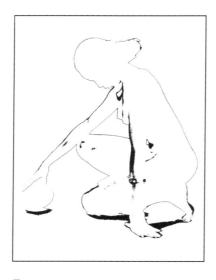

THE SOLARISED FILM WAS ITSELF CONTACT PRINTED ON FILM SO THAT THE WHITE MACKIE LINE PRINTED BLACK. THIS PRODUCED A LINE OUTLINE OF THE MODEL REACHING FOR THE EGG WHICH FORMED THE BASIS OF THE MASK.

THE COMPLETED FILM MASK.

A FINAL PRINT WAS MADE AND SCANNED INTO PHOTOSHOP FOR FINISHING.

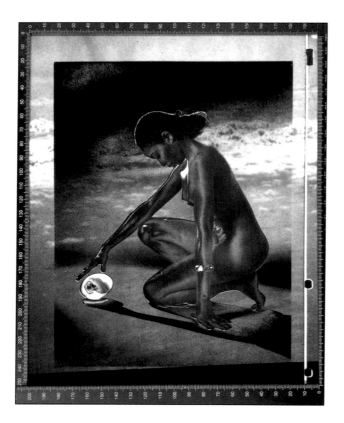

A SKY NEGATIVE WAS PRINTED ON FILM AS A POSITIVE

A TEST PRINT OF ALL THE COMPONENTS WAS ASSEMBLED ON THE REGISTER BOARD AND PRINTED ON BROMIDE PAPER.

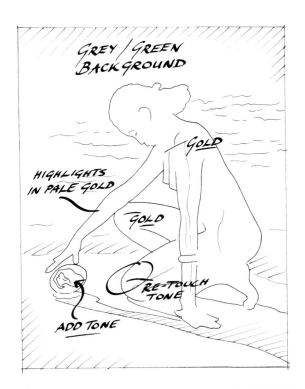

THE BLACK AND WHITE PRINT WAS TURNED INTO AN RGB COLOUR FILE (CHOOSE IMAGE> MODE> RGB) AND MANIPULATED TO PRODUCE A CUSTOM DUOTONE. THE SKY RECEIVED COLOUR FROM USING THE COLOR BALANCE COMMAND ON PRE-DETERMINED SELECTIONS.

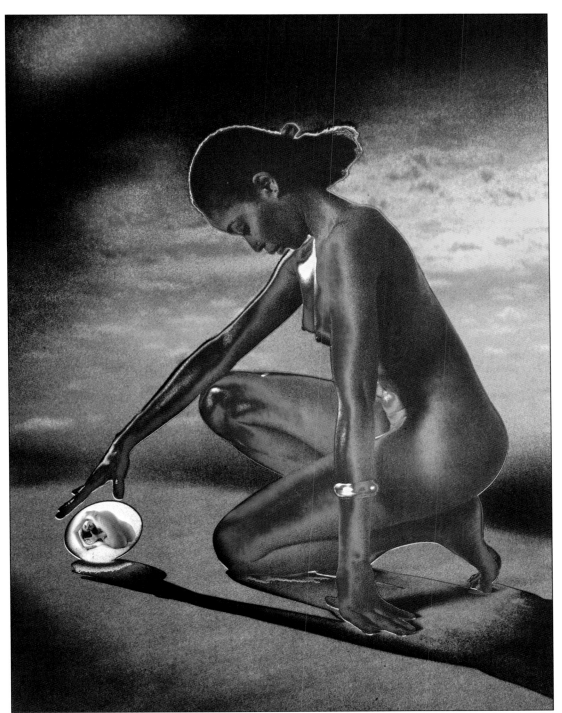

THE FINISHED IMAGE.

143

SEA GIRL

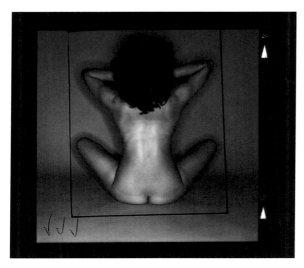

2. A POSITIVE REVERSAL WHICH HAS BEEN SOLARISED TO GIVE A BLACK LINE AROUND THE FIGURE AND NO DETAIL IN THE BODY.

3. A ROCKFORM WHICH HAS BEEN ADDED TO THE FIGURE.

1. CONTACT SHEET SHOWING SELECTED IMAGE OF GIRL WITH HER BACK TO CAMERA

4. AN EVENING SEASCAPE WAS ADDED AS BACKGROUND.

FINAL IMAGE ON SCREEN IS THE FULL COMPOSITE OF 3 COMPONENTS MERGED.

CALIFORNIA GIRL

2. A STUDIO
SHOT OF THE
MODEL.

1. THIS REMOTE PART OF THE
SOUTHERN CALIFORNIA COAST
ALWAYS ATTRACTED ME.

LATE ONE DAY I CAME UPON A
BLACK SAND BEACH AND MADE
SEVERAL TRANSPARENCIES IN
THE FADING SUNSET LIGHT.

THE MOTEL SIGN WAS VISIBLE AND
THE SEA HAD A GENTLE BLURRED
MOVEMENT WHICH I ENHANCED BY
A SLOW SHUTTER SPEED. IT BECAME
A NATURAL CHOICE FOR THE BACK
GROUND FOR CALIFORNIA GIRL.
IT WAS SCANNED INTO PHOTOSHOP
AND THE MASKED IMAGE OF THE
STUDIO MODEL WAS DROPPED IN.

THE FINAL IMAGE IS A HIGH
RESOLUTION COMPOSITE OF TWO
COMPONENTS MERGED.
THE COLOUR HAS BEEN HARMONISED
BY BALANCING BOTH TRANSPARENCIES
TO THE SAME SUNSET AMBIENCE.

THE MONUMENT

Element no. 2, work print selected from contact sheet.

This was an image for a large art poster and was to consist of two images from earlier black and white studio shots and a very colourful transparency of a diffraction grating about 15cm (6in) square. The reclining figure was photographed on white paper, while the two dancing figures and the grating had both been taken against a black velvet background. The first step was to scan all three and then import them into Adobe Photoshop for manipulation.

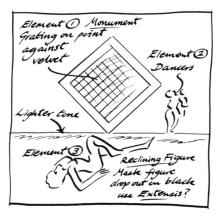

INITIAL CONCEPT SKETCH.

ELEMENT NO. 1 WAS A PHOTOGRAPH OF A COLOUR GRATING, SUSPENDED ON A CORNER AND PLACED AGAINST A BLACK VELVET BACKGROUND. IT WAS LIT WITH A SMALL SHARP SPOTLIGHT.

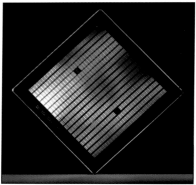

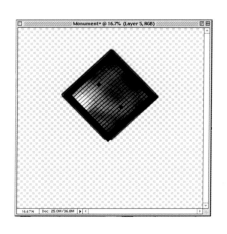

THE GRATING HAS BEEN CUT OUT FROM ITS BACKGROUND.

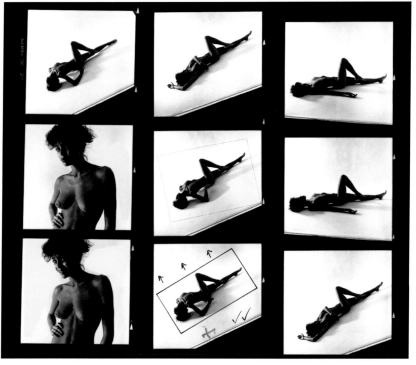

ELEMENT NO. 3, CONTACT SHEET.

A HIGH RESOLUTION FILE OF THE ENTIRE COMPOSITE.

Sky Diver

A client had need of a slightly surreal image for a brochure cover, and accepted my proposal of a diving nude backed by a strong cloudscape. For added impact, I included the piece of a Victorian cupboard to increase perspective. The nude figure began as a black and white image photographed on a white paper fall. Although only three elements were chosen for this composite, some very sophisticated work has been done in Adobe Photoshop and Extensis Mask Pro.

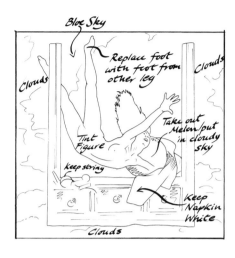

INITIAL CONCEPT SKETCH.

THE SELECTED IMAGE, WHICH WAS SCANNED INTO PHOTOSHOP AND ROTATED ALMOST 180 DEGREES, SO THAT THE FIGURE APPEARED AIRBORNE.

A GOOD SKY BACKGROUND WAS TAKEN FROM MY LIBRARY FILE AND SCANNED IN.

A STILL LIFE SUBJECT WAS CHOSEN, AGAIN FROM MY LIBRARY FILE AND SCANNED IN.

CONTACT SHEET FROM MODEL PHOTOGRAPHY SESSION.

AFTER SCANNING, MOST DETAIL WITHIN THE CUPBOARD WAS REMOVED BY SELECTION AND SUBSEQUENT DELETION. THE MELON WAS LEFT INTACT AND IN PLACE. THE SKY WAS ADDED AT THE SAME TIME.

THE FIGURE WAS IMPORTED AND PUT IN PLACE. NOTE THAT THE ARM HAS BECOME FLATTENED AND WILL NEED FURTHER WORK. THE LEFT FOOT APPEARS UNATTRACTIVELY DEFORMED WHERE IT WAS ON THE STUDIO FLOOR AND SUPPORTED THE ENTIRE MODEL'S WEIGHT AT THE MOMENT OF PHOTOGRAPHY.

THE ARM HAS BEEN PARTIALLY OBSCURED BY CLOUD. THE LEFT FOOT HAS BEEN REPLACED BY A SELECTION OF THE ANKLE FROM THE RIGHT FOOT AND JOINED SEAMLESSLY IN PLACE.

THE SURFACE OF THE MELON WAS REPLACED WITH SKY.

THE LEFT FOOT IS NOW PARTIALLY OBSCURED BY THE CUPBOARD. THIS STOPS A VISUAL COMPARISON BETWEEN THE FEET AND MAKES THE RETOUCHING SEEM MORE CREDIBLE. THE FIGURE NOW APPEARS TO BE DIVING THROUGH THE FRAME OF THE CUPBOARD AND THE IMAGE IS MORE DYNAMIC. THE MODEL'S BODY HAS BEEN GIVEN A FAINT TINT. THIS IS THE FINAL PREVIEW IMAGE AT LOW RESOLUTION.

SKY DIVER* @ 12.5% (Layer 6, RGB)

12.5%   Doc: 33.1M/118.6M

THIS IS THE FINAL FINISHED IMAGE IN HIGH RESOLUTION AND READY FOR REPRO. THE IMAGE MANIPULATION, INCLUDING THE SCANNING, HAS TAKEN 5 HOURS OF INTENSIVE WORK.

TO MAKE THIS COMPOSITE USING CONVENTIONAL DARKROOM METHODS AND A REGISTER BOARD WOULD HAVE TAKEN AT LEAST 8 DAYS AND EASY PREVIEWS AT EACH STAGE OF THE COMPOSITE WOULD NOT HAVE BEEN POSSIBLE.

NOTE THAT THE STILL LIFE CAME FROM A 13 X 18CM (5 X 7IN) TRANSPARENCY AND WAS MUCH FINER GRAIN THAN THE BLACK & WHITE OF THE GIRL. THIS IMBALANCE OF GRAIN CAN BE USED FOR ADDED EFFECT OR CAN BE HARMONISED BETWEEN ALL ELEMENTS BY USING A DESPECKLE FILTER OR A SMOOTHING FILTER ON THE GRAINIER ELEMENTS.

CHAPTER FOURTEEN

Making a Living

Everyone who photographs the female nude will become aware of two constant factors: it is an expensive activity and there exists an insatiable commercial market for good pictures of such subjects. It would seem sensible that the benefits from one could be used to subsidise the other.

THE MODEL RELEASE

Because these images are unlike ordinary photographs of ordinary subjects, some care and thought is needed before venturing into the marketplace or dealing with the buyers who offer the rewards. Before making any moves to gain commercial benefit from any pictures of the nude, it is wise to re-read the model release and, in the light of that information, discuss with the model the proposed use of the photographs. If there is no model release, do not proceed to any commercial or editorial negotiation until there is one. The use of photographs of the female nude without specific permission from the model can draw substantial legal and financial penalties.

A general advertising release which does not indicate any restrictions and is in favour of the photographer, will be the ideal model release, but few models are likely to agree to this except for very high initial fees. If such a general release does not exist, make sure that the model knows what photograph you have selected and to whom you are offering it and be sure to build into your financial negotiations with the client an agreed model fee, separate from the photographic fee.

EROTICISM

One of the most lucrative markets for photographs of the nude is one which most photographers and models studiously avoid and this is the publishing world of pornography which seeks only grossly erotic and tastelessly obscene images of women. These markets are highly exploitive of both model and photographer and there is nothing to be gained from them.

There are, of course, legitimate commercial publishing markets where eroticism, sensitively illustrated, will have its place and the photographer must apply good judgement on what is offered if this is to be one of the identified areas of interest.

This type of work also needs prior understanding from the model who should be given a choice of participating or not.

FINE ART

The fine artist who works with images of the nude need not submit to the commercial censorship of the markets and can produce photographs whose style and content is dictated entirely by the aesthetic judgement of model and photographer. Exhibition of such work will still require the permission of the model, so a release is necessary, but photographs of the female nude are much more acceptable to a larger segment of society than ever before, so such releases are usually given.

Photographers of the nude who choose to exhibit as fine artists will soon be aware that this is possibly the most difficult and financially unrewarding of occupations. The photographer can, of course, sell direct from the studio, but it is usually necessary to be represented by an agent or gallery, preferably one who can operate globally and who already has good contacts in art circles. Normally, such agents or galleries will take at least 50% of sales and pay the artist only when work is sold. To cover fine art sales, a contract is essential and the photographer would be well advised to ask for credit references.

The artist-photographer will usually need to work in large sizes, greater than 60 x 80cm. (24 x 32in), produce archival prints and mount them on archival material. With the latest developments in print technology, such as Aerosonic printing, very large sizes are achievable, printed electronically directly on to canvas, but input costs are high and must initially be met by the photographer.

PUBLISHING MARKETS

The photographic picture book is one distinct division of publishing, usually dealt with by specialist publishers, where the artist/photographer can hope to sell a number of related images. Photographs of the nude which are destined for this market should generally carry a theme, often be entirely in black and white in order to reduce production costs and be innovative in style and technique.

To find those publishers who exist to serve this market, the photographer needs to research the art book shops or specialist photographic galleries and their book shops, or to come to an arrangement with a literary agent who will undertake the search on his or her behalf. It should be understood that many literary agents are not necessarily skilled in visual matters, nor do they often understand the extremely heavy costs of producing photographs and it is wise to try to find an agent who both understands the publishing world and the visual arts.

For the artist using a camera to develop a book theme around the female nude, it would be tempting to accept a commission where the photographic expenses are paid for separately from royalties. Such an arrangement could endanger the photographer's copyright, particularly in the United Kingdom, where the owner of film material and the commissioning party obtains considerable control over copyright, unless specifically refuted in writing. Commissioned work and the expenses involved should not allow any prejudice of the photographer's copyright and it should be noted in all contracts.

To provide sufficient material for a book of photographs can be a time consuming and expensive exercise and it is one which cannot be generally counted on as a sole source of income. This will mean that a dedicated photographic artist must organise a very defensive living style, perhaps even taking on a job which has nothing to do with photography while the book is being prepared. Royalty cheques are often only paid once a year and even a successful book will not contribute very meaningful income for a long time. Unless earnings are augmented from other activities, it may be difficult to continue working with creative freedom.

A growing area for the fine artist in photography, is the self-published book and the portfolio. Obviously the need here is for sufficient money to finance each project, but if this is possible, the freedom to create and produce a sequential set of images can carry a tremendous artistic reward. Outlets for this type of book exist among specialist bookshops and gallery bookshops, particularly those in Germany and the USA. A distributor or wholesaler is essential for marketing such works.

The portfolio, on the other hand, is usually made from actual photo-print material, rather than reproductions from it and will generally consist of not more than 10 or 15 images, flawlessly produced, and presented in an outer box made from archival material and with each image separately mounted archivally with protective interleaving acid-free tissues between images. Gold embossing or other evidence of the bookbinder's art will frequently embellish the outer cover. Such portfolios can be offered direct by the photographer through the small ads in art magazines, through an agent or through a gallery.

Occasionally such portfolios are tested on the market by giving them to art auction houses to include in suitable sales, but this can sometimes be hazardous in a marketing sense. Should the portfolio fall far below the expected price, it could greatly damage sales in other areas such as galleries, who carefully monitor all art auction activities. It is considered mandatory that such portfolios represent the highest achievement in conceptual and photographic skills and that prints are processed to archivally perfect standards. Guidance on archival techniques can be obtained from Silverline Ltd of London, whose website is http//www.silverprint.co.uk.

PAYMENT FOR PHOTOGRAPHY

In the professional, or part-time freelance side of photography, care must be taken to protect the photographer from irresponsibility or misunderstandings on the part of clients. It will be helpful to take note of the following essentials:

PAYMENT TERMS

1. Be sure the client is aware of the copyright status of the images before agreeing a final fee.

2 State, *in writing* the rights awarded by the fee agreed and the precise number of reproductions permitted, their nature, size and the time limit on those rights.

3 Do not endorse a settlement cheque if your signature, in any way, is part of a waiver or disclaimer in respect of copyright.

4. Work only to a prior order or contract which covers the entire job or fee.

5 Avoid the 'work made for hire' contract or one where the client pays for all material costs. Both types may automatically award the copyright to the client, not to the photographer.

6 Invoice promptly and state the settlement terms and due date.

7 Do not hesitate to make strong requests for payment after the due date.

8 Do not allow any invoice to be outstanding longer than eight weeks, unless by mutual agreement between photographer and client.

PICTURE GALLERIES

Another growing market for photographs of the nude is the commercial picture gallery, distinct from fine art galleries. These are often run by framing manufacturers who serve the large number of people wanting to purchase limited editions or distinctive prints of a very high quality, but do not want to buy the more complex and expensive photographs provided by fine art galleries.

These commercial picture galleries may be found for the photographer by an agent, but it is mostly up to each artist to locate and talk to gallery management about potential schemes. Photographs may be given 'on consignment', which means they are taken on a sale or return basis, with no certainty that any will be sold at all. It is far better to come to an arrangement whereby the gallery is offered a number of images exclusively and these are bought outright.

The minimum size of such pictures is likely to be 50 x 60cm (20 x 24in) and to protect the photographer's copyright, each should be signed and dated, preferably within the image area. A separate letter from the photographer should accompany every consignment of pictures, listing each and noting its value, together with a clear statement of copyright and the terms under which each has been offered.

POSTERS

There exists also a somewhat over-lapping market to these picture gallery outlets and this is the poster shop. This is a modern retail phenomenon offering low priced posters to a youthful market. Whereas the picture gallery will at least have some pretensions towards an artistic image, the poster shop will be looking for images which reflect trends and styles of the moment and perhaps feature humour or very mild eroticism.

Most poster shops will obtain their supplies from main distributors and publishers and these can sometimes be identified by a small by-line on the poster itself or by asking the shop manager for information. A letter or a visit to the management of an identified publishing firm should be accompanied by a small portfolio of possible subjects. Each image in the portfolio must carry the photographer's name and copyright statement, preferably deep within the image area so that no piracy of the image is possible should the portfolio go astray. The letter should list submitted work and, if posted through the mail, should be registered. Return postage should always be included.

Calendars, of all markets, respond to a little humour.

CALENDARS

Poster shops will occasionally also sell calendars and the female nude is a favourite subject. Calendar publishers fall into widely different categories and each requires a specific type of image and even a specific type of model. For general release, fantasy subjects, graphic treatments, soft-focus nudes in landscapes, romanticism and very little overt sexuality, are the most acceptable treatments and models can be left to the photographer's own choice.

153

This is the build up towards the final picture. Light has been beamed in from the back of the set from a tight reflector, a star filter is in place on the camera and the model has been directed to cover the backlight with her body, but allow a few beams to escape around her to produce the halation and sunbeam effect. Overall a large diffused flood in a gold reflector box produces the summer ambience. The model at this stage is nervous and tense, awaiting direction.

This is an excellent example of a nude photograph which will interest most media buyers. The girl projects a sensual, outdoor presence, looks beautiful and relaxed. Her hands are elegant and manicured, her look is serene and direct to camera. The light is golden and poetic. Made with a 35mm camera and a 135mm lens.

Commercial calendars are another matter and much bigger business. Many printing houses offer commercial calendars as a service to industrial clients and imprint the client's own logo and text as desired. Such printers are usually looking for very low priced photographs and quality of concept is not a vital part of most of their needs. They tend to pay an outright fee which is fairly diminutive, but before accepting it, the photographer should understand what rights are given away by receiving such a fee.

A wise photographer will, in discussions with the printing management or publishers of calendars, define a time (for example two years) during which the photographs may be used and an area (such as United Kingdom or Europe or North America). When these time and area limits are to be extended at the request of the printer or publisher, extra fees should be negotiated for both model and photographer. It should be made clear that copyright is held by the photographer unless a

suitably large fee can be agreed by the publisher to cover outright purchase of copyright.

Specialist calendar publishers, often connected to graphic design studios, will undertake very high quality productions for commercial or advertising clients, or advertising agencies themselves may work with such designers, to produce something specifically for their own clients. Such calendars are almost invariably commissioned and carry quite large budgets; very often they take place in exotic tropical locations.

These clients will generally want control over copyright and will pay accordingly and for the professional photographer who has shown acceptable skills in photography of the nude, this market is of particular interest. Girls who are chosen for calendar work often have fuller figures than would be the case of the models needed by the fine art or editorial photographer and their faces should be particularly expressive and pretty.

For most calendars of 12 or 13 pictures, at least three girls would be chosen, sometimes appearing together but usually singly. Themes for these high value productions are often established after very lengthy discussions with all parties concerned, but the photographer can contribute considerably when the work is actually being done. The model will add much to the final concept of each image and it is particularly important that girls be chosen who have the ability to do this.

In order to find some of the specialist calendar publishers, a photographer could search through graphic arts magazines, catalogues of advertising exhibitions and annual books of awards to graphic designers. These generally have a special section on calendars, with examples and a listing of names and addresses of companies involved.

PHOTO LIBRARIES

Where a photographer is professionally engaged in making frequent pictures of the nude, it is often sensible to come to an arrangement with a reputable photographic library or picture agency, whereby they agree to take into their files all spare photographs which are not included in the original commission or those which arise out of any freelance assignments.

Occasionally, after working some time with a photographer, such libraries may commission a set of pictures, but this is rare. The photographs remain on file, usually for lengthy periods from two to five years and are offered from time to time to commercial clients, magazines, calendar publishers and advertising agencies. The fee obtained is split in an agreed way, usually 60 per cent to 40 per cent in the photographer's favour but, of course, it is paid out only when the photographic agency receives this money from the final client. The model in the picture should be made fully aware of the intent to submit to photo libraries or picture agencies, because some will not permit their photographs to be used in this way, even for a considerable share of fees.

ADVERTISING & EDITORIAL

The professional photographer who is mainly concerned with advertising and editorial work, particularly if specialising in fashion and beauty, will often be called upon to produce highly innovative photographs of the female nude. There is room also in this field for the submission of speculative photographs. The models are extremely important for this type of assignment and need to have expressive faces, especially good hands and feet and have excellent hair.

For unusual advertising photographs, the photographer must present very special creative skills. Here a polarising filter has been used against a late afternoon sky. Besides the characteristic darkening of the sky, the polariser has increased colour saturation in the 35mm Kodachrome original.

Editorial clients usually pay model fees and film and processing costs, but photographers again must be wary of the copyright position with this type of client. Normally the photographer only receives a page rate, which is only payable after publication and this is barely enough return for such pictures. Be careful not to sign work for hire contracts or in any other way jeopardise copyright; in submitting work always accompany it with a written clarification about what is being offered in the way of copyright and list every single image.

Advertising agencies will be much more positive in their dealings with the photographer because they will usually have a very clear brief from their eventual client and will have had internal discussions about the styling and concept of the picture long before approaching the photographer, usually to the point of actually producing a layout sketch. These agencies will select a photographer on the basis of past work concluded for the agency and on the evidence of current portfolios.

If the photographer has decided to specialise in nude photography, no doubt a portfolio will have been shown and remembered. Agencies will usually pay a higher fee to both model and photographer and expect to own the copyright of the image. They will also require a specific advertising release from the model.

BOOK JACKETS

Other occasional users of nude photography will be paperback publishers and even more rarely, record companies. The pictorials which are used on covers for such publishers and producers will be closely related to the contents of the work being sold and the models are especially carefully chosen in order to fit the style and type of girl to be found in the story or music. Usually for this type of photography it is necessary for specific rights to be sold to cover the identified market (for example book rights) and the fee is down-graded accordingly for both model and photographer.

THE PIN-UP

While all the above market areas have easily definable requirements as far as models, photographic style visual concept and so on are concerned, the one type of photograph which normally sells well in almost every market except fine art, is the pin-up. These innocuous pictures are eagerly sought by most publishers of the nude simply because they have reached a degree of acceptability with the general public not yet found with other pictures of the female nude and they are therefore much more widely commercial.

The models for this type of work are generally fuller of figure, very expressive and often good actresses. Colour photography is almost universally a requirement so models must be chosen for their complexion, hair colour, colour of the eyes and so on, as well as for attributes of figure and personality.

The pin-up market is one area which is open to receiving speculative work and many photographers, when they have found a particularly suitable model, will make a number of pictures in different situations and with different props and then submit these to poster, calendar or picture library sources. The one requirement to all such pin-ups made speculatively is that they should not be too overtly sexual and never be pornographic in their concept, otherwise they may be rejected.

When submitting photographs of the nude to publishers, printer or magazines, it is necessary to take particular care to protect original or reproducible material. Never send originals when copies will do, do not supply contact sheets or negatives through the post and, most importantly, list every image and put a value on each. State clearly the copyright position, model release information, rights offered and fee for each specific image and insist on insurance while in the keeping of the client.

If the model release is made out in favour of the photographer, it is the duty of the photographer to protect the model in the case of unauthorised usage, so it is essential to take every precaution to see that usage is only as agreed with all parties. If something untoward does happen and photographs do find their way into an unauthorised market, the photographer may be faced with a very unpleasant and costly legal problem.

In making out a detailed list which accompanies submissions, always state size of transparency, film type and an identifying phrase for each image. For example: 'girl with white horse', is a sufficient identity, provided the image is also given a number which relates to the list. Mark each cardboard mount of any transparency and the back of every print with a copyright statement and the name and address of the photographer. Always include return postage if using the mail for submission and have a return address on the outside of the package, which should be sent by special delivery or registered post.

Making a reliable income solely from the sale of photographs of the nude is not always easy and it will require persistence, patience and a high regard for administrative detail. It will depend largely also on a flair for directing models into interesting situations and the photographic skill to make flawless pictures of the result.

INTRODUCTION

The Masterclass has been arranged with several levels of complexity. The first third of the examples presented here are directed at those who are reasonably well acquainted with photography, who have read this book and understood some of its content. The photographs I have selected from my portfolio are presented as good aspirational examples that could be emulated by the majority of skilled photographers with some training in the subject.
None of them are attributed to luck.
The middle section of The Masterclass assumes an advanced level of skills, all of which are explained in the earlier chapters of this book. Attaining this level of image management calls for many hours of practice, considerable discipline and a broad understanding of both wet and dry photography. No special equipment is needed to reach this standard, but it helps to have easy access to a permanent darkroom set-up of professional standards, and a quality SLR (preferably medium format) camera with a normal and telephoto lens.
The final part of The Masterclass is deliberately aimed at a high level and I offer these images for your contemplation with no apology for their unusual style. Some of these images require very advanced competence in darkroom techniques, others a serious involvement with sophisticated image management. The main attribute needed for those who aspire to this particular level, is an avid curiosity about Life in general and photography in particular, together with a willingness to push personal experience of its art and craft to the limit. It has always been my belief that photography must be approached with both passion and imagination . By presenting my work in this very personal way, I hope it may encourage many others to make their own deep commitment to the subject as I have done, and be as fascinated and fulfilled with its infinite challenges as I continue to be.

STANDING NUDE

O f all the photographs of the nude which I have taken, this remains the easiest for beginners to emulate and at the same time attains the most classical in style. It requires of the photographer a complete understanding of light as explained in the Workshop pages of this book and a flawless competence in black & white processing of fine grain films. The model was given exact direction and a trench light, 2 metres in height was used to light the figure from head to toe. A white paperfall was used as a background, but given a grey tone by masking the light which fell on it from the trench light . The film used was Agfapan 100, 120 format, which was given 30% overexposure and 25% underdevelopment. The repro print from which this image has been made required no special printing technique and there has been no computer manipulation.

As the quality of light has played such a major part in the success of this picture it may be of interest to study the image for its lighting structure. The lighting core is the threshold in an image where light meets dark, in this instance very dramatically. The model looks straight at the camera and the lighting core is centred on her face ; her torso has been twisted towards the key light and the core retreats to the arms, allowing her body to be seen in a glowing, textural light. The abdomen and hips have remained facing straight to camera and one leg has been advanced, with the lighting core running down her left side and leg. A confident, graceful and dynamic photograph, attainable by most photographers who have a few months experience.

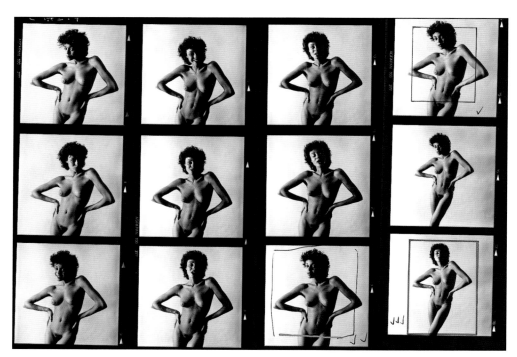

CONTACT SHEET.

THE LIGHTING CORE.

THE FINAL PRINT.

SEATED NUDE

The nude image is obviously very much concerned with texture. Once the deep structure of the body is suggested by the pose, and after contour is disclosed by the attitude of the body in relation to the key light, the visually tactile areas of skin, hands, feet and limbs are next in importance. Texture of the nude body is emphasised by the quality of the light, rather than its direction, although obviously, revelatory low angle lights placed at 90 degrees to the lens axis are also needed. Only meticulous processing will produce the rich detail and texture which is to be found in a successful print. There is usually a tendency of inexperienced photographers of the nude to print these body textures too light. Do not under expose or over develop either negative or print if the full tactile qualities of the body are to be expressed. Follow the steps outlined in Chapter 2 for extending scale by exposure and negative development.

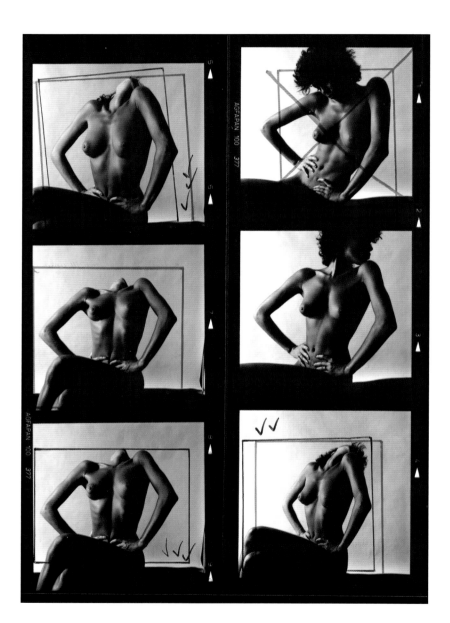

THE CONTACT PRINT OF THE SELECTED IMAGE.

THE MODEL WAS DIRECTED INTO ADOPTING VARIOUS POSES UNTIL THE FINAL TWO FRAMES PRODUCED THE DRAMATIC AND SCULPTURAL IMAGE WHICH WAS BEING SOUGHT.

THE FINAL PRINT.

STUDIO NUDE

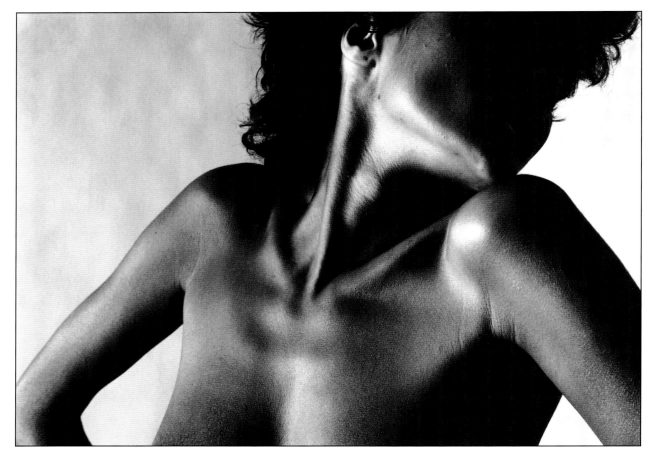

THE FINISHED PRINT.

A gain this is a very conventional studio photograph lit in a classical style and impeccably processed. The black & white repro print has been scanned on a Linotype Saphire Ultra flat bed scanner, imported into Photoshop on the Photographers Workstation and given a duotone colour treatment then printed out on an Epson Stylus Photo EX inkjet. The lesson here is more advanced in the sense that digital techniques have been added to basic and simple optical photography, but the digital work is completely elementary. A photographer who has made a fine print like this could have the digital enhancement carried out at very low cost at a bureau for digital processing.

ONCE THE WORKPRINT HAD BEEN MADE, A VERY CAREFUL CONSIDERATION OF THE FINAL IMAGE CROP WAS NEEDED. NUMEROUS CHOICES WERE POSSIBLE.

GOLDEN GIRL

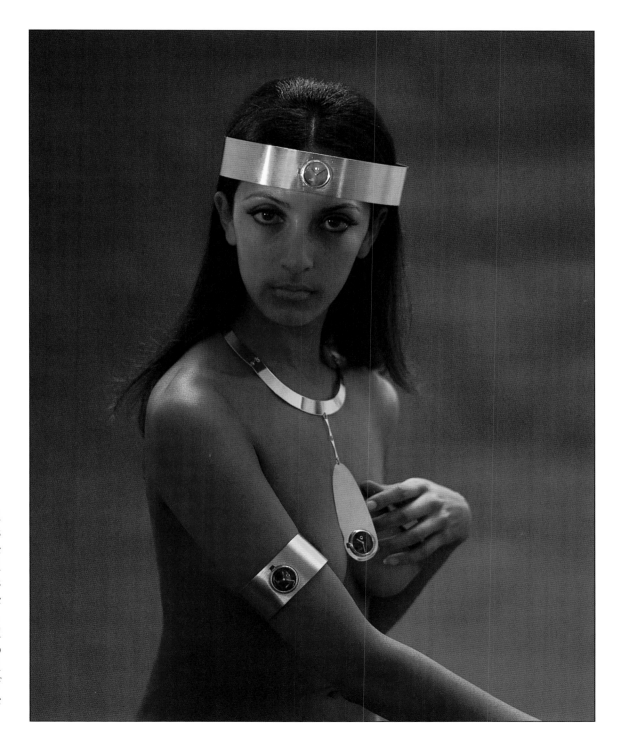

The brief for this picture stressed that, as the publicity was about gold, a golden ambience should be found in the image and all the fabulously expensive gold artifacts on the model, should make the metal's lustrous gleam very apparent. This was done by using a gold foil reflector in a broad diffuser as a top front fill light and a more directional key light to emphasise the contours of the body, beamed through a pale amber lighting gel.

PRISONER

R aw light from a projector, naked household lamps and sharp spots have been used to light the set. This has created dramatic pools of light and deep shadows to amplify a sombre mood to the theme. An actress was chosen to model the scene and a story line explained to her. Over several hours of rehearsal and actual takes, many excellent pictures resulted. This was the one I chose to best fulfil the client's brief.

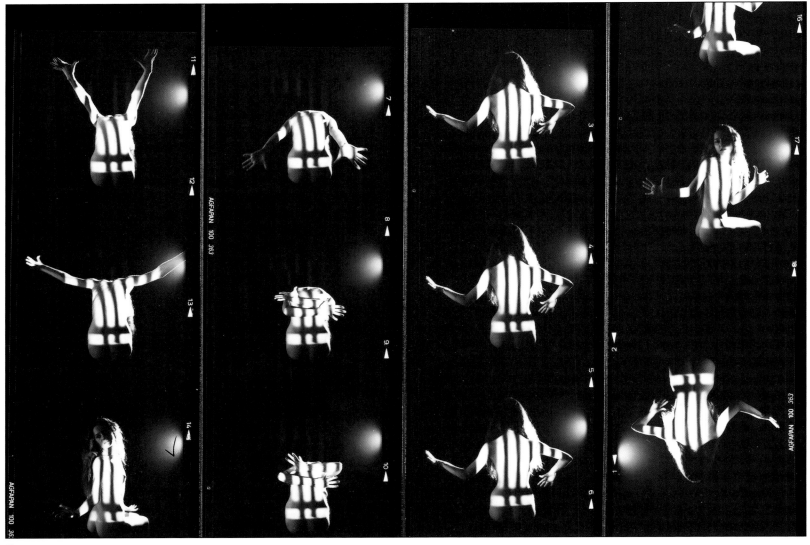

CONTACT SHEET.

THE FINAL PRINT.

BLUE NUDE

This picture was taken in a domestic room with all its furniture removed and a large seamless white paperfall fixed in place. Very tall windows lit the photograph with bright light. A tightly focussed 500 watt projector beam was aimed at the jewel and nothing from this source touched the model. The picture was made on a Contax 35mm camera with a zoom Zeiss lens. A fast tungsten film was loaded, which was perfectly balanced for the projector light and so rendered the jewel in correct colour, but because the daylight was about 6000K and therefore almost 50% colder than the tungsten light from the projector, everything except the jewel turned a moody blue. This is not particularly advanced photography, but it is very competent (and easily emulated). Mixing of coloured light sources in this image is better produced with conventional photography than with digital manipulation.

This may appear at first sight to be the result of a very difficult technical process, but it is not so. Also a major part of the work has been done by chance. This image is known as a Polaroid emulsion transfer and is explained fully in Chapter 11, where another version from the same image source appears. Compare the two results. The originations for transfer Polaroids were made from copying the source print on to 4 x 5 Polaroid Tungsten 64 film. The image was transferred to a tinted Pantone paper.

STORM

A montage was made by the method outlined below using conventional darkroom processing. The result was reproduced by photogravure and then copied on to 4 x 5 colour film through a colour filter.

Montages can be made by using a saw tooth vignetting mask to allow the chosen image element to print through on to the enlarging paper, while reserving unexposed areas for subsequent images. Usually these montages are not repeatable.

In order to make several montages exactly the same, a matte box is used. This acts like the vignetting mask, but can be precisely controlled to expose the same vignetted area every time. It is fitted to the enlarger lens and the masks adjusted differently for each element. A tracing rehearsal is needed to decide on layout of the montage.

A MATTE BOX.

THE STORM PICTURE WITH THE SELECTED AREA FOR MONTAGE.

THE WORKPRINT OF A TRIAL MONTAGE.

PENNY BLACK

The true title of this image is Penny Goes To The Photographer On A Saturday Afternoon, but for brevity's sake in this book, it has become Penny Black. It was one of the simplest images to actually make, but reaches layers of complexity which are unusual for something arising from very elementary photographic techniques. In Chapter 4, the silhouette is suggested as a simple starting point for beginners. Penny Black is just a collection of basic silhouettes, which have come to dynamic and graphic life by working in pure black and pure white as the colours of choice. The model Penny, an experienced dancer, became interested in the use of hands as graphic devices in the silhouette and was given minute and constant direction to shape the spaces in the image designs. The negatives were underexposed 20% and overdeveloped 30% to increase contrast, then contact printed as usual. Then the same

negatives were contact printed on to lith film, to give a reversed set of negatives. When these were contact printed on photo paper, one set of contacts had black silhouettes on a white background and the others had white figures on a black background. A selection was made and pasted together and then copied on line film. At that point a very unusual and creative image had been made and a large art print could be produced without further technical input from the photographer.

However, I decided to proceed further to refine the image and enlarged the copy negative on to 18 x 24cm. (8 x 10in) lith film and made a Tone Separation set (see Chapter 9), and combined these again on to a single lith film. This assembly was solarised and became my master negative for the final print. This then became a 75 x 100cm (30 x 40in) limited edition lithograph.

SECTION OF FIRST PHOTO SESSION.

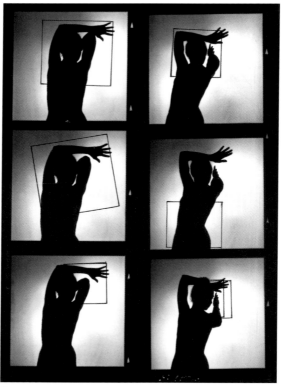

REVERSAL CONTACTS.

THIS IS A COPY NEGATIVE OF A PASTE UP OF 36 SMALL PRINTS. THIS WAS CONTACT PRINTED ONTO LITH FILM AND SOLARISED.

THESE ARE THE REVERSALS WHICH BECAME THE NEGATIVE FOR A SET OF CONTACTS WHICH WERE PRINTED ON TO BROMIDE PAPER TO SHOW A BLACK BACKGROUND AND SOME DETAIL IN THE BODY.

THIS IS THE SOLARISED LITH FILM OF THE PASTE UP.

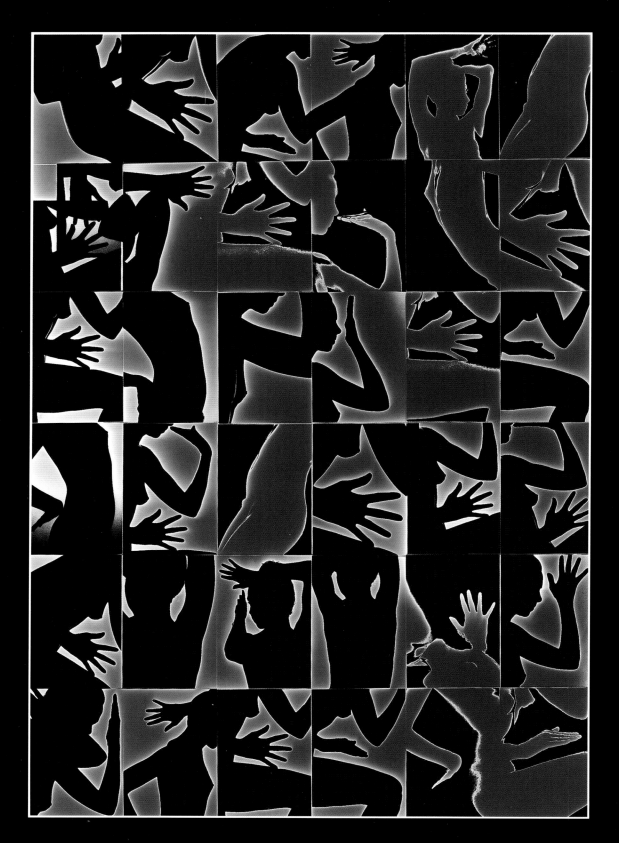

PENNY BLACK

THE FINISHED LITHOGRAPHIC PRINT.

172

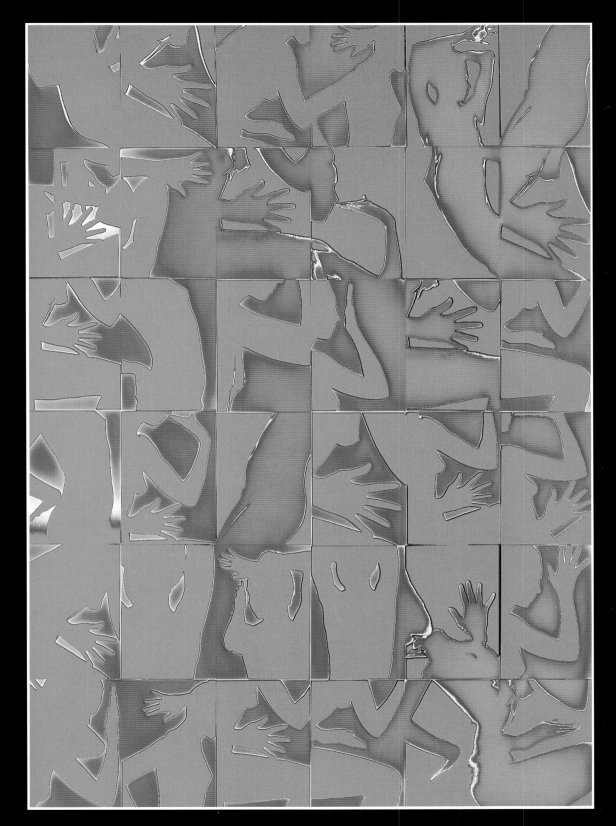

PENNY COLOURED

WHILE STILL A SOPHISTICATED
IMAGE, IT IS VERY ACCESSIBLE AND
NOT HEAVILY ABSTRACTED. USING
THE SAME SET OF SOLARISED
SEPARATIONS WHICH MADE THE
PREVIOUS IMAGE, EACH WAS GIVEN
AN EXPOSURE THROUGH A
SELECTED COLOUR FILTER ON TO
A SINGLE PIECE OF COLOUR FILM.
THE RESULT AS SEEN HERE,
IS VERY ABSTRACT AND EXTREMELY
SOPHISTICATED AS A FINE ART
IMAGE BUT MADE BY PURELY
MECHANICAL STEPS WHICH ANY
REASONABLY ADVANCED
PHOTOGRAPHER COULD MAKE IN
AN AVERAGE DARKROOM.

NUDE RISING

The model worked through a series of exercise routines, including crouching and rising very slowly in order to produce great tension. Responding to direction, the model has twisted her body toward camera, producing a further and different tension.

At the peak of her lift from the floor, the picture was made. Lighting was largely from an axis light from a studio flash. The negative has been enlarged on to lith film, processed in a weak print developer and partially solarised.

CHINA GIRL

A picture from an editorial assignment which is slightly enigmatic. Heightened dynamism has been achieved by the introduction of a very dark frame around the figure as an integral part of the image, which promotes a sense of voyeurism in the viewer.

DANCING ON GREY

This interesting image evolved exactly as planned. First the model was asked to perform dance routines on a black velvet backdrop, while lit by a sharp rim light which produced a highly structured, already abstracted image. A lith positive was made which itself became a successful limited edition print, but was given further treatment by printing on an Agfa high contrast bromide paper and solarised. A beautiful greytone separation and solarised form has been made as a natural consequence of the print solarising treatment.

THE FINISHED PRINT.

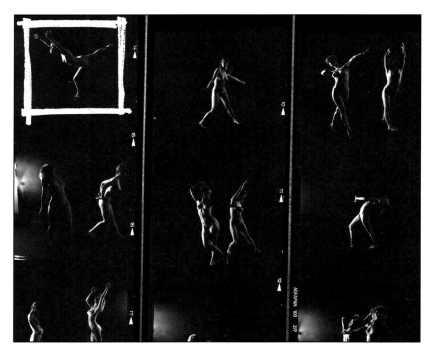

A SECTION OF THE CONTACT SHEET.

SOLARISED LINE CAN CREATE VERY ELEGANT SHAPES.

L ooking back at Chapter 3 you will find examples of how to use rim lighting. This is how this image was made. Having achieved a contrasty negative with the model harshly lit on a black cloth background a positive was made and solarised, with the first development allowed to continue longer than normal, before re-exposure. This affected only the body contours, leaving the background as fully developed silver. When a contact film reversal was made on lith film and developed in a two-bath lith developer, the purity of the line was maintained. The rich bromide print was subsequently laser copied to give a very striking exhibition artwork.

TRIAD

orking with three models in one frame requires of the photographer great concentration and quick reflexes, particularly if they are dancers as in this case. Earlier in the book (Chapter 9 page 97), I have suggested using slow shutter speeds and electronic flash.

By making several lith film masks, both positive and negative and solarising some of them, the image was changed dramatically even as a monochrome. By exposing the masks through pastel coloured lighting gels, the intriguing image opposite was made. It particularly pleased me because it was very photographic, showing action and blur, and very modern with the latest techniques of arbitrary colour masking. No computer manipulation was used.

THIS IS THE WORKPRINT MADE
FROM THE SELECTED FRAME.

THIS IS A CONTACT SHEET
FROM ONE SESSION.

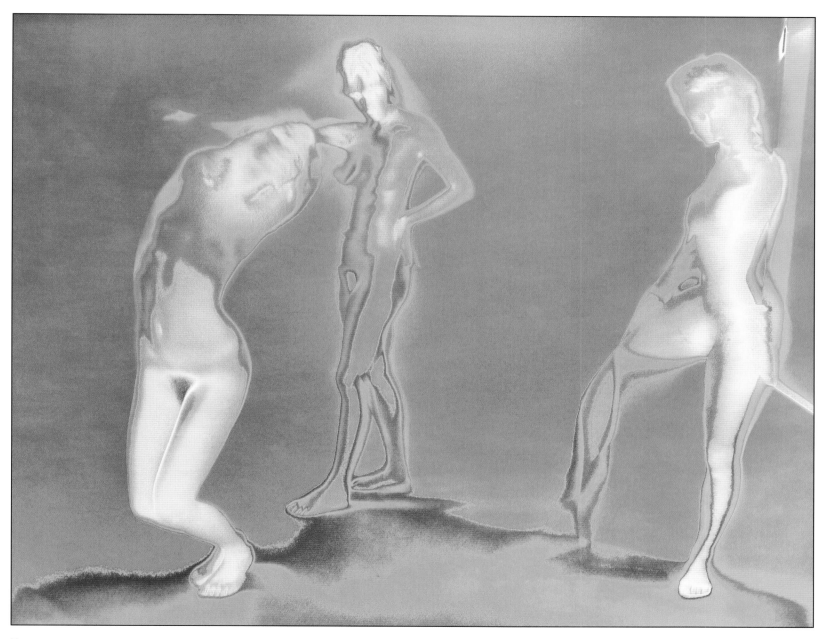

THE FINAL IMAGE.

STRETCHING NUDE

Earlier in this book there are examples of the model working in front of an acrylic mirror which has been flexed to perform distortions rather like a fun-fair mirror. This is a contact sheet from one such session.

The finished version used solarised masks and coloured filters to produce a final image for a limited edition art print.

ANOTHER DISTORTED IMAGE USING THE SAME TECHNIQUE.

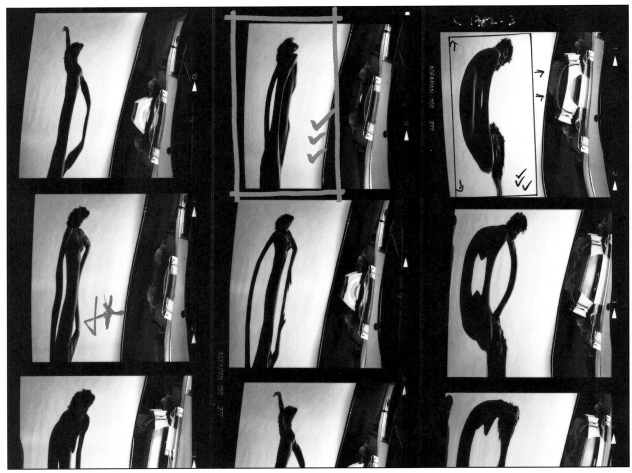

CONTACT SHEET.

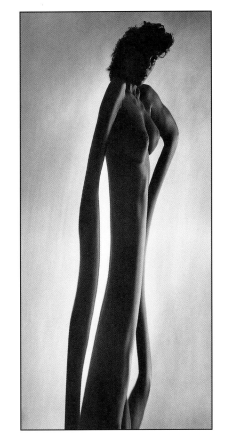

A TEST PRINT OF A SELECTED IMAGE.

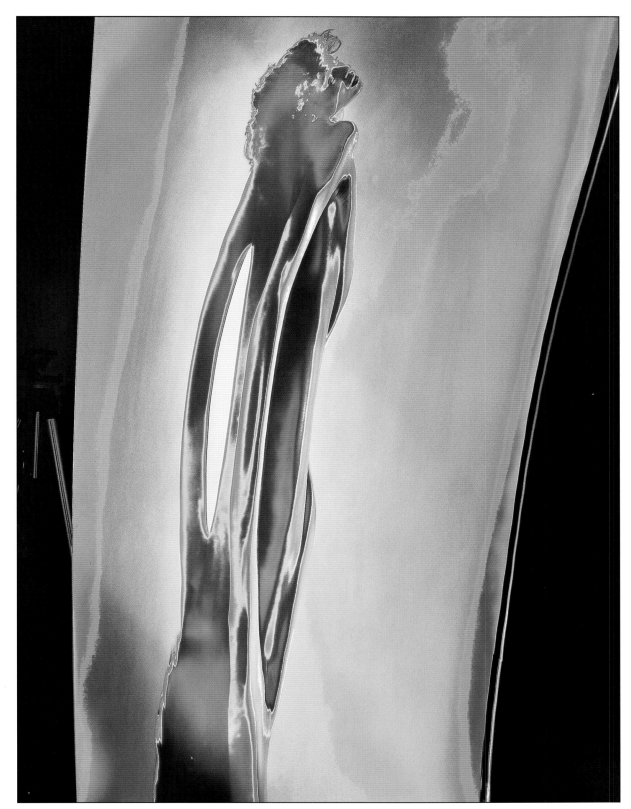

THE FINISHED PRINT.

TIME OUT

During a brief rest from photography, I noticed the model was standing with her back to me, while she rested. The line of her back and the delicate stance on high heels was striking, so we quickly produced some basic material for later dark room work.

SELECTED CONTACT.

THIS IS THE WORK PRINT FROM THE
BLACK AND WHITE NEGATIVES.

THE FINAL PRINT.

Marta was photographed with axis lighting to give the characteristic heavy outline shadow, so that it would respond to solarisation and tone compression in the darkroom. Four different separations were made from the solarised master negative and each given a colour overlay. Using the Kodak Register Punch for critical alignment, these were recopied by transmitted light on to Agfa Dupe film, exposing each colour separation on to the same piece of film.

POLAROID OF THE FINAL ASSEMBLY.

THE FINISHED TRANSPARENCY.

OCTOBER

Two film positives were made, one of which was flipped to give a mirror image and overlaid to produce this work print, which has been given some contrast enhancement in the developer. Areas of the print were given filter keys and notes kept. Lith separations were now made and the enhanced grain which came from using a high speed film, was allowed to print through, giving the sand - like texture. Lastly orange and green colour gels were applied directly to the film positives and, using a register punch, several separations were exposed on to one sheet of colour film.

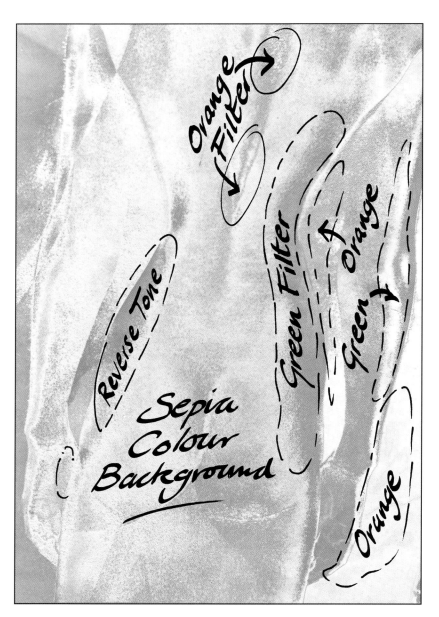

OVERLAY.

THIS IS THE STUDIO PHOTOGRAPH
FROM WHICH THIS IMAGE WAS MADE.

184

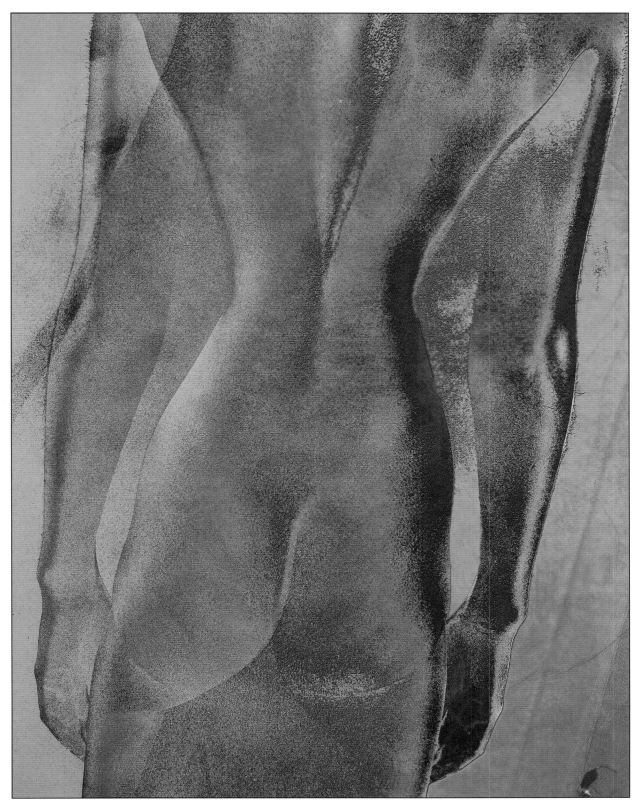

THE FINISHED IMAGE.

WORKOUT

Solarising six masks, some of which were negatives and some positives, very graphic separations were achieved. These emphasised the intense activity and the concentration of the lead dancer. Brightly coloured filters were used in the exposing light during the assembly on to lith film.

The contact sheet shows the activity encouraged for this session with experienced dancers. A selection was made and darkroom work commenced.

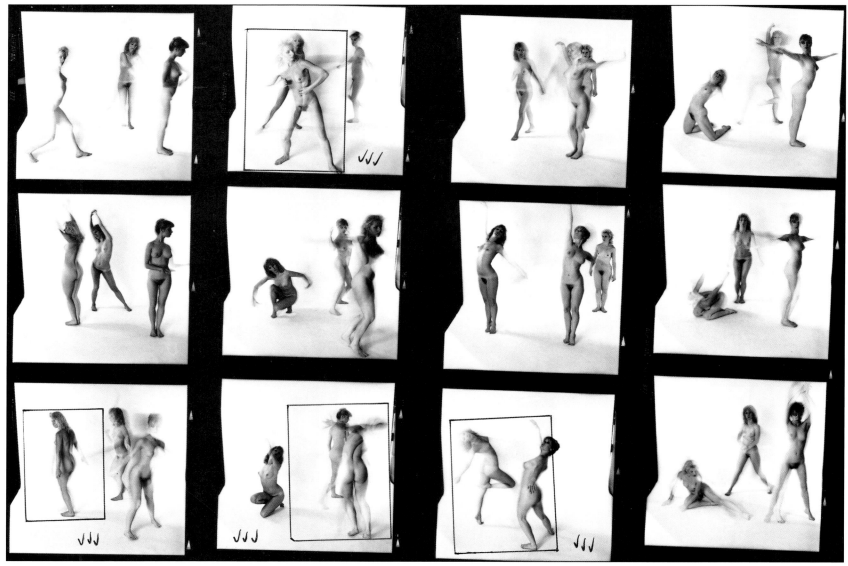

CONTACT SHEET.

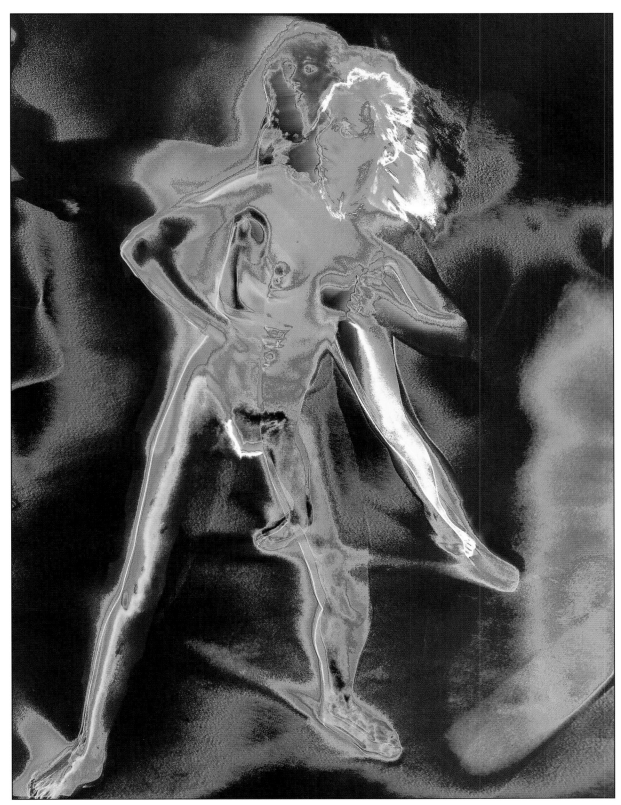

THE FINAL TRANSPARENCY.

Nude Fragmented

Nude fragmented is merely an extension of the simple silhouette technique explained earlier on page 50 yet it is the basis of very extensive and successful darkroom manipulation, which produced the intriguing image shown here. The original negative was enlarged on to lith film and solarised. From this (positive) a reversal (negative) was made. Sections of the reversal were painted out with photo opaque and contact printed on film. This created a mask which was partially clear film and elsewhere totally opaque.

MULTIPLE SPOTLIGHTS WERE USED TO CREATE MULTIPLE SHADOWS ON A GAUZE SCREEN.

THIS IS A DIAGRAM OF THE SET UP FOR THIS IMAGE. NOTICE THAT TWO LIGHTS HAVE BEEN USED TO PRODUCE THE MULTIPLE SHADOWS.

THIS IS A CONTACT PRINT FROM THE ORIGINAL NEGATIVE. NOTICE THE MULTIPLE SHADOWS AND THE SOLID SILHOUETTES, WHEREVER THE BODY TOUCHES THE SCREEN.

THE FINISHED TRANSPARENCY.

189

GENESIS

One of my most unusual graphic assemblies. It was very carefully planned on paper before any photography began and is a colour photogram directly on to colour reversal paper. First a model was photographed in black and white, with hand outstretched towards the camera and then enlarged on to lith film and developed in ordinary print developer. Sequential contacts, again on lith film, were made – both positive and negative and solarised in warm, dilute developer. After the first rapid, flickering of my hand in the solarising dish, the film was left for 30 seconds, completely still. This allowed a slow spread of bromide to attack the edges of the image. The hand seemed to grow and become somewhat demonic. A glass stage was laid over the colour paper in complete darkness and the solarised images, registered on register pins were placed in the enlarger. Each was given its own strong colour filter and projected through the glass stage on which were laid crinkled pieces of clear acetate and a piece of coarse twine. This particular technique is not for the faint hearted!

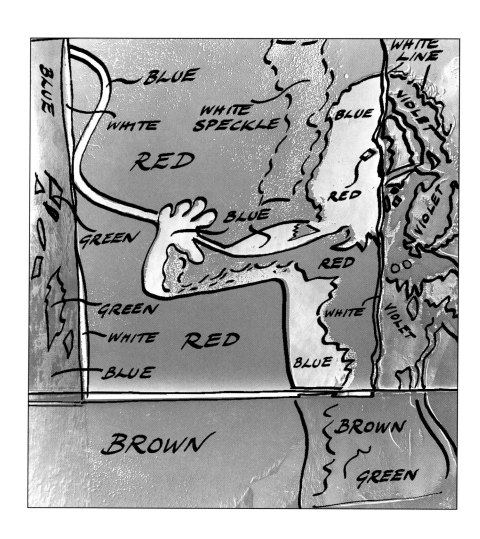

A WORK PRINT WAS MADE IN BLACK AND WHITE BY MAKING SUCCESSIVE EXPOSURES FROM FIVE LITH MASKS, USING A REGISTER BOARD AND EXPOSING ALL FIVE ON TO ONE SHEET OF PAPER. EACH MASK HAD BEEN SOLARISED.

USING THIS WORK PRINT AS A GUIDE, A TRACING WAS MADE AND COLOUR ZONES PLANNED. AGAIN USING THE REGISTER BOARD AS BEFORE, SUCCESSIVE EXPOSURES WERE MADE ON TO A SINGLE PIECE OF COLOUR FILM, EXPOSING THROUGH COLOUR GEL FILTERS TO CREATE THE REQUIRED COLOURS.

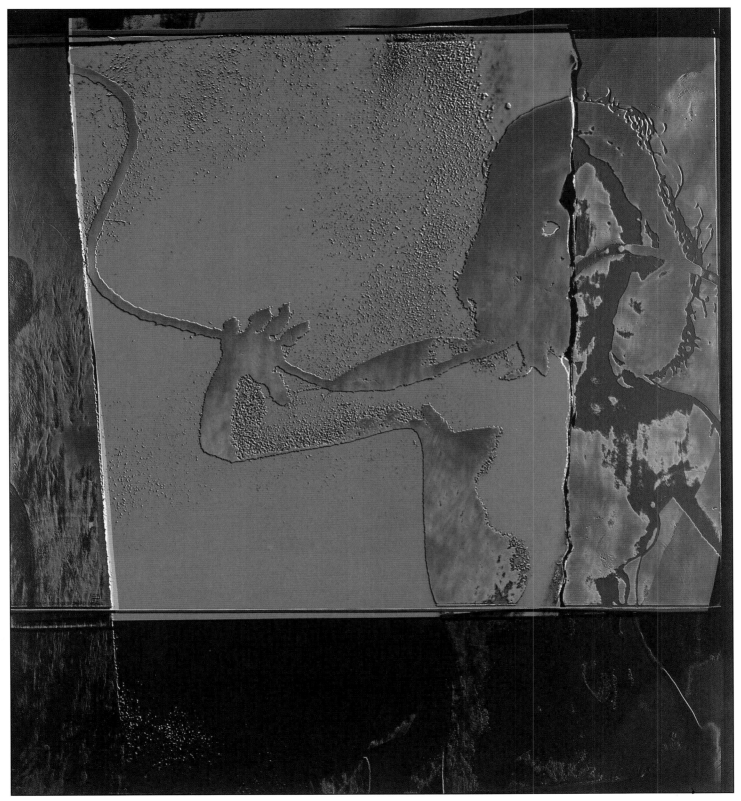

THE FINAL IMAGE.

The following sponsors have greatly assisted the compilation of this book and without their unstinting support, it would have been almost impossible to complete this project: Adel Rootstein Ltd, Shawfield House, Shawfield St, London SW3 – Display mannequins · Adel Rootstein Ltd, 205 W 19th St, New York NY10011 · Adobe Systems Europe Ltd, 1 Roundwood Ave, Stockley Park, Uxbridge UB11 1AY, UK, Website: www.adobe.co.uk. – Photoshop · Agfa UK, 27 Great West Rd ,Brentford, Middlesex TW8 9AX UK, – Manufacturers of Photographic Film and Digital Cameras · Dancing Bee Ltd, Website: www.dancing-bee.co.uk – Specialist graphic designers · Epson (UK) Ltd, Campus 100, Maylands Ave, Hemel Hempstead, Herts HP2 7T3, UK – Photo Studio Inkjet printers · Extensis Corporation Europe, Website: http://www.extensis com/ – MaskPro software · Fuji Photo Film (UK) Ltd, Fujifilm House, 125 Finchley Rd, London NW3 6HY – Manufacturers of Digital Cameras and Photographic Film · Hi-Grade Computers Plc, Hi-Grade House, 43 Thames Rd, Barking, Essex IG11 0HQ, Website: http://ww.higrade.com – Computer Manufacturers · iiYAMA Europe Ltd, 19 The Courtyards, Croxley Business Park, Hatters Lane, Watford, Herts WD1 8Y, UK – Professional Monitors · Ilford Ltd, P.O.Box 21, Mobberley, Knutsford, Cheshire WA16 7HA – Manufacturers and suppliers of fine quality photographic art papers and Cibachrome colour paper · Iomega International SA, 12, Avenue des Morgines, 1213 Petit-Lancy (Geneva), Switzerland, Website: http://ww.iomega.com · Kentmere Ltd, Staveley, Kendal, Cumbria LA8 9PB, UK – Manufacturers of fine quality photographic art paper · Kyocera Yashica (UK) Ltd, 4 Bennet Court, Bennet Rd, Reading, Berks RG2 0QX, UK – Contax Cameras · Linotype-CPS Ltd, Chelham House, Bath Rd, Cheltenham, Glos, GL3 7LR, Website: http://www.heidelberg-cps.com – Flatbed Scanners · maxx Aerosonic Ltd, studio maxx, 169 Tower Bridge Rd, London SE1 3NA – Giant electronic prints on canvas · Microsoft Manufacturing BV, PO Box 18100, Edinburgh, EH11 4WP, UK – Windows NT Workstation · Polaroid UK Ltd, Wheathamptead House, Codicote Rd, Wheathampstead, Herts, AL4 8SF, UK, Website: http://www.polaroid.com · Silverprint Ltd, 12 Valentine Place, London SE1 8QI, UK, Website: http:www.silverprint.co.uk – Specialist suppliers of photographic paper, film and chemicals

Registered and unregistered products and trademarks used herein are the exclusive property of their various owners. The author and publisher of this book make no claim to any such marks, nor willingly or knowingly have misused or misapplied such marks.